WHEN THE BRAVES RULED THE DIAMOND

FOURTEEN FLAGS OVER ATLANTA
2021 WORLD CHAMPIONSHIP EDITION

BY DAN SCHLOSSBERG
FOREWORD BY BOBBY COX

SPORTS PUBLISHING

T0109239

Sports Publishing books may be purchased in bulk at special discounts for sales promotion, corporate gifts, fund-raising, or educational purposes. Special editions can also be created to specifications. For details, contact the Special Sales Department, Sports Publishing, 307 West 36th Street, 11th Floor, New York, NY 10018 or sportspubbooks@skyhorsepublishing.com.

Sports Publishing® is a registered trademark of Skyhorse Publishing, Inc.®, a Delaware corporation.

Visit our website at www.sportspubbooks.com.

10 9 8 7 6 5 4 3 2 1

Library of Congress Cataloging-in-Publication Data is available on file.

Cover design by Tom Lau
Front cover photo courtesy of Getty Images
Back cover photo by Jeff Slate

ISBN: 978-1-68358-455-1
Ebook ISBN: 978-1-68358-273-1

Printed in the United States of America

To my dear departed friend Ed Lucas
Who shared my loves of baseball and laughter
For more than half a century
And who made this planet a better place.

ADVANCE PRAISE FOR *WHEN THE BRAVES RULED THE DIAMOND*:

"There's nothing better than a walk down memory lane, and *When the Braves Ruled the Diamond* is just that . . . a long, leisurely stroll with great conversation, inside stories and memories from the Braves' incredible run of 14 straight divisional titles. It's a must-read not only for Braves fans but for fans of baseball history."

—Chip Caray, Braves broadcaster

"How can a team that won year after year be underrated? That's the strange story of the Atlanta Braves dynasty. Dan Schlossberg, who knows more about the club than anyone, tells that story splendidly."

—John Thorn, official historian, Major League Baseball

"Dan Schlossberg puts his Hall of Fame Rolodex and encyclopedic baseball mind to work in profiles and chapters that move briskly and capture the essence of what it takes to be a winner."

—Steve Borelli, senior editor, *USA TODAY Sports Weekly*

"The years 1991-2005 are the greatest in Atlanta Braves history, climaxing in 1995 with a win over the Indians in a six-game World Series. Dan Schlossberg chronicles those years with grace and aplomb, telling the stories through the eyes of Cox, Mad Dog, Smoltz, Chipper and Glavine, whose one-hitter in Game 6 made a Justice homer stand up for the lone championship. Should the Braves have won more? You be the judge. Well done!"

—Barry Bloom, Sportico baseball columnist

"Like DiMaggio and Monroe, Ripken and The Streak, Aaron and Home Runs, it's Schlossberg and the Braves, a match and marriage never to be separated. Read it, love it, and enjoy the true passion of the author."

—Al Clark, Major League umpire, 1976-2001

"When it comes to knowledge of the Braves, there is only one sports-writer to go to and it's Dan Schlossberg. He's a real Atlanta Braves guru."
—**Jay Smith, president, Sports Travel and Tours**

"I've covered or been with an MLB team for more than 40 years and Atlanta's dominance during that 14-year title run was a special time in the game. Dan Schlossberg, as usual, has painted that picture so well in his book. It's a must-read."
—**Bob Ibach, author, sportscaster,
and former Chicago Cubs PR director**

"Dan Schlossberg has hit a grand slam! This is a fascinating, informative, and funny look at 14 great Atlanta Braves teams."
—**Doug Lyons, author of *100 Years of Who's Who in Baseball***

"Longtime SCD columnist Dan Schlossberg combines his passion for Braves baseball with his historian expertise to provide a first-class look at the amazing run of Atlanta title teams."
—**Tom Bartsch, former editor-in-chief, *Sports Collectors Digest***

CONTENTS

Dedication   *iii*

Introduction   *ix*

Foreword by Bobby Cox   *xiii*

Acknowledgments   *xxi*

PEOPLE   **1**

   1. The Conductor: John Schuerholz   3
   2. The Engineer: Bobby Cox   26
   3. The Fireman: Leo Mazzone   37
   4. The Survivor: John Smoltz   56
   5. The Hockey Player: Tom Glavine   70
   6. The Professor: Greg Maddux   85
   7. The MVPs: Terry and Chipper   96

SEASONS   **115**

   8. 1991: Worst to First   117
   9. 1992: Back-to-Back   134
 10. 1993: The Great Race   148
 11. 1995: Nirvana   160
 12. 1996: Power Plus Pitching   172
 13. 1997: Friggin' Florida   184
 14. 1998: Juggernaut   194
 15. 1999: Mr. Clutch   201
 16. 2000: Chipper, Andruw, and Andres   210
 17. 2001: Winning by a Whisker   220
 18. 2002: Maulers in the Outfield   224

19. 2003: Power to Burn   231
20. 2004: Rotation Reborn   237
21. 2005: Eighteen Rookies   244
22. After the Streak   255
23. The Miracle Braves of 2021   268
24. Cooperstown   282

Bibliography   302
Appendix   305
Index   315

INTRODUCTION

[Author's Note: Even though the 2021 Atlanta Braves won their first pennant since 1999 and first world championship since 1995, their 14-year title streak remains the team equivalent of Cal Ripken Jr.'s consecutive games playing streak. This is the only book to document that streak, year by year, and also detail what followed. –DS]

AS A BOY growing up in the New York bedroom suburb of Passaic, New Jersey, I had two passions: trains and baseball.

The electric train set in my basement was my favorite toy before baseball cards began to wean me away. I liked the color and design of the cards, not to mention the fact that I could carry them anywhere, hide them under my bed, and trade them with friends like a real-life general manager trading players.

Even now, after establishing a career as a professional writer and broadcaster, I still like trains and baseball. In fact, I consider the 14-year title streak of the Atlanta Braves not just a pro sports record but a living example of the ultimate express train.

Like the Phoebe Snow and the Orient Express, the Braves launched their streak after careful planning that parlayed mind and muscle into a juggernaut not seen before or since.

In railroad parlance, John Schuerholz, the general manager who arrived after the 1990 season, was the conductor.

Bobby Cox, the field manager for the entire 14-year run, was the engineer.

Leo Mazzone, the outspoken old-school pitching coach Cox discovered in the minors, drove him crazy with his nervous rocking but worked wonders with his charges, turning some into Hall of Famers and others into valuable supporting casts.

Beyond Cox and Mazzone, the only other man who wore a Braves uniform for the entire streak was John Smoltz, elected to the Hall of

Fame in 2015. He teamed with Greg Maddux and Tom Glavine, who reached Cooperstown a year earlier, to win a half-dozen Cy Young Awards and more pennants during the '90s than any other team.

Cox and Schuerholz also came to Cooperstown after election by Veterans Committees three years apart, in 2014 and 2017. When Chipper Jones joined them in 2018, that gave the Braves six electees in five years—an achievement almost as remarkable as the fourteen straight division titles.

Jones, whose 1995 rookie season coincided with the first world championship in Atlanta history, never left Atlanta during a career that lasted nineteen seasons. Although he could have departed via free agency, as all three pitchers did, Chipper won the hearts of Braves fans by choosing to spend his whole career with the team.

Like Terry Pendleton, another third baseman whose leadership pushed the team to several titles, Chipper won a National League batting crown and Most Valuable Player Award while wearing Braves livery. In fact, Chipper succeeded Terry at the critical position.

This is the story of a baseball express that roared through dozens of cities, stopping only to pick up helpful hands along the way.

It literally polevaulted from last place in 1990 to first place in 1991—and liked the rarefied air so much that it stayed there for 14 consecutive completed seasons.

Both the Braves and the Minnesota Twins, their '91 World Series opponents, went from worst to first—a feat never accomplished before—but Atlanta became the first team to do it after posting the worst record in both leagues the previous year.

That climb, coupled with the ability to stay at the summit, showed that the pairing of Cox and Schuerholz was a rare baseball marriage with lasting power.

Cox, who managed the Braves from 1978 to 1981 and the Toronto Blue Jays from 1982 to 1985, was hired twice by Ted Turner—once to manage a weak Braves team and again to rebuild the ballclub as general manager in 1985.

Emphasizing pitching, Cox and his scouts signed Glavine, traded for Smoltz, and found exceptional position players such as David Justice and Ron Gant. When he returned to the dugout during the 1990 season, all four were already blossoming.

Because he felt more comfortable in the dugout, Cox gladly gave up the GM's job to Schuerholz, who jumped across league lines from Kansas City to Atlanta after the 1990 campaign. The two not only knew and respected each other but had even made three trades. Both agreed that the best way to boost the franchise was to bolster a leaky defense.

Before the start of the '91 season, Schuerholz had signed seven free agents—most of them known for their defense—and traded for fleet centerfielder Otis Nixon, the final piece in his carefully crafted mosaic.

Reversing their 1990 record of 65–97, which left them last in the National League West and 26 games from the front-running Reds, the Braves went 94–68, good enough to beat out the Dodgers by a single game. Their young pitching, buoyed by confidence in their fielders, prevailed against the powerful Pittsburgh Pirates in the playoffs and set the stage for one of the most exciting World Series ever played.

Three games, including the historic seventh, went into extra innings. Four went down to the final pitch. And five were decided by a single run.

For the Braves, that was just the beginning. They won five pennants in the '90s—more than any other team—and brought Atlanta its first world championship.

They survived slumps, suspensions, strikes, and the never-ending salary spiral. Even a long-overdue switch from the National League West to the National League East didn't deter them.

This is the story of how the Atlanta Braves became baseball's most successful ballclub at a time when sustained excellence was unexpected and often unexplained.

It is the story of Antonio Alfonseca, whose hand had six fingers, and Andruw Jones, who kept in shape as a kid by swinging a sledgehammer.

It is the story of Fred McGriff, a towering left-handed slugger whose midseason acquisition ignited an offense on the same night the Braves stadium suffered a serious fire.

It is the story of Chipper Jones, a lanky switch-hitter who spent his entire career in a Braves uniform.

And it is the story of three remarkable pitchers who monopolized the Cy Young Award as they marched toward the Baseball Hall of Fame, along with their manager.

As a lifelong Braves fan who began following the club when Hank Aaron, Eddie Mathews, and Warren Spahn were the mainstays, I was thrilled to witness the half-dozen inductions of Braves legends that began in 2014.

Never have three pitching teammates been so good for so long.

Good pitching stops good hitting but *great* pitching? With Maddux, Glavine, and Smoltz in their rotation, the Braves rarely lost three games in a row. They were fun to watch—even from afar before Facebook and the Internet made following a distant team more feasible.

History may never see their like again—or a team that finishes in first place for 14 consecutive years.

—DAN SCHLOSSBERG
Fair Lawn, New Jersey

FOREWORD

FINISHING IN FIRST place over a 162-game season is tough enough. But doing it 14 times in a row? That's impossible, unheard of.

But the Atlanta Braves did it from 1991 through 2005, not counting the incomplete season of 1994 that ended in August because of a players' strike.

I was lucky enough to be the manager for all of those championship years. Fourteen straight—a pro sports record.

I remember sitting with Jim Leyland, Ned Yost, and a few other guys at the baseball winter meetings when Leyland brought that up. He said that record will never be broken. I'm not so sure, though; I never thought anybody would even come close to Lou Gehrig's record but look what happened.

There were a few years when players were injured and unavailable. We didn't know if we could keep the streak alive, to pull it off. We even had 18 rookies one year but still won.

For me, you have to have pitching. We made that our priority all those years. Without it, we couldn't have come close to winning 14 in a row. We were fortunate to have Paul Snyder as our chief scout. He could always draw somebody out of somewhere. So a lot of credit goes to our farm system.

I was a coach for the Yankees when Ted Turner hired me to manage the Braves in 1978. Working for Ted was fun—he was definitely out there.

He was right in the middle of forming his big empire. He bought the wrestling federation but needed more programming for WTBS (later

Photo courtesy of the National Baseball Hall of Fame and Museum.

SuperStation TBS, seen in all fifty states). So he bought the Braves for $10 million.

I had a blast with Ted. I loved him to death and miss him at the winter meetings. Along with Brad Corbett and George Steinbrenner, he made the meetings lively. You never knew where they were coming from but you knew something was definitely going to happen.

Ted was a laugh-a-minute. Unfortunately, so was our team. We did not have a lot of talent so Ted let me go after four years. He brought me back four years later as general manager.

I spent most of that time looking for pitching. We signed Tom Glavine, Steve Avery, Pete Smith, and a bunch of others and traded for a Double-A righthander named John Smoltz.

But I was a field guy from day one. I wanted to get back down there. In the middle of the 1990 season, with the team going nowhere, I did—but quickly found I couldn't be manager and general manager at the same time. It was totally impossible.

After the season, we got the perfect guy (for the GM job) when we hired John Schuerholz away from Kansas City. He and Paul Snyder, our scouting director, were instrumental in just about everything we did.

Even before the 1991 season started, I liked our club. We had signed Rafael Belliard, Sid Bream, and Terry Pendleton as free agents and picked up Otis Nixon at the end of spring training. That made our team; people who don't talk about defense on winning clubs are missing the boat. In order to have great pitching, you've got to have great defense. We just didn't; before we added those guys, our defense was horrendous, not good at all.

Pendleton was the perfect pick as the leader of that team. He was full of energy. We won the division by one game that year and Terry was instrumental in a lot of our wins. He had been at the top of our target list. We had tracked his fly balls in St. Louis, where the ballpark is pretty big, and realized they would have been home runs in Atlanta.

Terry not only won the batting crown but also the Most Valuable Player award that year.

The '91 season was one of the most exciting of my career. The city was energized, the stadium was packed every night, and we had several big series when the Dodgers came to town. That was a very special year.

We made it all the way to the seventh game of the World Series with John Smoltz pitching against Jack Morris. We had the bases loaded with one out at one point but didn't score. One bounce and we win the World Series but we never got that bounce.

We won another pennant in '92 when Francisco Cabrera pinch-hit a two-run single in the bottom of the ninth inning of Game Seven of the Championship Series against Pittsburgh. He wasn't very successful at the big league level but the one thing he could do was hit. He was a kid from the islands who swung at just about everything. We liked him as a hitter and I felt great with him up there.

In 1993, our season turned around when we picked up Fred McGriff from San Diego in July. The night he reported, he got to the ballpark a little bit late. He was hitting in our indoor tunnel when a bunch of guys started yelling, "The stadium's on fire." And it was. There was a major fire. We started the game about an hour-and-a-half late after they made sure the fire was out. That night, Freddie got hot, too, hitting two home runs. He never cooled off and we came from way behind to beat the Giants for the NL West title on the last day of the season.

We also added Greg Maddux to the team that season. We had enough money to sign one big guy and had to decide between Greg and Barry Bonds—the Cy Young Award winner and Most Valuable Player of the previous year. I don't know how different things might have been if we picked Barry but I was very pleased with the way things turned out.

When Maddux joined Tom Glavine and John Smoltz, it gave us three Hall of Fame pitchers on the same team. You could go way back in baseball history and not find that anywhere else. They stayed there, they pitched there forever. They loved the setting and liked winning.

All three of them were unbelievably great competitors. If I had to choose one, I couldn't.

Having those three workhorses helped us beat a hard-hitting Cleveland team in the 1995 World Series. We held them to almost nothing, especially when Glavine won the last game, 1–0, and yielded just a bloop single in eight innings. Good pitching will overcome good hitting just about every time.

That 1995 season was the best we ever had, winning the division by 21 games. It was our first year in the National League East, where we should have been from day one. When the league split into three divisions, that fixed the problem. It also created the wild card, giving a postseason spot to the second-place team with the best record. At first I didn't like it at all but I came to love it. Anything you can do to make it more interesting for a lot of cities and organizations is good.

It was also the year we added Chipper Jones to our lineup. He was one of those rare guys who spent his entire career with one club, like Tony Gwynn and Cal Ripken Jr. You almost never see that these days because of free agency and payrolls. Chip was always upfront with our front office people. He didn't want to go anywhere else. He was the one guy that we found a little bit more money for, even if we were over budget a little bit.

We signed Chipper in five minutes. All he wanted to do was play. That's what we wanted. Did we EVER get the right guy!

We knew he had big-time power from both sides of the plate. Managers would always turn him around to make him hit right-handed but it didn't matter to me. We knew he had a chance to be an All-Star caliber player when we signed him.

There were many times when he carried the club, especially near the end of the 1999 season when he was a one-man show against the New York Mets. He finished with 45 home runs, a record for a National League switch-hitter.

A few years later, Andruw Jones hit 51 home runs, a club record. He had unbelievable power. He took a lot of the plate away from the pitcher and he got up on the plate a little bit more that year. Andruw

Except for manager Bobby Cox and pitching coach Leo Mazzone, the Braves roster changed substantially between 1998 and 2005. But the team continued to win.
Photo courtesy of the Braves Museum and Hall of Fame.

was one of the best ballplayers I ever saw. He was a great centerfielder who could throw and run. He even had his own streak with 10 consecutive Gold Gloves. I never saw Willie Mays play that much but I always mention Andruw whenever anybody talks about Willie. That's pretty good company.

Javy Lopez was another slugger who helped us. He used to hit the ball a lot to right field but then started pulling the ball more. He got a little closer to the plate and wound up with 43 home runs, a record for a catcher.

We had so many different types of teams during our streak. We had slugging teams, speed teams, and really young teams but always had pitching. It was fun managing teams stacked with base-stealers: Otis Nixon, Deion Sanders, and later on Rafael Furcal. We had some pop in the lineup but I liked to turn the runners loose. And Ron Gant, whose second 30–30 year coincided with that worst-to-first season in '91, added a great combination of speed plus power.

I'm not only proud of every team I ever managed but proud of the fans and the organization. We only won five pennants and one World

Series but I thought we played as well in the World Series we lost as we did in the one we won. We always did as well as we could.

In 1996, after we won the first two games in the Bronx, we had the Yankees on the ropes. But we ran into some buzzsaw pitchers in Andy Pettitte and David Cone.

Three years later, after we almost swept the Mets in the playoffs, the Yankees swept us.

We won more pennants during the '90s than any other team but had to overcome lots of obstacles. Any time we had a problem in the clubhouse, I tried to get on it immediately. You can't let it grow—that's for sure. You don't have to like everybody to have him on the team but you can't forget that we're a team.

When somebody gets hurt, the players have to pick each other up. There's nothing else you can do unless you can make a trade—and that's almost impossible during the season.

We always had a pretty good bench. I always liked the guys who could actually play defense, too, instead of some cloggers who could hit but needed pinch-runners.

And finally, no manager can win without the right people around him. That starts in the front office, with the general manager and player development people, but also includes the coaches.

Leo Mazzone was with me for the entire 14-year run. I met Leo when he was in our farm system and liked him a lot. His throwing program proved to be workable for all

The Atlanta Braves won more games and more pennants during the '90s than any other team.

Photo by the author.

WHEN THE BRAVES RULED THE DIAMOND

our pitchers, starters and relievers, and the record bears that out. The Braves led the league in earned run average in almost every year of the 14-year streak.

Maybe the most amazing thing that occurred was the ability of John Smoltz to go from starter to closer to starter again. Nothing was impossible with John. If he set his mind to do something, he was going to do it. He's a scratch golfer, he could play basketball with anybody, and I would have loved to see what he could do as a quarterback. He was one of the most gifted athletes in the history of the game. What he did was not easy: saving 100 games over two seasons but still winning 213 overall.

It also made my life easier, since he was the only player to wear an Atlanta Braves uniform for the entire duration of the streak. The only other people who did that were Leo Mazzone and me.

My friend Dan Schlossberg, the author of this book, also witnessed the streak. A former AP sportswriter, he has managed to follow the team closely from his home outside New York and I always enjoyed our talks and interviews. His love of baseball in general and the Braves in particular is apparent in the pages that follow.

—BOBBY COX
Adairsville, Georgia

Editor's Note: Hall of Famer Bobby Cox won four Manager of the Year awards, five pennants, and one World Championship during a career that stretched from 1978 to 2010. Only three other managers won more games.

ACKNOWLEDGMENTS

AFTER HEARING NEARLY two-dozen different speeches in a five-year span at the Baseball Hall of Fame inductions, I know how important it is to thank the people who paved the path of possibility.

That being said, I owe a huge debt of thanks to my talented editor at Skyhorse Publishing, Julie Ganz. Even though she's an ardent fan of the New York Mets, the longtime archrivals of the Braves, she supported this project from the beginning. She also extended such complete artistic freedom that I got to pick the typeface of this book, as well as the picture placement.

Virtually all of the photos and artwork for *When the Braves Ruled the Diamond* was the result of fast friendships formed over the years, both inside and outside of baseball press boxes. Some were from my private collection but many were the work of Bill Menzel, one of the most talented baseball photographers I have ever seen.

After Clay Luraschi and Heather Greenberg of The Topps Company granted permission to reprint ten cards between these covers, I had the difficult but enjoyable task of sifting through my extensive collection of Atlanta Braves cards and making choices as difficult as those that faced Bobby Cox when he cut his roster to the 25-man limit every spring.

Thanks also to Ronnie Joyner, the best baseball cartoonist since Amadee, for allowing me to use the Tom Glavine and Greg Maddux panels he originally created for my book *The 300 Club* and for crafting new ones on John Smoltz and Bobby Cox exclusively for this book.

Bill Goff, founder of goodsportsart.com, came through, too, asking his artists if I could reprint their paintings in these pages. Goff's guys were great at painting pictures that looked like photographs—especially in the Hallowed Ground calendars he produced every year. I was almost as sorry to see the calendar retire as I was to see Chipper reach the end of the line with the Braves.

But life goes on, as I found out while collaborating with colorful and innovative umpire Al Clark on his 2014 book *Called Out But Safe: a Baseball Umpire's Journey.*

A year later, Chris Lucas and his dad Ed included me in their inspirational book *Seeing Home: the Ed Lucas Story.* I continue to enjoy their friendship, support, and laughter—especially at baseball events like the All-Star Game and World Series. Kudos also to Allison Lucas for helping Ed get through triple-bypass surgery during the 2018 baseball season.

Thanks to Brett Knight and Daniel Kleinman, who signed me as a baseball writer for forbes.com in 2018; to *Sports Collectors Digest* editor Bert Lehman; to Latino Sports founder and president Julio Pabon; and to Steve Borelli of *USA TODAY Sports Weekly* for sending regular work my way—keeping me sharp for various baseball book projects, including this one.

Most of all, heartfelt thanks go to my baseball friends: John Schuerholz, who once called me from Italy to fulfill an interview request; Tom Glavine, who was overly polite when I met him during his rookie year and never changed; the always articulate and thoughtful John Smoltz; Braves managers Fredi Gonzalez and Brian Snitker, whose humor and honesty in the face of adversity was remarkable and refreshing; Leo Mazzone, who deserves to be the first pitching coach in Cooperstown; and especially Bobby Cox, whom I have known since he first joined the Braves in 1978 and who generously provided the foreword for *When the Braves Ruled the Diamond.*

Thanks also to Ron Gant, Chipper Jones, Dale Murphy, Fred McGriff, Terry Pendleton, Eddie Perez and the many Braves players, managers, and broadcasters who appeared as guests on *Braves Banter* during a seven-year run that I started in 2011, and to Chris Mascaro, Art Minsky, and Jason Hyman, who served as co-hosts of the Thursday night show, and to Roger Noriega, my producer at NDB Media.

Thanks also to the following, in alphabetical order: B.B. Abbott, Jenny Ambrose, Marc Appleman, Tom Bartsch, Kevin Barnes, Evelyn Begley, Bruce Campbell; Wayne Coleman, Tom diPace, Bob Faller, David Fenster, Jim Gates, Vince Gennaro, Brad Hainje, Tom Hufford, Bob Ibach, Bill Jacobowitz; Maggie Linton, Clay Luraschi, Brad Hainje, Mark (Muggs) Hamilton, Milo Hamilton, Brad Horn, Jeff Idelson, Bob Ibach, Morgan Johnston, Sharon Jones, David Kaplan, Gene Locklear, John MacLean, Kevin MacDougall, Bruce Markusen, Gary Matthews, Adrienne Midgley, Bob Moscatell, Bob Nesoff, Bill Purdom, Linda Rosen, Jim Schultz, Carolyn Serra, Glen Serra, Howie Siegel, Jeff Slade, Jay Smith, Don Sutton, John Vorperian, Chris Wheeler, Bill Williams, Rob Wilson, and the late Kal London, Pete Van Wieren, and David Vincent.

Last but certainly not least, thanks to Phyllis Deutsch, Sandy Geiger, Ali Nolan, Sophie Nolan, Jenny O'Rourke, Samantha Schlossberg, and other family and friends who couldn't understand why I turned into a hermit, especially near the end of this intense writing process, but hopefully will be happy to see their names in this book.

PEOPLE

PEOPLE

1

THE CONDUCTOR: JOHN SCHUERHOLZ

L ESS THAN A handful of baseball general managers have won world championships in both leagues. But only one has guided a team to 14 consecutive division titles.

John Schuerholz, whose world titles came 10 years apart, won first with the Kansas City Royals and then with the Atlanta Braves. It was only at the second stop, however, that he established and cultivated a reputation as a creative genius.

A one-time Baltimore school teacher who took a pay cut to work for the Orioles, Schuerholz found his Atlanta tenure roughly equivalent to playing a game of whack-a-mole that lasted 15 years (the 1994 season, stopped by a player strike, was never completed).

When sudden injury struck, he had to fill the void. When salary arbitration forced him to spend too much on one player, he had to shave salary by shedding another. When a player suddenly slowed because of age or injury, he had to reach into his farm system.

He changed players only when he had to. During their title run, the Braves never used more than 47 players (2000 and 2001) and employed as few as 31 (1994), 33 (1993), and 34 (2003). Never did they use the same basic lineup in consecutive seasons.

At first base alone, the cast of characters included Sid Bream, Brian Hunter, Fred McGriff, Andres Galarraga, and even Julio Franco, an ancient bastion of fitness plucked from the Mexican League when nobody was watching.

"What the Braves have done without overwhelming economic advantage over their competitors is one of the most remarkable achievements in the history of professional sports," said broadcaster Bob Costas after Atlanta's streak finally ended. "And it's all been achieved without histrionics. When they've lost, there's been no excuse-making, no radical reassessments, knee-jerk housecleanings, or crazed personnel changes."

Schuerholz had a knack for finding good players in strange places, once trading a dozen bags of bats and balls to the independent Minneapolis Loons for Kerry Ligtenberg, an unknown commodity who morphed into a solid big league reliever.

A skilled negotiator, Schuerholz not only could hold the company line when negotiating player salaries but fleece an opposing team in trade talks by dangling prospects that were more like suspects. Rivals liked and respected him but also feared his superior intellect.

"Unless you've been inside and worked with him," said longtime Braves scouting director Paul Snyder of Schuerholz, "there's no way you can appreciate the man's baseball intelligence."

During his tenure as Atlanta general manager, Schuerholz had a well-established persona as a polished executive who dressed well, spoke well, and could ante up anecdotes about world-famous cellist Pablo Casals.

According to him, Casals practiced six hours a day even as he approached his 100th birthday. Asked why, the cellist said, "Maybe I can get better."

That philosophy guided Schuerholz throughout his career.

Before he left Kansas City to take the Atlanta job, Ted Turner was the owner, Stan Kasten was team president, and Bobby Cox was both manager and general manager. Then Kasten met Schuerholz in New York late in the 1990 season when both were working on the same committee for Major League Baseball.

"When Stan and I began talking," Schuerholz said, "he asked me to recommend potential general managers because he intended to keep

It Started in Milwaukee

Bill Bartholomay has more longevity with the Braves than any other executive. He became chairman of the Milwaukee Braves in 1962 and convinced the board of directors to relocate to Atlanta four years later.

A former director and shareholder with the Chicago White Sox, Bartholomay was chairman of the Atlanta Braves board of directors from 1966 to 2003, when he became chairman emeritus and chairman of the team's executive committee.

He served as a member of the Major League Baseball Executive Council and its financial and legislative committees. He has also chaired MLB's equal opportunity and ownership committees.

A director, trustee, or officer of numerous civic and business organizations, Bartholomay was inducted into the Braves Hall of Fame at Turner Field in 2002.

Bobby in the dugout. I thought that was a wise thing to do based upon my admiration and high regard for Bobby.

"Fast forward a couple of weeks and Stan offered me the job. He asked me again how I felt about Bobby managing the team and I said, 'I don't think I could consider this job without Bobby Cox in the dugout.' That's how highly I regarded the man. We started off on that basis and had a great 17-year partnership."

Most outsiders thought Schuerholz would never leave Kansas City, where he had worked in the front office for 23 seasons, but ownership changes with the Royals created unexpected tensions for the executive. But a different set of problems awaited his arrival in Atlanta.

"I had to somehow get rid of the losing mentality the organization suffered from," he said. "I had to defeat and eradicate apathy. Before I took the job, I analyzed the team's strengths, assets, and deficiencies.

The decision I reached was made after analyzing all the things I'd found to be good, not so good, and even downright disappointing about the Braves.

"I knew we had a manager who was absolutely in lockstep with me and with the kind of team we wanted to create. But I wanted to create the same kind of administrative organization. That was my vision—to create a world championship organization, top to bottom."

Even the concessions needed to be improved. Hot dogs were not supposed to be gray and cold.

"Some of my friends thought I was crazy to come to Atlanta," said Schuerholz, remembering the massive overhaul required both on and off the field. "But I knew Bobby and Paul Snyder had put together a robust minor league system and brought some good young arms to the Braves. I also noticed that when those young pitchers would make a good pitch, balls would go through legs, balls were thrown into the stands, and there were a lot more bad hops than good hops.

"The first thing I did was to improve the infield itself. I had heard from a number of general managers that it was far from a major league caliber playing surface. I hired Ed Mangan to be chief groundskeeper and then went out and signed three free agent infielders: Terry Pendleton, a third baseman who won a batting title and an MVP award in his first year with us; Rafael Belliard, who couldn't hit much but caught everything at shortstop; and Sid Bream, who never let anything get by at first base."

The Pendleton signing drew the ire of Furman Bisher, sports editor of the *Atlanta Journal*. He suggested in print that Schuerholz should be drawn and quartered, among other unpleasant things.

"He was our first and harshest critic when we signed Terry," Schuerholz said years later. "He finally began to cut me some slack after about 13 straight division titles."

The outspoken Bisher, a proud man who hated to admit defeat, eventually apologized for lambasting the general manager in print. He wrote, "You must keep this in mind: never sell Schuerholz short. Never."

Along with catcher Mike Heath and relief pitcher Juan Berenguer, also signed as free agents, the Braves had many new faces on the first day of 1991 spring training. But the biggest new face belonged to the new GM.

"Nobody knew John Schuerholz very well," said broadcaster Pete Van Wieren, "and nobody knew (assistant GM) Dean Taylor very well. We were all tiptoeing—John was too. Everybody was waiting to see how other people responded to certain situations. Bobby was careful what he said because he didn't want to upset Schuerholz and John was careful what he said because he didn't want to upset Bobby."

It didn't take long for the players, coaches, and manager to stop walking on eggshells. For his part, Schuerholz was still reshaping his roster.

Articulate, affable, and conservative, John Schuerholz was also a shrewd general manager who often guessed right in making player transactions.

AP Photo/Rogelio Solis

"We shared our spring training complex in West Palm Beach with the Montreal Expos," he said. "When they decided Otis Nixon wasn't going to be in their plans, we made a deal for him. We gave them a minor league catcher named Jimmy Kremers and put Otis in center field. So our defense got dramatically better from the time I took the job until we left Florida."

The revived defense made a huge difference in the morale and performance of Atlanta pitchers.

According to Schuerholz, "With more confidence in the men behind them, our pitchers gave us a chance to win every night. Although we were nine-and-a-half games back at the All-Star break, we played well down the stretch and finished with 94 wins—good enough to win the National League West by one game."

The first team in baseball history to finish first after posting the worst record in the majors the previous season, the Braves quickly erased the memory of seven straight losing seasons and attendance of under a million per year.

The streak was on, though neither Schuerholz nor anyone else realized it at the time. "We never dreamed it would happen this quickly," he said during the euphoria of the obligatory champagne party, "but since it has, it's my job to make sure we stay on top."

Invariably polished, professional, and reserved, Schuerholz finally succumbed to the party atmosphere he created. As the Atlanta team plane winged its way toward Minnesota for the 1991 World Series, he actually danced in the aisle with rap-loving reliever Marvin Freeman.

The general manager preferred the street corner harmony of doo wop music but also found golf a great stress reliever. An annual team spring training outing quickly picked up the initials of "SWT," short for Schuerholz Wins Tournament.

"When the outcome of the SWT event no longer lived up to its initials," he said, "someone must have had real good job security because my team started losing. It went the way of all good ideas. But it was always a fun time. It was all about fostering close personal relationships with the people you work with every day, you grind with every day, and you're shoulder-to-shoulder with every day."

Schuerholz gave his blessing to golf-loving pitchers Greg Maddux, Tom Glavine, and John Smoltz, who seemed to spend every free minute either on the links or planning their next visit. "Any time you can foster a bonding of relationships and personalities, and get them to spend more time with each other, the better it gets," he said.

Although Maddux did not arrive in Atlanta until 1993, Glavine and Smoltz were mainstays of the pitching staff that allowed the Braves to become the first team in National League history to vault from last place one year to first place the next. In fact, had Minnesota not ended a scoreless tie with a tenth-inning run in the seventh game of the World Series, the Braves might have become world champions.

John Schuerholz, the creator of that cast, sat on the edge of his seat as five of the games—including the 1–0 finale—were decided by one run.

"It was the most exciting World Series I've ever been involved in," he said. "Obviously, I'd rather win than play well and lose. But I remind people that we were the outdoor world champions that year. Unfortunately, four of those games were played inside the Metrodome."

With the decibel levels and a sea of white handkerchiefs on their side, the Twins made history repeat: in 1987, against the favored St. Louis Cardinals, the home team also won all of its games—making Minnesota's home-field advantage tip the scales in its favor.

Unlike the '91 Braves, the Twins wouldn't make a return appearance. But Game Seven starter Jack Morris would; he signed with the Toronto Blue Jays as a free agent and came back to face the Braves again when the Jays won the American League pennant in 1992.

In the meantime, Atlanta's arms kept the team on top in the National League.

Thanks primarily to the prowess of their pitchers, the Braves duplicated their 1991 margin by finishing first by a single game in two more seasons: 1993 and 2000. Those races were just as nerve-wracking—not only for players and fans but for the GM who put those clubs together.

"The '93 race was incredibly stimulating," Schuerholz admitted. "It was our last year in the National League West. We made up substantial ground on San Francisco before finally winning on the last day of the season. The two biggest factors were signing Greg Maddux as a free agent and trading for Fred McGriff in July. Looking back, it's fair to say that Maddux and Pendleton were my best free agent acquisitions and McGriff was the most significant player obtained in a trade."

After debating whether to sign Maddux or Barry Bonds, who both hit free agency after the 1992 season, the pitcher won out.

"Greg was the most intelligent pitcher I've ever been around," Schuerholz wrote in his book *Built to Win*. "He would find a way to succeed. Greg went about pitching as if it were a chess match, crafting sequences of pitches and locations tailored for each hitter to set up an out pitch. Greg could hit the target more consistently than any pitcher I had ever seen."

He cited one game where Maddux beat the Yankees by fanning 11, walking none, and throwing fewer than 100 pitches. Ironically, Maddux had spurned a sweeter offer from the Yankees because he preferred to stay in the National League, felt more comfortable relocating to the South than the Northeast, and thought he could earn a World Series ring sooner in Atlanta. Three years later, he did.

Maddux was already an Atlanta mainstay in mid-July when Schuerholz sent three minor leaguers to San Diego for McGriff, who homered in his first game and never stopped hitting. "He was a great hitter, a wonderful asset, and a beautiful man," the GM said of the first baseman. "I am proud and honored to have been the general manager who was able to acquire a guy of that caliber, not only as a player but as a human being, and to have him wear our uniform and represent our organization in such fine fashion."

Led by McGriff and Maddux, who both started their Braves careers in 1993, Atlanta won 104 games, one more than the Giants, in the last true pennant race. Just three years after the Braves became the only team in the majors to miss the million mark in attendance, the once-moribund ballclub drew 3,884,720.

Slick Dealer

Other general managers were wary of trading with John Schuerholz. "John is one of my idols but he's shrewd," said Walt Jockety, who served as GM in St. Louis before moving to Cincinnati. "I've watched how he's operated over the years and no general manager has had the success that he's had. But you've got to be a little cautious going into a deal with him because you know he's had so many great deals. The thing I like about him is that he's right up front. A lot of guys talk and try to do different things but I prefer to deal straight, right up front. That's the way John operates."

San Francisco drew well also but their fans weren't happy at the sudden end to their season. After Giants fans complained that their team should have proceeded into postseason play, baseball introduced the three-division format that included the wildcard (which the Giants would have won had it existed in 1993).

Even with the new alignment, which moved them from the NL West to the NL East, the Braves made a habit of playing deep into October, winning more pennants during the '90s than any other team. Their best year was 1995, when Chipper Jones was a rookie. They won their first NL East title easily, finishing with a 21-game margin, and went on to beat the Colorado Rockies in the Division Series, the Cincinnati Reds in the Championship Series, and the Cleveland Indians in the World Series.

"It was a very complementary team, a team that was well-balanced, and a team that had the pitching, offense, and defense that were always a hallmark of Bobby's teams," Schuerholz said. "The players came through when we had to win games and win series. They were relentless and consistent in coming up big at the right time."

Jones, drafted and signed as a shortstop when Cox was still general manager of the Braves, was supposed to make his major league debut in 1994 but tore up his knee during spring training. "He was a big, strong,

---

"Team of the '90s"

According to Ron Gant, who played for both bad and good Atlanta teams, "The Braves were definitely the Team of the '90s. Most people in baseball will tell you that one of the hardest things to do is put together a winning ballclub and see that success continue for a long period of time. Look at teams like the Marlins and other teams that have won the World Series and are then dismantled in the next year or two. For me, the Braves were definitely the Team of the '90s."

---

athletic guy who had put up big numbers in the minor leagues, just bursting through the roof," said Schuerholz of Jones. "Bobby believed Chipper could play anywhere. He had good hands, a strong arm, and was a smart player who knew how to play hitters well. As he continued to grow and get bigger, we felt he was going to be a power hitter. We never thought he'd hit 45 home runs in a season but he was a hard worker who was determined and knowledgeable. He was a thinker who had good mechanics from both sides of the plate."

Though still in the minors for the first three years of Atlanta's title streak, Jones wasted little time in becoming the face of the franchise, as Dale Murphy was before him. Like Tony Gwynn and Cal Ripken Jr., Jones wound up playing his entire career with one team.

"That happened because Chipper wanted it to happen," Schuerholz said in retrospect. "It's a two-way street. You've got to have a player who cares so much to remain in the organization that signed him. He has to tell his representatives, 'I want to remain a Brave for my career. Get the best deal you can make but get it done.'"

Chipper, McGriff, and rookie Andruw Jones gave the Braves three solid sluggers that carried them into the 1996 World Series, which the Yankees won after losing the first two games at home. Though determined to return in '97, Atlanta encountered the enormous strike zone of portly umpire Eric Gregg in Game Five of the NL Championship Series.

"McGriff was 6'5" tall and had the wingspan of a giant condor," Schuerholz said with a grimace. "He had a long bat in his hands but couldn't reach pitches that were being called strikes."

Livan Hernandez ended with up with 15 strikeouts, an NLCS record, and a 2–1 win over Maddux. The Marlins, nine games behind Atlanta during the 162-game season, went to the World Series as the first wild-card team to win a pennant.

The Braves wouldn't return to the Fall Classic until 1999 but Schuerholz never quit trying. "We picked the right players," he said of his scouts. "The front office people did a great job analyzing them."

He said baseball ability was the primary consideration but not the only one. "We also considered what a person's character was, what his makeup was," said the longtime executive. "We wanted to know his aptitude, his competitive spirit, his personality, and whether he was a team player. We learned that the highest-paid players don't always guarantee a winning season."

Having the Three Horsemen of the Hall of Fame on the mound helped the Braves a lot, said Schuerholz, who retained the GM title before becoming president of the team in 2007. Maddux, Glavine, and Smoltz combined for six Cy Young Awards and often helped the Braves lead the league in earned run average.

"Our scouts deserve a lot of credit for getting the guys, drafting them, and signing them," Schuerholz said. "So do our minor league pitching coaches, which Leo Mazzone was before he became our major league coach. He did a lot of things to help our young pitchers get refined, polished, and finished up and kept that string going for a long time."

Cox, who made three trades with Schuerholz when they were general managers, got the most credit from the executive.

"The most important relationship that exists in baseball is the one between the manager and general manager," he said. "There were very few times we disagreed on player decisions but there were times we both had to defer to the other's opinion. The vast majority of the time, however, we were on the same page.

"I can't say enough about Bobby. He had such admiration for the people who put on the uniform and were able to perform at the major-league level. He treated people with honor and respect and had high expectations of individuals and teams. That was very clear to the people involved with him and people played up to those standards.

"Bobby had great passion for the game but mostly passion for his team winning. He wanted umpires to make the right calls on behalf of his beloved Braves and that's why he went out to argue so often. If they gave a trophy for ejections, he'd have it locked up. I have no doubt that

---

Kind Words

Former Mets general manager Omar Minaya was dutifully impressed by The Streak. "If they were to give a Pulitzer Prize in baseball, Bobby Cox and John Schuerholz and their whole organization deserve it," he said. "What they've done is more than impressive."

---

there will ever be a human being who sets foot on this planet that has a chance to take that trophy away from Bobby Cox."

The 14-year run was possible because Bobby was so adaptable. Playing the hand Schuerholz gave him, he won with different types of teams: some dominated by pitching, some loaded with sluggers, others with speed merchants, and still others with veterans. One year, the Braves even used 18 rookies but still managed to win.

Making those changes was not easy, according to Schuerholz.

"When you sit in the chair of the GM," he said, "you're going to face things that are uncomfortable, that are disquieting to you, that make you feel bad because of the personal relationships you have with the players, plus their excellence and productivity in your uniform.

But you have the responsibility of building the next best team, not reflecting back on the previous best team."

Players who failed to fit into the businesslike clubhouse had to be disciplined, if not dealt. John Rocker, a power-pitching closer of considerable ability, finally talked his way off the team.

"John had a cannon for an arm," said Schuerholz. "He was as dominant and intimidating as any lefthanded pitcher we ever had in Atlanta. I still see the pitch he threw at Mark Grace, coming right at his neck at about 100 miles per hour. His helmet went one way, his body went another, and his bat went flying up into the air. He landed with a thud as the ball rocketed into the catcher's mitt.

"John was not afraid to pitch inside. He was a real asset to our organization but got off-track after he said some controversial things to

Sports Illustrated after the 1999 season. He was never able to get it back and we traded him to Cleveland."

Not all trades—made by John Schuerholz or any other general manager—are good ones.

Seeking to fill the lineup void created when slugging right fielder Gary Sheffield left via free agency, Schuerholz set his sights on J. D. Drew. But the St. Louis Cardinals wouldn't move him without receiving Adam Wainwright—Atlanta's top pitching prospect—in return.

"In retrospect, the Wainwright deal was a bad one," Schuerholz admitted, "but we used the same processes and evaluations that I've used in every trade I ever made—the good ones and the bad ones. I asked the opinions of the people responsible for making evaluations, analysis, projections, and judgments on players and trades. Of the half-dozen people in the room before we made the Wainwright deal, only one said 'Don't do it.'

"It was also tough to trade Charlie Leibrandt and Kevin Millwood, who had been solid starting pitchers for us, to accommodate our budget needs. Only a handful of organizations had unlimited budgets but they didn't win as many games as we did. We managed our budget, made our decisions appropriately, brought in players that helped us win, and offloaded players who were making more money than we could afford to keep on our payroll."

Keeping Maddux, Glavine, and Smoltz as long as he did was a tribute to the GM's creativity in balancing the budget. When he traded David Justice and Marquis Grissom to Cleveland on March 25, 1997, for example, Schuerholz told stunned media members that he needed to free up money for the pitchers. Fans also howled when he traded Kevin Millwood to Philadelphia for little-known backup catcher Johnny Estrada, who turned into an NL All-Star in 2004 after the Braves lost Javy Lopez to free agency.

The lure of free agent dollars persuaded several Atlanta icons to sign elsewhere. Losing Glavine was especially tough for Schuerholz.

"That was really tough," he said of Glavine's wrenching decision to sign with the rival New York Mets. "It was one of the least favorite times in my life. But it was part of the business of baseball.

"It was tough for Tom and it was tough for us. We were hoping he'd stay but it didn't happen. He went to New York and had four good years under his belt. But we were concerned about his age. You've got a key guy who was a winner, a leader, and had the Braves in his heart. But he wanted more money than we thought we could afford and it didn't work out."

Although Maddux, Glavine, and Smoltz all rode free agency out of Atlanta, Chipper Jones stayed put. He spent his entire career with the Braves.

"We were lucky we were able to keep Chipper Jones for his entire career," Schuerholz said. "It happened because Chipper wanted it to happen. It's a two-way street. You've got to have a player who cares so

Big Shoes to Fill

Terry McGuirk began his association with the Braves shortly after joining Turner Broadcasting System as an account executive for WTCG. Instrumental in the launch of the TBS SuperStation, which beamed Braves games across the country by satellite, McGuirk later became president of Turner Sports. When TBS merged with Time Warner in 1996, he succeeded Ted Turner as chairman, president, and chief executive officer. In 2001, he became CEO of three Atlanta sports teams owned by the broadcast giant: the Braves, the Hawks (basketball), and the Thrashers (hockey).

As chairman and president of the Braves, a role he assumed after the 2003 season, he had oversight of all team operations, including trades, team operations, and Turner Field. The Bayshore, New York, native sits on the board of directors of several corporations and educational institutions.

much to stay in the organization he signed with that he tells his representatives, 'I want to remain with the Braves for my career. Get it done and makes the best deal you can.' It has to come from the player."

During their 14-year title run, the Atlanta Braves tried to maintain consistency—a difficult feat in an era of free agency and salary arbitration. The team had the same manager and pitching coach throughout the streak but only one player stayed from start to finish.

Glavine was there at the start and Jones was there at the end but Smoltz was the only athlete who rode out the whole streak. Even Maddux couldn't say that.

With Cox already enshrined in Cooperstown, Schuerholz could soon follow. They finished first in all but the last three seasons of their 17-year partnership. They consulted daily on player personnel decisions and then sought final approval from ownership, though the purse strings got tighter after Turner left.

Every GM wins some and loses some when it comes to transactions. Schuerholz, better than most of his brethren, hit home runs with the following moves:

- Jimmy Kremers and Keith Morrison to Montreal for Otis Nixon, 1991
- Joe Roa and Tony Castillo to the New York Mets for Alejandro Pena, 1991
- Donnie Elliott, Vince Moore, and Melvin Nieves to San Diego for Fred McGriff, 1993
- Roberto Kelly, Tony Tarasco, and Esteban Yan to Montreal for Marquis Grissom, 1995
- Denny Neagle, Rob Bell, and Michael Tucker to Cincinnati for Bret Boone and Mike Remlinger, 1998
- Damian Moss and Merkin Valdez to San Francisco for Russ Ortiz, 2002
- Brian Jordan, Odalis Perez, and Andrew Brown to Los Angeles for Gary Sheffield, 2002

- Juan Cruz, Dan Meyer, and Charles Thomas to Oakland for Tim Hudson, 2004

Since even the best batter has a bad day, Schuerholz also struck out on occasion:

- David Justice and Marquis Grissom to Cleveland for Kenny Lofton and Alan Embree, 1997
- Jermaine Dye and Jamie Walker to Kansas City for Michael Tucker and Keith Lockhart, 1997
- Ryan Klesko, Bret Boone, and Jason Shiell to San Diego for Wally Joyner, Reggie Sanders, and Quilvio Veras, 1999
- Adam Wainwright, Ray King, and Jason Marquis to St. Louis for J. D. Drew and Eli Marrero, 2003

Never afraid to make a move, Schuerholz always acted in the best interests of the team. Although the outcome of a trade is often hard to predict, he pulled the trigger with confidence time after time. If a deal turned out to be a clunker, it didn't stop Schuerholz from clamboring back into the saddle and making another swap.

Key Players: A GM's Take

During his long tenure as general manager of the Atlanta Braves, John Schuerholz added, subtracted, and observed many players. His comments on some of them follow:

Bret Boone—"Dynamic player. Good second baseman from the great Boone family. I had his dad in KC as a catcher with all that great young pitching. Bret was a hard-nosed player and good offensive player who improved himself defensively."

Sid Bream—"We had to outbid San Diego to sign him to a three-year contract for $5.6 million. He had some of the same positive characteristics as Terry Pendleton. And he played for a winning team."

Vinny Castilla—"He was in the organization as a shortstop when I got here. We lost him to Colorado in the expansion draft. He played very well for the Rockies and earned his buck."

Julio Franco—"In 2001, we needed another solid hitter to bolster our playoff push. It would be safe to assume no other team ever reached into the Mexican league for a 43-year-old first baseman and pinch-hitter. He had played for seven different teams and then played in Japan before going to Mexico. Plus his .427 average for the Mexico City Tigres was leading the league. We needed to sign him before the August 31 date for freezing playoff rosters but his team was eliminated from the playoffs two days before that and we rushed him to Atlanta. Ned Yost, one of our coaches, saw him put on his uniform and said he was a strong-looking dude, maybe in better shape than anyone else in the clubhouse. Julio hit .300 for the final month that season and continued to defy Father Time with solid production."

Andres Galarraga—"The Big Cat, a gentle giant. Power beyond measure. Delightful man. Fought and survived cancer. Another man who made our organization better and stronger because he was in it."

Mike Hampton—"Small but strongly-built left-handed pitcher. Great athlete, great competitor. I felt he had a chance to win every time he took the mound. Then he started having some physical problems and wasn't the same. At full strength, he was as tough a cookie on the mound that we have ever sent out there."

Andruw Jones—"A remarkable two-way player, both offense and defense. A Gold Glove center fielder almost every year. He could go after balls. He could play shallow. He could run into the gap. He could throw guys out. At the plate, he would hit home runs, doubles, and triples and steal bases. He was a really dynamic player who made a big impact on our organization for the years he was with us."

Brian Jordan—"Great athlete. Two-sport star. NFL player. Homeboy for me since we're both Baltimoreans. Great guy. Trading Brian was a tough thing for me. I always had great admiration for his winning spirit."

Charlie Leibrandt—"Acquired by Atlanta for Gerald Perry, he was a veteran left-handed starter who became a free agent after the 1990 season and re-signed with the Braves for $8 million over three years. He pitched well before we traded him to Texas to make room for Greg Maddux in 1993."

Kerry Ligtenberg—"Recommended by Greg Olson, who used to catch for us. He said, 'We've got a guy up here pitching in a league I coach in. He can really pitch.' I said, 'We'll take him on your recommendation. What do you want?' He said, 'We're short on bats and balls.' So I sent a couple of dozen bats and balls up to him and that was the acquisition cost for Kerry Ligtenberg."

Javy Lopez—"He was a big, strong guy who looked like Adonis—a movie star in a baseball uniform. When he connected with the ball, it went a long way. He really made himself into a good hitter. The year he hit 43 home runs epitomized the combination of his power and hitting ability."

Greg Maddux—"I would put him in the category of Sandy Koufax and Bob Gibson, different style pitchers who had the same bottom line of consistent excellence and success. Greg was a remarkable pitcher."

Otis Nixon—"I had a great relationship with Otis. His teammates loved him. When he was suspended for substance abuse during the last month of the 1991 season, I was crestfallen for him as well as our organization. It was a damaging blow from which we couldn't recover and did hurt us a great deal."

Greg Olson—"Baseball is a tough game, a physical game. When guys go after things hard, they put themselves at risk of suffering injuries. They play to win, they play at all costs. That's why you like them. They're championship-caliber players who get hurt sometimes. That's what happened to Oley."

Deion Sanders—"The second-best athlete I've ever seen in a baseball uniform behind Bo Jackson. A heck of a baseball player. An exciting player and dynamic game-winner with his bat or his legs."

Gary Sheffield—"Great talent. A stick of dynamite guy. He came over to us and handled himself in a completely professional manner from the first day he stepped onto the field until the last. He was a real pro, an exciting player, and contributed a lot to our organization."

Lonnie Smith—"A lot of people blame Lonnie's baserunning for costing us the seventh game of the 1991 World Series. But playing in the Metrodome, you couldn't hear yourself think. You certainly couldn't hear the third-base coach. Plus the fans were waving those white hankies. It was hard to see, it was hard to hear. The lights were designed for football games and were blinding the outfielders. And it was hard to see the ball against that goofy dome. When the ball came down on the artificial turf, it would bounce like a ping-pong ball. Lonnie was on base with nobody out but our third, fourth, and fifth-place hitters couldn't knock him in. That was a rough environment to play in. So I give Lonnie a pass on that (Minnesota won, 1–0, in 10 innings)."

More familiar with suspenders than spikes, John Schuerholz was the conductor whose baton never missed a beat, changing the cast continually as age, injuries, trades, player development, payroll limitations, and the uneven interleague scheduling dictated.

Such a successful and prolonged juggling act is not likely to be repeated. "I don't think it will ever be accomplished in any of the sports that exist on Planet Earth today," Schuerholz said. "There are just too many variables."

After the 2014 San Francisco Giants won their third world championship in five years, brother Jerry Schuerholz called John from Baltimore to say what a difficult feat that was.

A day later, after thinking about his comment, Jerry sent John an email that said, "I know what the odds are against winning the World Series three times in five years but the odds of winning 14 consecutive division titles are far greater."

During that streak, the Braves had three straight 100-win campaigns, a feat matched previously only by the Philadelphia Athletics of 1929–31, the St. Louis Cardinals of 1942–44, and the Baltimore Orioles of 1969–71. No, the Yankees of Babe Ruth and Lou Gehrig vintage never did it.

What the Atlanta Braves did from 1991 to 2005 was so remarkable that it could become the team equivalent of Cal Ripken's consecutive games streak or Joe DiMaggio's hitting streak.

John Schuerholz, the architect, certainly thinks so.

Like a proud papa whose son was just named magna cum laude, Schuerholz fielded similar sentiments from both constituents and opponents. "We heard it from our fans, we heard it from the media, and we heard it from visiting players and management people who said, 'You just can't do that. It's impossible in this day and age.' We're very proud of that."

Schuerholz was not only the Executive of the Year in 1991 but the executive of the decade. "John Schuerholz was the best general manager of our time," said Jim Bowden, who served the Reds and Nationals in the same role. "If we had a GM award, it should be named the John Schuerholz Award."

Mouth of the South

According to John Schuerholz, Ted Turner was an enigmatic but imaginative boss.

"Working for him was stimulating," said Schuerholz of Turner, who owned the Braves from 1976 to 1996. "He was a brilliant man with vision and ideas.

"If you were drawing a cartoon, Ted would be sitting behind a desk and talking to you when a bubble would pop up with another idea. His eyes would flash and he would smile.

"You could almost see him intellectualizing, thinking, and going through the process of listening to what you're saying, hearing your plans, and wrapping his brain around them. It was a great time. He was a great boss who became a good friend, including Karen and me in our private vacation time together. It was a real joy, a real honor, and a real pleasure to work for him as long as I did."

Turner, a 37-year-old Cincinnati native who had inherited his father's billboard advertising empire, bought the Braves for $10 million when he needed programming for WTBS, a local Atlanta channel that soon became the first superstation, carrying games to all fifty states. Since the team was terrible, broadcasters Pete Van Wieren, Skip Caray, and Ernie Johnson became more popular than the players.

Anxious to boost attendance and keep the franchise in Atlanta, Turner followed Bill Veeck's adage that said, "Give 'em a show if you can't give 'em a ballclub." A variety of zany promotions, including Headlock & Wedlock Night and a wet T-shirt contest won by a minister's daughter, didn't help. Nor did Turner's ill-fated decision to make himself manager for a day (before he was bounced by baseball commissioner Bowie Kuhn).

He also found time to win the America's Cup yacht race in 1977, launch Cable News Network three years later, and marry actress Jane Fonda in 1991. The Braves' title streak outlasted the marriage, which ended in 2001.

Ted and Jane's wedding, at his 8,100-acre Florida estate, came four days before Christmas, on the exact same day the Soviet Union collapsed. "Today's my birthday," Jane told friends, "and I'm getting Ted Turner."

Variously called Captain Outrageous or Mouth of the South, the impulsive Turner was never a wallflower. On his desk was a sign that said LEAD, FOLLOW, or GET THE HELL OUT THE WAY.

Only when he learned to delegate did he reverse his baseball fortunes; he let his baseball people run the team without interference—partially because his assorted other ventures were demanding more of his personal attention.

"Ted left it all up to Stan Kasten and Terry McGuirk to get my contract done," John Schuerholz said of his negotiations to join the team. "Hiring a new GM was their job and Ted chose to let them do it.

"He was a man who knew about competing. He didn't necessarily know about baseball but was willing to let others do the things that needed to get done."

Kasten, an attorney who first met Turner at an Atlanta Hawks basketball game, was the one who told Ted he had to change his approach. "I told him we had to stop with the free agents and start building from within," he said. "He said, 'Stan, just do it. I'm so tired of not winning that you should do whatever it takes.'"

Although he took a back seat in baseball operations, Turner still had a front row seat at the ballpark. Ted and Jane became ballpark regulars, often sharing their front row box with former president Jimmy Carter, joining other fans in chanting and chopping, and trying to stay awake during late-starting World Series games.

With the billionaire philanthropist as sole owner, the Braves could afford to pay their players well and acquire new ones on the free agent market. But that started to change in 1996, when Turner Broadcasting merged with Time Warner. Turner became vice chairman of the board, running cable and production operations for the new company, but his role with the Braves diminished. Terry McGuirk became the team's president and chairman of the board.

Off the field, Turner's star also dimmed. He couldn't stop the sale of the Los Angeles Dodgers to rival media magnate Rupert Murdoch, whose FOX network got regional and national deals that hurt TBS. He later failed in an attempt to succeed Steve Case, whom he had helped depose, as chairman of the struggling AOL Time Warner. With both his pride and his pocketbook wounded, Turner resigned as vice chairman in 2003.

In 2015, eighteen years after the opening of Turner Field, the Atlanta City Council considered naming a street in his honor. The owner of the largest private buffalo herd in the United States, he sponsored numerous environmental initiatives and gave $1 billion to the United Nations. The former owner of the Atlanta Hawks remained chairman of the Turner Foundation and Turner Enterprises, founder of the Ted's Montana Grill restaurant chain, and a member of the Braves' board of directors.

2
THE ENGINEER: BOBBY COX

CONNIE MACK WON 3,731 games. John McGraw brought his New York Giants home first 10 times and second 11 times. Casey Stengel won 10 pennants in 12 years with the Yankees, the same team Joe Torre brought to the postseason 12 straight times, with six pennants and four world championships.

But none of those managers finished in first place 14 years in a row.

Bobby Cox did that, guiding his Atlanta Braves to more consecutive regular season championships than anyone else in the history of professional sports. In fact, nobody else has come close.

No other club has even reached double digits. The Yankees of 1998–2006 rank a distant second in baseball with nine straight, while the Boston Celtics, Los Angeles Lakers, and Colorado Avalanche managed nine apiece in winter sports.

Only one other major league team has even reached double digits in consecutive playoff outings: the Yankees, with the generous boost of the wildcard, had 11 in a row from 1995 to 2005.

The Braves won because they had Bobby Cox, a director with the tenacity, talent, and fortitude of Steven Spielberg. When he talked, people listened (with the possible exception of the umpires).

It didn't matter whether the Braves played in the National League West, as they did when the streak started in 1991, or the National League East, which they dominated after realignment in 1994.

In every complete season from 1991 through 2005, Cox and the Braves finished first (a strike stopped the '94 campaign in August).

An Ump Who Liked Bobby

"Bobby Cox was ejected more than any manager in major-league history. But maybe that's because he managed for so many years.

Bobby was a great old-school manager. Like Ralph Houk, he was a guy who felt that today's game is today and yesterday's was yesterday. There was never any carryover.

"I knew Cox since he was a coach with the Yankees and later during his tenure with the Toronto Blue Jays. He had that great run with the Braves, when he and general manager John Schuerholz put together 14 straight division titles. That was unheard of and unparalleled.

"Bobby Cox deserves to be in the Hall of Fame as much as Babe Ruth does. He was a baseball lifer who deserved all his accolades. Perhaps I'm talking from a stump that's a little taller and a little long of tooth but I appreciated and respected those tough old managers very much. They were what baseball was all about."

—Al Clark
MLB UMPIRE 1976–2001
IN *Called Out But Safe: A Baseball Umpire's Journey*

Like a master magician, Cox pulled rabbits out of the hat, sawed opposing teams in half, and managed to elevate himself, his coaches, and his players above the fray.

He won with fast teams, slow teams, speed teams, power teams, veteran teams, and even one injury-riddled team that required the influx and influence of 18 rookies. Ability mattered more than experience, with Andruw Jones and Rafael Furcal shining examples of players promoted to the varsity with resumes shorter than Sarah Palin's.

When Bobby banned music in the clubhouse, a rarity in baseball, he said he was doing it for several reasons: to create a businesslike

Illustration by Ronnie Joyner.

atmosphere, to allow his players to concentrate on baseball, and to prevent arguments. There were no Latin quarters or neighborhood hangouts in his clubhouses. Everybody was treated equally.

Obviously, the system worked.

A third baseman who signed with the Dodgers but played for the Yankees, Cox found his calling after the Yankees gave him a chance to manage in the minors in 1971. Six years later, he served as first base coach of a world championship team in the Bronx and attracted the attention of Ted Turner.

Even though they had a few good men in Dale Murphy, free agent signee Gary Matthews, and future Hall of Famer Phil Niekro, the Bad News Braves of 1978 wouldn't have won for Houdini. After four years of poor play and poor attendance, the impatient Turner canned Cox in favor of Joe Torre. The former Braves catcher immediately won a division title with the team he inherited.

Cox did not sit still. He crossed league lines again, landing in Toronto as manager of a Blue Jays team he would take to the 1985 American League Championship Series. Turner, who had second-guessed his initial decision to dump the dedicated young manager, then brought him back to Atlanta as *general* manager—and gave him ample money to rebuild the moribund minor league system.

With pitching his proclaimed priority, Cox acquired future Hall of Famers Tom Glavine via the amateur draft and John Smoltz via a trade for Doyle Alexander, Atlanta's top pitcher at the time.

Working in concert with scouting director Paul Snyder, Cox also scoured the amateur ranks for infielders Mark Lemke and Jeff Blauser, slugging outfielder David Justice, and left-handed pitcher Steve Avery—all key players in the worst-to-first team that started the 14-year title streak in 1991.

By then, Cox was managing the Braves again. He had returned to the dugout before the 1990 All-Star break at the behest of team president

Tall Paul

Paul Snyder was one of the true unsung heroes of The Streak. A player, coach, and scout for the Braves starting in 1958, he was regarded as one of the best talent evaluators in the major leagues. Snyder was inducted into the Braves Hall of Fame in 2005.

Stan Kasten, who vetoed Russ Nixon as field general while allowing Cox to keep both jobs for the rest of that season.

According to Terry McGuirk, who later became the team's chief executive officer, "Bobby might have showed his best talent as GM. He took an absolutely bankrupt situation and put together the talent, the coaches, the scouts, and the support system. But I don't think he was ever really comfortable in the role."

For the last half of the 1990 campaign, Cox kept his foot in the front office but his heart in the dugout. He even promoted an innovative but outspoken minor league pitching coach named Leo Mazzone.

Plagued by poor defense, the Braves didn't do any better for Bobby in 1990 than they did for him during his previous tenure. But that was before Kasten convinced John Schuerholz to leave the Kansas City Royals after the season.

The new GM rebuilt the infield, giving the young pitchers confidence that ground balls and pop-ups would become outs, and the Braves were on their way.

"My first taste of victory was the 1991 season," Cox said years later. "We had gone so bad for so many years. We improved our defense with Terry Pendleton, Sid Bream, and Rafael Belliard. Even though we were 10 games back at the All-Star break, we came back. It was the first time since 1982 our fans had anything to cheer about. They came out in droves. The city was completely energized. It was electric. It was the greatest experience."

The '91 Braves were the first team to reach the World Series just one season after posting the worst record in the major leagues. They won another pennant in '92 with a three-run rally in the last inning of the National League Championship Series. Then, after signing star pitcher Greg Maddux, they won 104 games, taking the 1993 NL West by one game over San Francisco in a title chase that went down to the final day. Two years later, Cox led the Braves to a world championship.

Having Maddux, Glavine, and Smoltz on the same staff helped; together with the Braves from 1993 to 2002, the threesome produced a staggering 648 victories—and would have won more if Smoltz had not spent three-and-a-half years as the closer.

"What made him a great manager was that he was so good at handling his players," Glavine said of Cox. "He was so good at getting the best and most out of his guys. He treated everybody with the utmost respect and made everybody understand that whether you were a superstar or the 25th man coming out of spring training, you were going to be at important piece of the puzzle. He made guys not only understand that but believe it.

"At one point people thought Bobby was digging his own grave by having three former managers (Jimy Williams, Don Baylor, and Pat Corrales) on the bench with him. But that's Bobby. He was comfortable in what he was doing. He wanted the best people around him to try and make the team as successful as he could. It turned out to be a pretty good formula."

In his book *Starting and Closing*, Smoltz also sang the praises of the pilot. "While Bobby helped lay the framework for our [14-year] run, he also deserves a ton of recognition for sustaining our run. You don't win any division for 14 years straight without finding ways to win games that you have no business winning, statistically speaking.

"Bobby's moves were always calculated, made with the intention of preserving a lead, preserving his athletes, or generating some offense when the run support well had run dry. He knew things the rest of us didn't know, saw things even the best in the game didn't see."

Thanks primarily to their future Hall of Famers, the 1998 Braves won 106 times, a franchise record, but Cox would add three more triple-digit seasons. The only previous pilot to post six 100-win seasons anywhere was Joe McCarthy, nicknamed "the push-button manager" because his Yankees seemed to win without much effort from the bench.

Cox worked hard, especially after the Braves lost Glavine and Maddux to free agency. Smoltz was actually the only player to share the entire 14-year run in uniform with Cox and Mazzone.

In 2005, the last year of the streak, the wily manager employed 18 rookies, with all but six making their major league debuts. Forced to fill in for injured regulars Chipper Jones and Johnny Estrada, plus ailing pitchers Tim Hudson, Mike Hampton, and John Thomson, Cox proved himself a master juggler. He still produced a 90-win season for the 14th time and finished first for the 15th straight time (counting his last year in Toronto but not counting the incomplete seasons of 1990 or 1994).

His teams won 2,504 games—fourth all-time among managers—in a 29-year career that stretched from 1978 to 2010. The Bobby Cox resume included 15 division titles, five pennants, two knee replacements (perhaps from making so many trips to the mound) and a world championship—not to mention a record 158 ejections.

"He was thrown out more than any manager but that's because he took the game to heart and stood up for his guys," said Fredi Gonzalez, who succeeded Cox as manager of the Braves after the 2010 campaign.

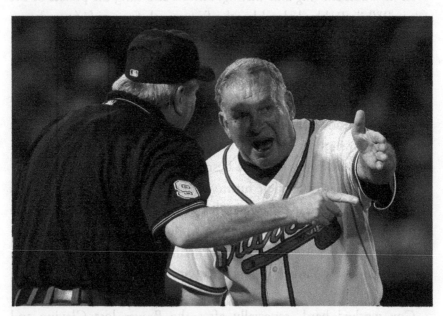

The cool composure of Bobby Cox often exploded when he argued with umpires. He was ejected more often than any other manager.

AP Photo/John Bazemore

"I grabbed him one night," said longtime Cox lieutenant Pat Corrales, a former manager himself. "I could see him starting to blow. So I grabbed him around the chest. He said, 'I'll fire you if you don't let me go.' I said, 'Then you're going to have to fire me because I'm not letting go.' I just hung on until I realized he wasn't going to do anything."

Another Cox coach, Ned Yost, told writer Jayson Stark that Cox had two personas. "He's the nicest guy in the world," he said. "Just don't get him mad at you. If he ever gets mad, he turns into Mike Tyson. He doesn't care who you are or what you are."

After Cox sprayed Jerry Crawford with tobacco juice during an argument, he always made it a point to take whatever he was chewing out of his mouth before going out to argue. "It just happened," said Crawford, "and he was upset about it and wanted to make sure it didn't happen again."

Although he argued with umpires often, Cox was a player's manager whose rules were simple: show up on time and play hard. It was not uncommon for stars of other teams to express a desire to play for him.

Because of rapid changes in baseball economics, Cox was handed a new deck of cards every spring. But he always managed to make the most of what he had. On the rare occasions when he found a joker in the deck, Cox cut ties quickly.

Players like Deion Sanders, Kenny Lofton, John Rocker, and Bret Boone did not fit the Cox formula of a businesslike clubhouse devoid

Series Boots

Bobby Cox, whose 158 ejections during the regular season may be an unreachable record, was also the only manager to be ejected from a World Series game more than once. He was kicked out of Game Three in 1992 for arguing a call on a checked swing and from Game Six of the 1996 Series over a stolen base safe call that went against the Braves.

of such distractions as the raucous rock music that permeates and often divides other locker rooms. Bobby Cox teams did not have cliques or controversies other than the usual moaning and groaning from players perplexed by his penchant for platooning.

Cox protected his players, never complaining about them publicly, and took the blame himself when things went badly.

When they did, however, even star players didn't escape the manager's scrutiny. In 1998, Cox replaced Andruw Jones in the middle of an inning after the star centerfielder made a halfhearted effort to catch a fly ball. The lesson, though embarrassing, was learned: Jones won 10 consecutive Gold Gloves and earned comparisons to Willie Mays for his spectacular defensive play.

"The greatest compliment I could ever give a manager is to say I would have loved playing for him," said Hall of Fame pitcher Don Sutton of Cox. "As much as any manager I've been around, Bobby had loyalty from his players and coaches—a commitment from every one of them to do the right thing. That's something very few managers can say."

The first man named Manager of the Year in both leagues, Cox won the official award from the Baseball Writers Association of America four times. When *The Sporting News* polled his peers, however, Cox won the honor six times—twice as often as anyone else.

His best performance might have come in 2004, when his Braves won 96 games—topping the division by 10 games— after losing Greg Maddux, Gary Sheffield, Javy Lopez, and Vinny Castilla to free agency and Marcus Giles and Horacio Ramirez to injury.

Before both he and Cox were inducted into the Baseball Hall of Fame in 2014, Tony La Russa recalled his initial impression of Bobby.

"When I was with the White Sox and Jim Leyland was one of my coaches, we used to face Billy Martin, Sparky Anderson, Earl Weaver, and Gene Mauch," he said. "But all of a sudden this new guy goes to Toronto and after a series or two, we looked at each other and said, 'Hey, this guy's pretty good.' It turned out to be Bobby Cox.

"In 1996, when I got to the National League for the first time, the Braves were the world champions and Bobby was on that incredible run of division titles. I had known him during the winter—he's a terrific guy, sociable and fun—and I was looking forward to saying hello when we went to play his team. I saw him standing at first base. I was expecting a big hug and a nice conversation. He waved but that was it.

"He made it real clear that it was his team against your team and there was a score. I've always felt that Bobby was the very best at sending the message that said, 'If I see you this winter or in the restaurant after a game, I'll say hello and ask how your family is and wish you well since you're in a different division.' But playing against him, he and his team competed and they were going to beat you."

Jeff Torborg, who managed three different teams against Cox, agreed. "What I liked about Bobby was that he was so consistent," said Torborg, a former catcher who served as pilot of the Mets, Expos, and Marlins. "No show, down to earth, very genuine.

"That streak (of 14 titles) was unbelievable. He called me one time, asking about somebody in the administrative level, and the next thing you know, we're trying to make a trade. But he wasn't going to give up one of those young pitchers if his life depended on it. Avery was the guy we thought might be available. No chance. When you think about what he did—how he set it up, then went down to the field to make it work—his career was just incredible."

Bobby Cox did more than push buttons; he had a gift for meshing many different personalities and persuading them to maximize their potential.

According to John Schuerholz, who succeeded Cox as general manager and retained the position throughout the 14-year run, "Bobby had such great talent: his instincts for dealing with people, his ability to communicate in his own inimitable fashion, plus the respect he has for the game and the players who play it at the highest of all levels. It's so clear and obvious to them that they gave back to him in double or triple measure the same amount of respect. He held them in such high

35

esteem, and expected so much of them. That was the attitude and professionalism he brought to the ballpark every day.

"I don't think anyone will ever win 14 consecutive titles again. I had the great pleasure of working side-by-side with him to marshal our plan and keep it in place. It's a remarkable feat no one will see in our sport or any other sport in our lifetime."

Bobby Cox spent 29 years as a manager and five as a general manager, mainly with the Braves, in his Hall of Fame career.

Photo by Bill Menzel.

3

THE FIREMAN: LEO MAZZONE

BEFORE BOBBY COX made him the pitching coach of the Atlanta Braves, Leo Mazzone was marooned in the minors.

Bobby must have seen something, as Mazzone, a career minor leaguer as player, coach, and manager, made such an impact in the majors that he could become the first pitching coach in the Baseball Hall of Fame.

He did it without benefit of a computer or even a notepad.

A disciple of Johnny Sain, another innovative coach whose unorthodox but time-tested theories ran counter to traditional baseball thinking, Mazzone managed to ride out the entire 14-year title run in Atlanta—even though the cast of characters changed constantly.

Mazzone's ties to Cox dated back to 1979, when the young manager—then in the first of two terms in Atlanta—brought the coach into spring camp as a batting practice pitcher for Dale Murphy, Bob Horner, and Chris Chambliss. "I remember watching 'Miracle on Ice' in Bobby's little office in West Palm Beach," Mazzone recalled. "I also remember the respect he showed for minor league coaches. He cared a lot about the coaches and managers in the farm system."

That feeling never wavered, even though Cox spent four years as manager of the Toronto Blue Jays after Ted Turner fired him as Braves manager in 1981. Five years later, the mercurial owner brought Cox back but kicked him upstairs.

"Bobby was general manager in 1986 when he called a meeting at Fulton County Stadium," said Mazzone. "He said he was going to turn an offense-oriented organization into a pitching one. He wanted to know who could take care of the pitchers. There were four or five minor league pitching coaches there and he let us all talk. I had a history of keeping arms healthy in the minor leagues so after I talked, Bobby said, 'Let's use Leo's program.'

"I had to shut a few people up but gladly did it. I had met Johnny Sain in 1979, my first year with the Braves organization, when he was in charge of all the minor league pitching. I figured if I'm going to improve my ability as pitching coach, why not do it with the guy who had the greatest track record in the history of baseball?

"Johnny took me under his wing. He had an RV that he parked at a campground in West Palm. Every night, I went over there, we'd have a little sip of vodka, he'd cook a meal for both of us, and we'd talk pitching for hours. He was so far ahead of his time and so advanced. He taught me a great deal about proper pitches and proper spins on the ball but also how to deal with management and some of the different things I was going to face down the road.

"A lot of people didn't like Johnny—they feared his knowledge. They knew he was smarter than anyone else in the room when he was talking about the game of baseball and especially the pitching aspect of it. I thought he was amazing; I wish I would have known all that when I was pitching in the minor leagues."

According to Mazzone, Sain had more success than any other pitching coach. "He had the most 20-game winners and went to the World Series with three or four different teams," he said of Sain. "Why would I not pick that man's brain and do everything I could to learn from him?"

The concept of throwing twice between starts, widely attributed to Mazzone, was actually started by Sain. "I got the idea from him," said Mazzone, a West Virginia native who spent much of his life in neighboring Maryland. "Under the four-man rotation, you would pitch, take a day off, throw on the side, take a day off, and then pitch. When the baseball world went to a five-man rotation, we had an extra day. I wanted to get my pitchers to get a better feel for the ball and to throw more often with less exertion. With that extra day, I was going to have them throw."

Hank Aaron, then Atlanta's farm director, gave Mazzone carte blanche. "He said, 'You take care of these pitchers, Leo, and I don't care how you do that.' Instead of taking the extra day off, why shouldn't a starter spend another 10 minutes in the bullpen acquiring a little touch on the ball?"

The theory worked out well. "My record for healthy arms was the thing I was always the most proud of," said Mazzone, whose Atlanta staffs led the league in earned run average or ranked second in all but one year from 1992 to 2005.

"We were able to do that because we didn't miss any starts," he said. "Our guys took great pride in going to the post. Each one would say, 'I'm not going to be the first one to miss a start.' I never talked to them about wins or numbers or used the term velocity, which is ruining arms today."

A stocky man with big ideas and a voice to match, Mazzone made sure relief pitchers also subscribed to his throwing theories. "If a guy didn't get into a game for two days, I went down to the bullpen and gave him a 5–10 minute tune up, just as I would for a starter," he said. "The so-called geniuses said, 'You can't do that.' I wanted to know why not? They said, 'He might get into the game tonight.' I said, 'That's what we're prepping them for.'"

Leo Mazzone's outspoken style and unorthodox methods as pitching coach were key reasons the Braves won 14 consecutive division titles.

Photo courtesy of the Atlanta Braves.

When Mazzone coached Atlanta pitchers, the tenth or eleventh man on the staff would get as much attention as the top starter. "The No. 11 guy got as much attention as the No. 1 guy," he said, "mentally as well as physically. I always felt if the low guy on the totem pole felt good about himself mentally and you gave him attention, he would perform better."

Like the Milwaukee Braves teams that reached the World Series by relying on the powerful pitching troika of Warren Spahn, Lew Burdette, and Bob Buhl, the Atlanta Braves rode the arms of Greg Maddux, Tom Glavine, and John Smoltz.

"They had one thing in common," Mazzone said of his megastars. "They loved to throw a baseball. In 1992, we had a great year pitching-wise and then we added Maddux to the equation. We had meetings in Atlanta and Ted Turner said he had one bullet to fire. It was Maddux or Barry Bonds. Bobby Cox had the final say. 'If we take Maddux,' he said, 'I don't think we'll ever have a losing streak.' He was right, of course, but he asked me and I said, 'You're talking to a pitching coach. Who the hell do you think I'm going to pick?'"

The 1992 staff, without Maddux, had thrown 24 shutouts. He simply made the strongest staff stronger.

All Maddux did was win Cy Young Awards in his first three seasons with Atlanta. "When Bobby was inducted into the Hall of Fame, he said he wouldn't be there without his Big Three. They had the greatest pitching run in the history of baseball. Somebody said we should have had more 20-game winners. If we had used a four-man rotation, we would have."

Under Mazzone's tutelage, the Braves had nine 20-game winners, including Glavine five times, Maddux and Smoltz once each, and even such add-ons as Denny Neagle and Russ Ortiz. Sain's teams had 16.

"It started in spring training," Mazzone said. "Nothing got done in spring training until the pitchers got their work in. That is what separates Bobby from other managers in the Hall of Fame: his ability to understand pitching, to handle pitching staffs, and to realize what they're going through.

"Nothing changed from the first day of spring training til the end of the year. We didn't cut back on anything, we didn't slow anything down. We were consistent, day in and day out, for eight months."

Trading information with each other was essential to the success of the staff, said Mazzone. "Maddux would watch Smoltz throw, Glavine would talk to Damian Moss, a left-hander from Australia. We all coached together, exchanged ideas, and had a nice little thing going on. A lot of guys came down to the bullpen for a side session even if it wasn't their day to throw."

When the team brought in promising pitchers like Kevin Millwood and Horacio Ramirez, Mazzone urged them not only to watch the established veterans but to talk to them. "I told them to pick their brains," he admitted.

Maddux was a master, Mazzone said. "He was amazing. He was one of the very few pitchers I talked to who had the answer before the fact. He could predict where a guy was going to hit a pitch. He was a real quiet guy, an unassuming Peabody out there on the mound before he got his contacts in. But he'd cut your heart out.

"He had the greatest control I've ever seen in my life. He would be practicing down in the bullpen. If he missed by an inch, he was pissed. Any other pitcher would have said, 'Wow, that's a great pitch.' After the strike zone changed, I would say, 'That pitch looks good, Mad Dog.' He'd say, 'No, Leo, that's not a strike anymore.'"

Maddux wanted opposing batters to hit the ball. "He wanted them to hit it on the handle or on the end of the bat," Mazzone explained. "There are a lot of pitchers who pitch away from contact. They don't have much success."

Glavine, following a similar formula, not only became the first man to throw two shutouts at Denver's Coors Field but authored a 1–0 shutout at Houston's Minute Maid Park, another hitters' haven, when it was still called Enron Field. He threw only fastballs and changeups in that game, Mazzone remembered.

Perfect Percentages

During his tenure with the Braves from 1993 to 2003, Greg Maddux went 194–88 for a .688 winning percentage—the best in franchise history. Tom Glavine, with the team from 1987 to 2002 and in 2008, had a .624 mark (244–147) that was the best by a left-handed pitcher, topping Warren Spahn's .609 (356–229).

Smoltz not only owned the best slider Mazzone ever saw from a right-handed pitcher but also a combination of control, great stuff, and a classic delivery. He threw six pitches for strikes from a variety of arm angles. "There's no pitch he couldn't throw and no arm angle he couldn't execute," said Mazzone of Smoltz.

Avery, a fourth starter who pitched like an ace in the playoffs, threw a fastball, curveball, and changeup thrown so hard opponents thought it was a sinker. He was also adept at changing speeds.

For all of them, durability was vital. From 1991 to 1993, the top four Atlanta starters missed exactly one start—after Maddux suffered a swollen elbow when hit by a line drive.

In 1993, when the Braves won 104 games, Glavine, Smoltz, and Steve Avery were NL All-Stars but the snubbed Maddux wound up with the Cy Young Award. The Big Four threw 973 innings, leaving only 91 for fifth starter Pete Smith, and helped the staff compile a best-in-baseball 3.14 ERA. In his first year with the team, Maddux led the league in ERA and complete games and finished third in strikeouts while Glavine tied for the NL lead in victories.

The pitching peaked during a four-game August sweep of the Giants in San Francisco. "Glavine made a great pitch to Will Clark with the bases loaded, getting him on a grounder to second," Mazzone said. "He always killed us; he was one of the best hitters we ever faced.

"Barry Bonds had great respect for us. He told Maddux one time that if he pitched to him, he wouldn't try to steal but if he walked him, he would.

"Bonds was the greatest hitter I ever saw. Early in his career, we could get him out down-and-away but later on, he didn't have a hole anywhere. When we went over their lineup, I said, 'Okay, our goal is to have Bonds come up with nobody on.' He hit a lot of home runs against us but a lot of them came before the sixth inning."

More than once, Cox ordered him walked with a runner on first base, Mazzone said. He added that his aces also had trouble with Tony Gwynn, winner of eight National League batting titles.

Like Bonds, Gwynn was a left-handed hitter with a great batting eye.

"After Tom Glavine finally got Gwynn out, he came back to our dugout and said he just threw it down the middle and said 'Here, hit it.'"

But Gwynn, a lifelong member of the San Diego Padres, lacked the power of Bonds, who moved from Pittsburgh to San Francisco as a free agent during the 1992 Baseball Winter Meetings.

"The '93 Giants were the best team we faced in that entire run, except for the Yankees in the World Series. But we shut them down completely. Had we lost that series in San Francisco, we would have been 10 or 12 games out. But once we swept them, we felt we were going to win the damn thing."

Adding Fred McGriff's bat the previous month helped Atlanta. "Bonds said we got him too late," said Mazzone, "but when he hit that bomb to left-center the first night, we knew we were in business. It just snowballed from there."

Five years later, the team's five starters all won at least 16 games and produced a combined ERA of 2.97—1.27 better than the league average. Glavine won the Cy Young, Maddux and Smoltz tied for fourth in the balloting, and Maddux, Glavine, and Smoltz finished first, third, and sixth in earned run average. Glavine won 20, Maddux 18, Smoltz and Kevin Millwood 17 apiece, and Denny Neagle 16.

During the 1995 season, when Maddux went 19–2, the pitcher went to the coach. "He had made about four or five starts already," Mazzone remembered, "but wanted to ask some questions about certain situations. I always had answers for him; I felt he couldn't stand a 50–50 coach. You say what you believe. There were no maybes with him. Do you think it will work or not? I loved that about him and felt confident enough that he knew I was going to be honest with him and try to help him."

One day, Maddux was coasting with a three-hit shutout in the sixth inning. After he retired the first hitter, the pitcher peered into the Atlanta dugout. Cox caught the glance and said, 'Leo, get your butt out there and make sure he's okay.' So I went out and he said, 'I don't want to talk to Chipper. I don't want to talk to the umpire. The catcher doesn't speak English.' I said, 'You look great to me.' So he said, 'Is the bullpen going to need any work? My approach would be different in the seventh if you're going to take me out or leave me in.' I said, 'Think nine.' He said, 'Thanks for the visit' and I went back to the dugout."

Maddux, known for his economy of pitches, had his own theory about a complete game. "He used to tell me you either go seven or you go nine," Mazzone related. "He said eight was like kissing your sister."

Although Maddux won 355 games, more than any living pitcher, he never hesitated to take himself out when necessary. "One time, he got tired after 70 pitches and said, 'I'm done.' I said, 'You sure?' He said, 'Yeah, I'm done. I got embarrassed by my last start at Shea Stadium— I'd never given up so many runs so early. I made up my mind that was never going to happen to me again. I just got mentally tired.'

"I learned what the great ones go through. Hell, when those guys give up three runs or so, you wonder what the hell is going on."

Glavine, like Maddux, depended upon location rather than velocity. "With him, it was always steady as she goes," Mazzone said of the great left-hander. "Day in, day out, everything was the same. It was the same work ethic, nothing changed. He never gave in to the strike zone. He walked a guy in spring training on purpose once. When I asked him about it, he admitted it. I said, 'It's spring training. It doesn't count.' He said, 'I don't care. I don't want to give up any runs.'

The pitcher often had problems in the first inning. "Cincinnati had the bases loaded with two outs and Kevin Mitchell hitting," said Mazzone. "Tom was already down, 1–0. I went out and said, 'Don't give in to this guy. You've got a base open.' Glavine couldn't believe it. 'I don't know what you're talking about, Leo. The last time I looked, the bases were loaded. You mind telling me which base is open?' I said, 'Sure—home plate.' He ended up walking Mitchell on a 3–2 changeup that was down low. We're down 2–0 but he got the next guy out, retired 18 in a row after that, and we won, 5–2."

As for Smoltz, his career could have taken a turn for the worse in 1991. "The main reason John Smoltz got into the Hall of Fame is that Bobby Cox did not take him out of the rotation when he was 2–11 at the All-Star break in 1991," Mazzone insisted. "There were people from within who wanted him taken out. But Bobby did not change one pitcher in the rotation the whole year, regardless of won-lost record.

"When those pitchers saw the faith Bobby had in them, whether they won or lost, they all jumped on the bandwagon together. They knew the manager had their back. And off we went."

That same year, Avery won 18 games during the regular season and then pitched a 1–0 gem in the playoffs at Pittsburgh. "Before the game, he started to warm up and then sat down," Mazzone said. "When I asked what he was doing, he said, 'Would you tell me when there's five minutes left?' Ave was an ornery bugger but I loved him like a son. When I told him he had five minutes, I saw fastballs, breaking balls, and changeups. I thought to myself, 'I hope he takes that stuff out there.'"

By that time, Mazzone was a confirmed rocker—though neither a singer nor a relative of the controversial closer whose comments would create a divisive atmosphere years later.

"I rocked because my wheels were turning," said Mazzone, who soon acquired his Rockin' Leo nickname. "I was never nervous late in the season or in the postseason. My anxiety would always set in during the first two months, making sure everybody got out of the gate healthy and making sure we had a record good enough to compete for a title. By the time we got to the All-Star break, I wanted to be sure we had a chance to win the pennant."

After Mazzone's arrival just before the 1990 All-Star break, the young pitchers improved dramatically. Like the team, the staff ERA went from worst to first—4.58, worst in the majors, in 1990 but 3.14, topping both leagues, by 1992.

Preparation was the key. With the permission of Bobby Cox and John Schuerholz, Mazzone got the jump on spring training by inviting pitchers to a pre-camp throwing program in Atlanta just after Super Bowl Sunday.

"I was getting ready for my first full spring training in '91 when I saw the Dodgers working out at Chavez Ravine in Los Angeles," he said. "I thought we should do something like that. We started bringing some in and before you know it, they were saying 'We can't wait to get there.'"

Camp Leo, as it came to be known, lasted as long as the coach was there. It obviously worked.

In 1995, the Braves won everything: the division title, the first Division Series, the NL Championship Series, and the World Series.

"We won the division by 21 games but were underdogs against Cincinnati in the NLCS because the Reds had such great team speed," said Mazzone, dubbed "the Rock of Atlanta" by ESPN.com in 2005. "The reporters asked how we would stop their running game. They asked if we were working on slide-steps, pickoff plays, or upsetting their rhythm or timing. After I said no to all of that, they asked what we were going to do. I said, 'If we make our pitches, they can't get on base.' We did and the running game meant nothing.'"

Cleveland was next in line. "They had a lot of power with Albert Belle, Jim Thome, and some other sluggers," according to Mazzone, "but the whole key to that lineup was Kenny Lofton. He's the one who made them go. We tried to keep him off the bases because we knew he was going to go and we couldn't stop him."

With the Braves needing one win to clinch, Glavine got the call. Though he pitched brilliantly, yielding only one bloop single and no runs in eight innings, the lefty ran out of gas. "He came in and said, 'I'm done,'" Mazzone said. "I said, 'You sure?' And he said, 'Leo, I'm shot.' Bobby said, 'I heard you. Tell (Mark) Wohlers he's in.'"

The flamethrowing right-hander finished the game, and the Series, with a perfect ninth. "They made him a reliever in the minors because he worried himself to death between starts," said Mazzone with a laugh. "When he came to the ballpark not knowing when he was going to pitch, he picked up speed on his fastball because he didn't think about things so much. He let his natural abilities take over."

Smoltz did the same four years later, when he was preparing for the postseason with a bad elbow. "He dropped down to low three-quarters," said Mazzone, "because he said that didn't hurt compared to throwing over the top. He asked me if I thought it would work and I said, 'If you do, I do.' He had practice sessions on back-to-back days.

"He started against Houston and the Killer Bees, struck out seven, and only gave up a run or two. Craig Biggio said later, 'We heard he might drop down but we didn't think he would be this nasty.' The only thing was he couldn't throw his split from that angle.

"Before the fourth game of the World Series against the Yankees, he and I were walking to the bullpen together. He looked at me, I looked at him, and I said, 'You're going on top, aren't you?' He said, 'Yep, I'm going on top. I need the split against the Yankee hitters.' He went on to strike out 10 but we lost the game."

Maddux and Glavine were so good for so long that umpires routinely gave them strikes that were borderline. After rival teams squawked, Major League Baseball introduced QuesTec, a machine intended to monitor umpire performance at the plate. It squeezed the east-west strike zone almost immediately.

"We're in spring training and Maddux was pitching," said Mazzone. "Jerry Layne, who was behind the plate, called the first pitch a ball. Right away, Bobby wanted to know what the hell is going on. Jerry comes over and shows him a piece of paper in his pocket. He told Bobby they couldn't call that pitch a strike anymore."

Maddux and Glavine were the poster kids for QuesTec. "It was because of the way they owned the corners," the coach said. "We couldn't get a called strike on Bonds, Gwynn, or Wade Boggs. Before QuesTec, if you showed you could hit a spot all the time, you got credit for a strike."

Mazzone always emphasized the importance of strike one. "We taught our pitchers to pitch inside; we owned the down-and-away strike," he said. "We could pitch inside selectively, effectively, and when we wanted to. And if we owned down and away, we could do whatever we wanted."

That's how Kent Mercker threw his no-hitter in Los Angeles early in the 1994 campaign. "It was his first start of the season," Mazzone said, "so he said he was getting tired. I said, 'Are you out of your friggin' mind?' He said, 'Whaddya mean?' I said, 'Look at the scoreboard.' When he saw it was the end of the seventh, he said, 'I ain't tired no more,' he said.

In a game at Philadelphia, Mercker was victimized by four gopher balls in five innings. He said, 'Hey, Leo, you know that theory you've got that a starter can give up four solos and still go nine? I'm cutting it a little close, ain't I?'"

Current coaches might not be so relaxed. "Coaches are always looking at their notes," Mazzone said. "They've got the book out; you can read the top of his cap the entire game. I never had one note in my hand. I didn't need notes. My computer was in my brain."

With Sain and Cox as mentors, Mazzone didn't need mechanical assistance. "I had the two greatest teachers you can possibly have," he said. "Bobby knew how to handle people and handle pitching staffs. I've always said he was the greatest influence in my life of any male figure with the exception of my father.

"I had Sain out to Wrigley Field when Maddux and Glavine were scheduled to throw on the side. I wanted to make sure he saw them both. As he watched, he said, 'You know what I love about Glavine?

He can hang that ball on a string and right when it gets to home plate, he pulls that string. And Maddux has some of the best movement on a baseball I've ever seen.'

"Maddux, not one for making speeches, asked to do just that early in spring training camp one year. Speaking to an assemblage of 28 pitchers, he asked, 'You know why I'm a fucking millionaire? Because I can throw my fastball where I want to. And you know why I have beachfront property in Los Angeles? Because I can change speeds.' Then he said, 'That's it, Leo.'"

As usual, Maddux was right on target, Mazzone said. "There's nothing more to pitching than fastball command and changing speeds. Anything after that is cake."

The coach appreciated the simplicity of their game plans. He said Maddux threw a moving fastball, a changeup, a cutter, and an occasional slider; Glavine offered a fastball, change, and occasional breaking ball; and Smoltz had three above-average pitches: a fastball, breaking ball, and split, though he did throw a knuckleball in the 1999 World Series.

"With Smoltzie, you had to have different approaches when you wanted to critique something," he said. "With Maddux, you had to have answers and be confident in your answers and your decision-making. You could get on Glavine but he was really strong-minded, with thick skin. You had to be a little firm with him.

"I had to have a sense of humor with Smoltzie. One time I went out to the mound and told him to get his head out of his ass. He said, 'Leo, the catcher just told me exactly the same thing.' I said, 'You don't need to hear it twice. I'll go back in.'"

Avery was a different breed of cat, the pitching coach revealed. "I had to tell him to stand on the mound when I came out because he'd back off," said Mazzone. "We were in Colorado, a tough place to pitch, and he was overthrowing. He hit Larry Walker and Andres Galarraga. When Mark Lemke and Jeff Blauser went out to the mound, I came out too. He said, 'What the fuck are you doing here?' I said, 'Now that I'm out here, I'm out here to tell you to go fuck yourself. How do you like that?' He said, 'Now that you're here, are you going to leave?' I said, 'No. Go fuck yourself, you fucking asshole. NOW I'm going to leave.'

"Bobby Cox said to me, 'What the hell was going on out there?' I said, 'Oh, nothing, everything is fine.' Meanwhile, Skip Caray, up in the booth, was saying, 'Leo is trying to settle Avery down.'"

Later on, Avery apologized. "We were a very close unit so when you have moments like that, it was no big deal," Mazzone said. "I told him, 'I have a tremendous amount of respect for what you do out there on the mound. Just have a little respect for me when I come out to the mound. I don't care if you don't hear a word I'm saying. Just act like you do.'"

During the torrid title chase of 1993, Avery approached Mazzone. As the coach remembers, "He said, 'We got 'em now, Leo.' I said, 'Really, Steve? Last time I looked, we were about seven-and-a-half games behind.' So he said, 'Yeah, but (John) Burkett and (Bill) Swift are talking about a little fatigue setting in after 150 innings. I got news for him: we don't kick it in until after 150.'"

After Avery's career ended prematurely, agent Scott Boras accused the Braves of overworking the pitcher before he was ready. "My rebuttal is simple," Mazzone said. "If 9–10 years in the big leagues and 1,600 innings is a short career, we'll take it."

Mazzone never believed in pitch counts. Kent Mercker threw 130 in his 1994 no-hitter, for example. "Before they put the pitch count up on the board," he said, "I kept track of it with a little clicker in my hand. Somebody would ask how many he's got, I'd answer, and they'd say, 'Is that your count, Leo, or the real count?' If Maddux threw a first-pitch sinker to get somebody out or Glavine popped somebody up with a changeup, I wasn't counting those.

"One time Smoltzie was throwing a shutout in L.A. when he said he was getting tired. I said he was under par but he said, 'I thought I had more (pitches) than that.' I said, 'No, you're under par, you're fine.' Of course I wouldn't tell him what the actual number was."

Mazzone made no secret of his opinions.

When Marvin Freeman arrived from Philadelphia, he started learning to throw his sinker 90 percent of the time. "He said, 'Oh, we're going to do it your way, huh?' I said, 'You see No. 6 down there in the dugout? He agrees with me 100 percent.' Freeman started throwing some nasty sinkers and had several good years with us."

So did pitchers like Jaret Wright, John Burkett, John Thomson, Mike Hampton, and Russ Ortiz—castoffs from other organizations who prospered under Mazzone.

"Ortiz came over from the Giants, who told him he was walking too many guys," Mazzone remembered. "I told him I don't give a fuck how many he walked—all I cared about was how many of them scored."

Burkett was struggling when he landed in the Land of Mazzone. After winning 22 games with the '93 Giants, he had pitched so poorly that he lost more than he won over a three-year span. Released by Tampa Bay during 2000 spring training, Burkett was ready to retire.

He was throwing in the bullpen when Mazzone took notice. "Aside from Maddux," he told the new acquisition, "you have the best control I've ever seen on the side."

That psychological boost—plus a strong suggestion that he junk his slider for a down-and-away fastball—made Burkett a 36-year-old All-Star in 2001, when he posted a career-best 3.04 ERA. No wonder writer Roger Kahn once dubbed Mazzone "the Pope of pitching."

Paul Byrd, another reclamation project, said of Mazzone, "Leo helped me reinvent myself."

Ditto Jaret Wright, who had a 15-win season and 3.28 ERA, both career bests, in 2004 after rebounding from shoulder troubles. That was the same season John Thomson, a journeyman jolted by exposure to Mazzone, contributed an equally unexpected 14 wins.

"I didn't care about velocity," Mazzone mentioned. "If Wright was throwing 94, I told him I'd rather have him locate at 91. If Burkett was throwing 85, I'd rather have him throw more fastballs than sliders because everybody gets away from their fastball when they get into trouble. Then they resort to super-power and super-control. Super-power means you're throwing the ball harder than you can and super-control means you're trying to hit the black so you're going to get behind in the count.

"When we rejuvenated those guys, we had them practicing on their fastball command 90 percent of the time. Then we figured out the amount of effort we wanted them to put on the fastball in order to locate it the way we wanted to. The only way to do that is to go down to the bullpen and practice it."

Mazzone never tired of teaching. The coach converted lefthander Mike Remlinger, a struggling starter with the Reds, to a successful reliever with the Braves. Like Burkett, he even went to the All-Star Game.

Hampton gave the Braves two strong seasons before his elbow barked. "He was embarrassed by his contract," said Mazzone of Hampton. "One time he said to me, 'A dumb organization like Colorado gave this stupid-ass left-hander $125 million.'"

Whatever pixie dust the coach sprinkled only worked for pitchers while they wore the same uniform. Before and after their Atlanta stints, they just weren't the same.

"I went into every season thinking our starting pitchers were going to pitch 220 innings," Mazzone said in his book *Tales from the Braves Mound*. "That excludes the fifth starter, who got skipped every so often because of the schedule.

"The record I'm most proud of is the innings pitched by our starting staff—not just the 20-game winners or Cy Young guys. When you have the innings pitched, everything else just takes care of itself."

Burkett was a solid case in point. During the pitcher's first spring training with the team, Mazzone predicted he would pitch 220 innings.

He came close. "We were going up the tunnel at the end of the season," the coach said, "and I said, 'Burkie, I have to apologize to you. I said you were going to pitch 220 innings this year but you only pitched 219 1/3.'"

Always outspoken and prone to dropping more F-bombs than Tony Soprano, Mazzone never blended into the background with the Braves. "I don't think you'd call Leo a diplomat," said former team president Stan Kasten. "Some people don't like how direct he is."

For every Jason Marquis, who didn't realize his talent before Atlanta sent him to St. Louis, there were dozens of others who responded to the siren call of the diminutive but combative coach. He got the most out of men like Kerry Ligtenberg, a closer acquired from an independent team for bags of bats and balls, and Greg McMichael, whose changeup plunged so precipitously that it looked like it was falling off a table.

"I didn't know anything about him before (1993) spring training," Mazzone wrote of McMichael. "He was one of our spring invitees on Field Two. Since every pitcher who comes to spring training gets to pitch, he came in and had a 1-2-3 inning. Then he had another perfect inning. And he's throwing a pretty good changeup.

"He graduated to Field One and started pitching against better hitters. We set it up so that he would pitch before the other team brought in their Double-A and Triple-A guys at the end of the game. He did great. So we put him in against the Mets to face their top left-handed hitters. He not only retired the side but made them look sick. As Mac was walking off the field, Terry Pendleton came over and said to me, 'If you guys don't put him on this pitching staff, you ought to be shot.'"

After McMichael's pet pitch paralyzed a pair of left-handed Yankees named Wade Boggs and Don Mattingly, he made the staff. Pressed into service as a part-time closer, the rookie finished the year with 19 saves and a 2.06 ERA, and had several more seasons as a quality setup man.

Mazzone said Smoltz was the best closer he saw during his tenure, with Mark Wohlers second and John Rocker third. But others had their moments.

"Juan Berenguer was our closer in 1991," he recalled. "He always had to have the bases loaded and get the last out on a deep fly to the base of the wall. When he got hurt, we acquired Alejandro Pena. He did the job as quietly and efficiently as anybody. Kerry Ligtenberg saved 30 games one year but people wondered how he was doing it. How did Kent Mercker or Mike Stanton save games? How did McMichael save games throwing 83? They just felt it wasn't that big a deal to get three fucking outs.

"Rocker was high maintenance, whether it be physical or mental. He'd come flying through that bullpen gate and Maddux would start hollering, 'Whoopee! Here he comes, Leo. Look at that crazy son of a bitch.'

"One time Bobby came out to take him out of a game and Rocker made a face at him. If we kept him out there, we wouldn't have been

Bullpen Deficit

Broadcaster Jim Kaat, who had a long career as a pitcher, said a weak bullpen kept the Braves from winning more than one world championship. "That Atlanta team had everything except a quality closer," said Kaat, the last active player from the original Washington Senators. "If you could put somebody like Mariano Rivera on that club, they would have been unbeatable. When you look back on those great Braves teams, that's what they were lacking: an automatic, lockdown guy coming out of the bullpen."

It took a lot to upset the manager, who tilled the rudder with a steady hand—and the assistance of aides like Leo Mazzone.

"It was a privilege to be around those guys, with the atmosphere we had and Bobby Cox running the show," Mazzone said. "We'll never experience that again no matter what we do. The most incredible aspect of the streak was our pitching run, which came during the era of revived offense in baseball."

able to use him the next day. We'd work his butt off for nothing. So Rocker came in and sat down next to me and said, 'Did you lose confidence in me?' I said, 'No. Some days, you just don't have it. You might have 10 good ones and one so-so. Why stay out there and work your butt off when we wouldn't able to use you for a couple of days?'

"In the meantime, Bobby said to Rocker, 'If you ever make a face at me again when I come to the mound, I'll break your fucking neck.' And then he walked away. So I said to Rocker, 'I think coach Cox is pissed.'"

Mazzone's Mistake

According to baseball rules, managers must change pitchers if they make more than one trip to the mound in the same inning. In one game during the 1991 season, Steve Avery got into trouble and Bobby Cox paid him a visit. Later in the inning, pitching coach Leo Mazzone thought he detected an injury to the pitcher. Without notifying the umpire that his was an "injury" visit, he charged out to the mound. The umpire joined him and asked who was coming in. Since no one was warming up, Mazzone found himself in a ticklish spot—especially when the manager joined him on the mound. "Who could come in without warming up?" the manager asked the coach. Mazzone thought for a minute, and then said, "Mike Stanton." The surprised pitcher entered the game, took his eight warm-up pitches, and then retired the batter on a sharp line drive for the third out. The Braves hung on to win the game—and finished the season with a one-game lead.

4

THE SURVIVOR: JOHN SMOLTZ

OTHER THAN MANAGER Bobby Cox and pitching coach Leo Mazzone, the only man who wore a Braves uniform throughout the team's streak of 14 consecutive titles was John Smoltz.

Like rotation mate Tom Glavine, he reached Atlanta when the team was struggling but became a vital part of its success after a few years in baseball purgatory.

A Michigan native who idolized Tigers shortstop Alan Trammell, Smoltz played the accordion before he played baseball. He turned pro only after his grandfather, a longtime member of the Tiger Stadium grounds crew, tipped off an area scout about a high school prodigy in Lansing.

Worried that he might choose basketball or college over baseball, the Tigers did not draft Smoltz until the 22nd round of the amateur draft. He delayed signing, playing for the U.S. Junior Olympic team instead, and put his signature on a contract only one night before he was set to start classes at Michigan State.

During a minor league stop in Lakeland, a sleepy town in Central Florida, he took up golf as a diversion. That hobby would eventually help him reach the Baseball Hall of Fame, where he arrived a year after the man who traded for him.

It was Bobby Cox, then general manager of the Braves, who insisted on Smoltz in exchange for veteran starter Doyle Alexander. Detroit got immediate dividends—Alexander went 9–0 the rest of the season as the Tigers reached the playoffs—but Atlanta got an ace who would last for a generation.

Powered by an overwhelming need to succeed at anything he did, Smoltz was the most competitive player Chipper Jones ever saw. That's quite a compliment from an Atlanta icon who spent his entire career with the Braves.

"I want to win a ring," Smoltz said. "I wanted to win more than one. That drove me for 21 years."

Illustration by Ronnie Joyner.

The 6-foot-3, 210-pound right-hander won his major league debut at New York's Shea Stadium in 1988 and eventually won a World Series ring, a Cy Young Award, five pennants, and 14 trips to the postseason. He also became the only pitcher with at least 200 wins and 150 saves.

Even before he reached the baseball pinnacle with a Cooperstown plaque, Smoltz had no trouble filling his trophy room. It started with the MVP award for the 1992 NL Championship Series but continued with the both the Cy Young and the National League Pitcher of the Year Award from *The Sporting News* four years later. He also won the NL's Rolaids Relief Man in 2002 and took three humanitarian awards: the Lou Gehrig Memorial Award and the Roberto Clemente Award, both in 2005, and the Branch Rickey Award in 2007.

Like fellow Hall of Famer Dennis Eckersley, Smoltz was a successful starter who became a quality closer. Unlike Eckersley, however, he later returned to the rotation and picked up where he left off.

"It was the hardest thing I ever did," said Smoltz about going to the bullpen. "I had to learn on the job and I failed miserably at the beginning [eight runs in two-thirds of an inning against the Mets]. I got booed in my own ballpark.

"I struggled that whole month of April with a thumb injury but things eventually worked themselves out. By the end of the year, I had [a league-record] 55 saves so that answered a lot of questions. It also made people forget about me as a starter, which was a little tough to swallow at that time."

It was Smoltz himself who conjured up the closer move. The team had been struggling, especially after controversial John Rocker talked his way out of the league, and Smoltz needed to protect an elbow that had just been repaired by Tommy John surgery. The idea, at the outset, was to pitch fewer innings and loosen the burden on the balky joint.

"I tried everything," Smoltz said of his five arm surgeries. "I changed arm angles, I threw sidearm, I threw knuckleballs, and I pitched under circumstances that probably weren't ideal."

Trying to find ways to avoid pain, the pitcher even dropped down, throwing with a sidearm motion. "I was trying to fake it," he admitted, "and knew I was heading for surgery."

After the Braves lost the first three games of the 1999 World Series, Smoltz decided to throw over the top—no matter how painful—in Game Four. Though he fanned 11 Yankees in seven innings, the Braves failed to support their starter with even a modicum of offense. He spent the winter throwing knuckleballs, and hoping, but came to spring training in March knowing his elbow wouldn't cooperate.

Although Atlanta maintained its title streak without him, Smoltz had plenty of time to reflect during his year-long rehab.

He thought about the worst-to-first season of 1991, his scoreless duel with Jack Morris in the seventh game of the World Series, the Francisco Cabrera hit that won the '92 pennant, and the big games he won as a starter in 1995, the world championship season, and 1996, which nearly resulted in a repeat.

For Smoltz, who had started the '91 campaign with a 2–11 record, the loyalty of Bobby Cox helped. While writers, fans, and even some front office officials were insisting Smoltz be moved to the bullpen or even sent to the minors, Cox kept handing him the ball.

"The All-Star break couldn't have come at a better time," Smoltz said. "I had just gone through a difficult contract negotiation, had recently gotten married, and had my first newborn. There were a lot of changes in my life. I changed my perspective of how I viewed what I was doing. I was out to show (general manager) John Schuerholz why I deserved my contract. I was going to prove something to him in ways I never should have done. I lost my confidence and went 2–11.

"I was the best 2–11 pitcher you ever saw but I just couldn't get out of an inning. I let the thing go on longer than it should have."

Enter sports psychologist Jack Llewellyn, who gave Smoltz pointers and then attended every game clad in a red shirt so the pitcher could spot him. "Nobody interviewed me the entire year," Smoltz said with a laugh years later. "They interviewed him."

Big-Game Pitcher

Capping the worst-to-first season of 1991, John Smoltz pitched the division clincher, the pennant clincher, and shutout ball into the eighth inning of World Series Game Seven.

Whatever the shrink said must have worked; Smoltz went 12–2 over the second half. "I felt unbeatable," he said. "I don't think I lost any of my last 15 starts. It was crazy. If you would have told me when I was 2–11 that I would go 12–2 and pitch the seventh game of both the Championship Series and the World Series, I would have thought you weren't all there."

The experience proved invaluable. "It proved to me that you can overcome some things even when it seems you can't," said Smoltz. "One game is not worth two, four, or five victories. You have to plod your way along. Ultimately, it changed my way of thinking and my career."

Entrusted with a potential division-clinching game during the last weekend of the season, Smoltz went all the way to beat the Houston Astros. "It was one of my greatest games," he said. "I remember (catcher) Greg Olson jumping into my arms afterward. Here we were, headed to the playoffs after a long drought. That was *the* playoff game for me. I was put into a position, thanks to the brilliance of Steve Avery, to pitch Game Seven on the road in Pittsburgh. I went all nine and Greg jumped into my arms again. There's no greater feeling than finishing something you started. Bobby knew I wasn't giving the ball to anybody."

Had the Braves managed a single run against Jack Morris in the World Series finale, Smoltz would have finished the season by pitching three nine-inning clinchers. "That would have been the ultimate scenario," said Smoltz, who cultivated a reputation as a no holds barred competitor.

"Game Seven was just like I remembered it as a kid. I was 46 feet from my house and throwing against a wall. I must have done that 100 times. I went through every single detail in my mind. And I won just about every game I pitched in that situation. So when I went out there for the real Game Seven, everybody else freaked out. My family was nervous—no one talked to me. But I thought it was a dream come true.

"Not everybody has that thought process. They just think of what could happen. When I stood on the mound during warmups, I thought, 'This is exactly where I want to be.' I never felt nervous, never felt out of place, and never felt like I was going to give up a run."

Minnesota eventually prevailed, 1–0 in 10 innings, although the game had been scoreless when Smoltz left with one out in the eighth.

Hoping for a better outcome in '92, Smoltz beat Pittsburgh ace Doug Drabek in the first and fourth games of the Championship Series. When they met again in Game Seven, the Pirates scratched out two runs and held the Braves scoreless through eight. Then the Braves filled the bases with nobody out in the ninth.

"I was pouting," Smoltz reported. "We had been up three games to one and I was ready for Game One of the World Series. I pitched really well, giving up two harmless runs, and we're down 2–0 in the ninth. I thought I was going to lose and we were going to go home.

"I was in the back corner of the clubhouse saying, 'This can't be happening.' Then all of a sudden I saw (Cabrera's) swing and line drive. I ran about 200 yards—that's how far it was to the field—and jumped on the pile at home plate. I didn't see the play until two weeks later. If Sid (Bream) had been called out, I might have been the fool who ran onto the field in a tie game because I had so much momentum."

Writers recognized that momentum, voting Smoltz the most valuable player of that NLCS. But his shot at a World Series ring evaporated when Jeff Reardon surrendered a two-run, ninth-inning homer to Ed Sprague in a game Smoltz had started. The World Series against Toronto had to be anticlimactic after the euphoria of the Francisco Cabrera game but big challenges lay ahead.

In 1993, the San Francisco Giants sprinted to a 10-game lead by mid-July, convincing the Braves to acquire slugger Fred McGriff from San Diego for three prospects.

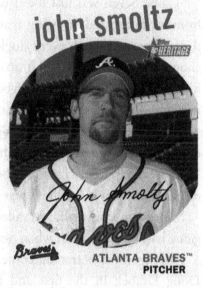

ATLANTA BRAVES™
PITCHER

Courtesy of The Topps Company, Inc.

"I thought we could chase down the Giants because we had been there, done that," Smoltz said, noting that the worst-to-first team of 1991 had been nine-and-a-half games back at the All-Star break. "Their pitching staff was going through it for the first time. There was some talk that they were getting tired, that innings were piling up. McGriff infused us with some incredible momentum. When we got him, we started to believe we could win."

With a victory in the final game of the season after the teams had been tied atop the standings for three consecutive days, the Braves finally finished with 104 wins, then a club record, and the Giants with 103. The playoffs against the Phillies, which followed, paled in comparison.

After a players' strike wiped out the 1994 postseason, Smoltz yearned to return to the World Series for the first time in three years. He got his wish, as the Braves won for the first time as a member of the National League East, where they had moved in a 1994 realignment that split each league into three divisions and introduced the wild-card format.

Rebounding from the worst year of his career, the soft-spoken fireballer went 12–7 during the season and pitched well in the playoffs except for one shaky start against Cleveland in the World Series. It was the worst postseason appearance for Smoltz, whose 15 October wins rank second only to Andy Pettitte's 19.

"What happened in 1995 gave us the greatest feeling of accomplishment," Smoltz said. "To win that World Series was the result of an awesome team capping off a great season," he said. "We were the team that won the last game. To win that championship was something special."

The best memento he received, with the possible exception of the World Series ring, was a putting green for the clubhouse. Team president Stan Kasten agreed to install one after the Braves won a world title. Made of artificial turf, it was ten feet long and twenty feet wide, occupying a choice spot under a mural of the 16th hole at Augusta. It was perfect for the golf-loving pitcher, who later honed his game against Tiger Woods.

Maybe all that putting helped; Smoltz enjoyed his best season in 1996. He even matched his uniform number—29—in victories when the All-Star Game and postseason were factored in.

Healthy all season, he went 24–8 with a 2.94 earned run average, leading the league in wins and strikeouts, before adding three playoff wins against the Dodgers and Cardinals plus a World Series victory over the Yankees. He was also the winning pitcher in the All-Star Game.

"That was the first year I didn't spend an offseason in rehab," he revealed. "I was coming off a pretty good 1995 campaign after having surgery early in the year. I'm not a cocky or arrogant guy but I remember going into spring training and saying to the coaches, 'This is my year.' I felt completely at peace with myself and physically felt really good. I lost my first game but won my next 14. Everybody said the Cy Young was mine to lose.

"Many people had predicted I would win the award three or four times based on expectations but as a guy who had never won, it was hard to hear that."

It was also hard for Smoltz to wind up on the short end of another 1–0 game in the World Series. "It was my greatest postseason run," he said. "I went 4–1 with an 0.87 ERA. I felt dominant, almost unbeatable. I still can't believe I lost that game to Pettitte. It was an unearned run. To this day, those games against Morris and Pettitte were two of the best games I ever pitched. And they didn't result in a win."

In 41 postseason games, Smoltz went 15–4 with a 2.67 earned run average and 199 strikeouts, a postseason record, in 209 innings. He had a perfect 7–0 mark in the NL Division Series, 6–2 record in the

Without a 1–0 loss in 1996 World Series Game Five and a scoreless duel in 1991 World Series Game Seven, John Smoltz would have been even better than 15–4 in postseason play.

Photo by Jeff Slate.

Championship Series, and 2–2 mark in the World Series despite a 2.47 ERA.

"I wasn't afraid to fail," he said, explaining his success under the postseason spotlight. "I had dreamed of pitching every one of those games. I had gears that I could go to in terms of velocity and stuff that other guys couldn't.

"Not that the rest of the season wasn't important to me—if I would have pitched 10 regular-season games like I pitched a postseason game, I wouldn't have made it through the season. Every inning you pitch in the postseason is like two or three innings in the regular season. After pitching 270 innings, you're already maxed out. But you don't know if you're pitching another game so you pour everything into it.

"The greatest part of our 14-year run was that it allowed me to show-case my ability as a big-game pitcher. That's how I always want to be known."

Smoltz followed Glavine and Greg Maddux, inducted in 2014, into the Baseball Hall of Fame. Never has one team had three stalwart pitchers pitch so well for so long.

"In 10 years, we exceeded everyone's expectations as we got older," Smoltz said. "We were all different. But we spent time on the golf course talking about things that helped us become as good as we were. Those two guys maximized their ability and were more prepared than anyone else. If we had been cars, I probably had more thunder in the engine and maybe higher expectations but maybe that was a little unfair given some of the predicaments I was in.

"The bottom line is that we had a great seat every time one of us pitched. It was an enjoyable run and it will never happen again. Economics and all kinds of other things will prevent it and that's too bad. My only regret was seeing them leave. When I went to the bullpen, I had looked forward to saving the 300th win for both of them. To me, that would have been the ultimate."

The last of the 16 pitchers to reach 3,000 strikeouts, Smoltz twice led the National League in strikeouts while working his way to the top of the Atlanta club list. Teammates, rivals, and scouts said his stuff was electric, allowing him to top the NL with a career-high 9.792 strikeouts per nine innings during his Cy Young season of 1996. A power pitcher whose slider was probably the league's best, the two-time NL strikeout king topped the team in strikeouts per nine innings three times. He never mastered the changeup favored by Maddux and Glavine but was willing to try anything, including a late-career knuckleball he felt would alleviate the strain on his troublesome right elbow.

Golf was the great enabler for John Smoltz. "There was nothing better than getting to bed after a game, waking up, playing golf, and enjoying the day and the fruits of that city," he said. "When you start every five days, the structure of that is so great. It was hard to give that up when I went to the pen."

Bobby Cox, a golfer himself, encouraged him. "There are a lot of things organizations get wrong in baseball based upon the mindset or perceptions of what the game is and what it takes to play successfully," he said. "Bobby understood what the long season was like and what outlets we needed. He also understood that we were responsible and professional about everything we did.

"I loved being active—I wasn't one of those guys who was going to visit museums or look at architecture. I developed one of the greatest black books in history, with all the golf courses, the names of members and pros. I was the golf concierge of the Atlanta Braves and I was pretty good at it."

He was pretty good at pitching, too. He won 159 games as a starter, converted 154 of 168 save opportunities in three-and-a-half years, and then averaged 15 more wins and 222 innings over three more years in the Atlanta rotation. He even had 100 saves over a two-year span from 2002, when he led the league with 55, to 2003, when he finished second with 45. He had 44 more in 2004.

The last remnant of the great troika, Smoltz won 14 games for the Braves as they wrapped up their title run in 2005 (he would have won more if his bullpen replacements hadn't blown numerous opportunities in their hapless attempts to save his starts).

Two years later, while trying to ignite a new streak, he notched his 200th career victory by beating the Mets, 2–1. The losing pitcher, defeated by Smoltz for the third time that season, was former Braves icon and golf buddy Tom Glavine. "I can't say who I beat for my 200th," Glavine said years later, "but I'm sure John will remember whom he beat for his 200th."

The first Hall of Famer who had Tommy John surgery, he was also the first to reach Cooperstown after starting his career as a high-round draft choice.

Like Maddux and Glavine, Smoltz never pitched a no-hitter but came close.

"Tony Gwynn was certainly the greatest hitter I ever played against," he recalled. "I didn't have a clue how to get him out. I was pitching in San Diego, had a bunch of strikeouts, and it was a gem. With two outs in the eighth, Gwynn hit a fly ball to right. Ryan Klesko couldn't catch it and they scored it a double. He ran 20 or 25 steps and the ball

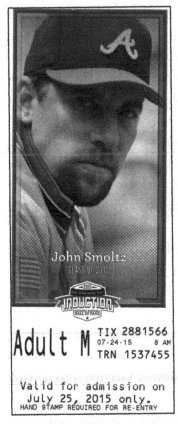

Michigan native John Smoltz wanted to pitch for the Tigers but was glad to be traded to the Braves.

Photo courtesy of the National Baseball Hall of Fame and Museum.

hit off his glove. I knew it was an error, especially that late in the game. To me, if there ever was a no-hitter to be had, it was that game."

Earlier in his career, at Philadelphia's Veterans Stadium, Lenny Dykstra ended a Smoltz bid with a late-inning single. "I was looking for any idea, any suggestion, that might help me prepare for the game better," Smoltz said. "Somebody said pitching on an empty stomach made them feel a lot better. So I didn't eat. By the sixth or seventh inning, I'm starving. I'm at a point where I think I'm going to pass out. I got everybody out in the bottom of the eighth but went inside to grab a sandwich. Then I gave up a hit in the next inning."

For his career, Smoltz had more strikeouts (3,084) and fewer hits allowed (3,074) than innings pitched (3,473). No wonder the Braves eventually retired his No. 29.

"That was just the number they gave me," he said. "I was actually trying to change it for years. I knew I couldn't win 29 games so I wanted to switch to 20 or 21. Warren Spahn had 21 so that was retired. Then in 1996, I won 24 games, four post-season games, and an All-Star Game—matching my number—so I figured I should keep the number that gave me such good luck."

Good luck did not always accompany John Smoltz. Articulate with the media and affable with his teammates, he was widely considered the hypochondriac of the clubhouse—always complaining about something.

As Tom Glavine explained, "The joke in the clubhouse was that if Smoltzie came in the day he was pitching and said something was wrong with him, we knew he was going to have a great game. When he came in and nothing was wrong, we were worried. He was one of those guys who wore his emotions on his sleeve. He let you know what was going on."

In his book *Starting and Closing*, Smoltz said "The No. 1 rule in baseball is you can't make the club in the tub. I think I might be the exception. I had to invest a lot of time in the trainer's room—way more than I would have liked—but it was essential to keeping me at the level I needed to be in order to pitch.

"I think I missed the least amount of time I could have missed with five surgeries. I missed all of 2000 after Tommy John surgery and there was no way to avoid that. But when you think about the big picture, I really didn't miss that much time."

Considered the most emotional member of the Big Three, Smoltz felt his return to the rotation in 2005 allowed the Braves to maintain their streak even though Maddux had followed Glavine into greener pastures via free agency.

"I don't think we could have won otherwise," Smoltz said. "Our rotation had drastically changed. When I was in the bullpen, we didn't win the Series. They didn't even get to me a lot. So the conversation became 'What's better?'

"I honestly believed that having me start gave us a much better chance to win. It was like adding another frontline pitcher and making us good enough to get to the playoffs. I had a great year and followed up with another good year. We didn't get to the World Series but I won a game in the postseason. You can't win forever as a team; sooner or later, every streak comes to an end."

Although Smoltz never planned to leave Atlanta, he divided his last season between Boston and St. Louis after he and management disagreed on the right time to retire. Only three of his 213 wins came when he wasn't wearing a Braves uniform.

JOHN ANDREW SMOLTZ
ATLANTA, N.L. 1988-99, 2001-08; BOSTON, A.L. 2009; ST. LOUIS, N.L. 2009

A WORKHORSE POWER PITCHER, TRADED HIS STARTING DOMINANCE TO DEVELOP INTO PREMIER CLOSER BEFORE RETURNING TO ROTATION. BECAME THE FIRST PLAYER IN HISTORY WITH 200 WINS AND 150 SAVES. WITH A DYNAMIC FASTBALL, A DECEPTIVE SLIDER AND A DARTING SPLITTER, FANNED 3,084 BATTERS AND WAS NAMED TO EIGHT ALL-STAR TEAMS. THE 1996 N.L. CY YOUNG AWARD WINNER AND 1992 NLCS MVP. SET N.L. RECORD WITH 55 SAVES IN 2002. PITCHED BEST WHEN GAME WAS BIGGEST, RECORDING A 15-4 POST-SEASON RECORD, HELPING BRAVES TO 1995 WORLD SERIES TITLE.

Photo courtesy of the National Baseball Hall of Fame and Museum.

"Playing for one team was my desire," he said, "and I gave up a lot of money over the years to stay in Atlanta."

The Braves and their fans are glad he did.

5

THE HOCKEY PLAYER: TOM GLAVINE

LONG BEFORE ANYONE beyond Billerica, Massachusetts, heard of Tom Glavine, *SPORT* magazine published his picture and predicted he'd blossom into a future star.

He looked like a kid—too young to shave, vote, or buy himself a beer but bubbling with the potential to become a pretty decent pitcher. He lacked both size and strength but compensated with stamina and stubbornness—traits that would make him one of the most successful southpaws in the history of the game.

Just months before his picture appeared, Glavine had to decide whether to go to college on a hockey scholarship or whether to become a professional athlete. He also needed to make a difficult choice between baseball and hockey—sports in which he excelled at his suburban Boston high school.

Hoping he'd pick sports over college, the Atlanta Braves drafted him in the second round of the baseball amateur draft in June 1984. Days later, the Los Angeles Kings tried to make Glavine a professional hockey player. The 69th overall pick in the NHL draft, he was actually chosen ahead of Brett Hull.

Thanks in part to his father's stories about Hall of Fame left-hander Warren Spahn, the young Tom Glavine decided a ball was a better bet than a puck.

"Spahn was a very big influence on me without my realizing it," Glavine said years after he retired. "My dad was a big Boston Braves fan when he was a kid and liked Spahn a lot. Whatever pitching advice my dad gave me as a kid was usually followed with, 'I heard Warren Spahn say this.' My dad would repeat things to me that he heard Spahn say. I had to figure out if they worked.

"As I got older and got into the game, I knew who Spahn was, what he meant to the game, and certainly what he meant to the Braves franchise. When you start getting mentioned in the same sentence with guys like that, it's the kind of thing that motivates you to continue to try and do well."

By the time he retired in 2008, Glavine had won 305 games, trailing only Spahn, Steve Carlton, and Eddie Plank on the list of lifetime victories by a left-hander.

The big league trail began for Glavine in 1987, when the Bad News Braves were based in Atlanta as well as the basement of their division. It was trial by fire: the infielders couldn't catch much more than a cold, the hitters hardly hit, and the pitchers received such pathetic support that they reported to the park without a drop of confidence.

His August 17 debut could only be described as disappointing. The Houston Astros pounded him for six runs on ten hits in three-and-two-thirds innings. He finished the year with an unsightly earned run average of 5.54—exactly two full runs over his eventual career mark.

Although a contender might have given up on him, the Braves were beggars, not choosers. In his first two seasons, Glavine staggered to a 9–21 record, showing only occasional flashes of the familiar form that eventually led to the Hall of Fame.

Glavine's Cache

Longtime Braves star Tom Glavine revealed in 2014 that he has a memorabilia collection that includes souvenirs from his 200th, 250th, and 300th wins, his two Cy Young trophies, and baseballs signed by Mickey Mantle, Whitey Ford, and Ted Williams.

But the on-the-job training helped the studious left-hander gain invaluable experience. Glavine threw his first four shutouts during a 14–8 campaign—his first winning season—in 1989.

Things were changing for the team, too.

Bobby Cox, the general manager whose scouts found and signed Glavine, moved into the dugout in 1990; new general manager John Schuerholz found some fielders on the free agent market; and the once-moribund franchise rebounded to become the best in the National League.

Glavine was a huge part of that revival.

In fact, he was Atlanta's No. 1 starter in both 1991, when the team started its streak of 14 straight titles and he won the first of his two Cy Young Awards, and in 1992.

The even-tempered Glavine hardly blinked when the Braves signed Greg Maddux before the '93 campaign.

"Every winter, you assess your team, and try to play along with the front office to see what we could do to get better," he recalled. "That winter, all the talk was that we were going to get Barry Bonds. The Maddux stuff came out of the blue.

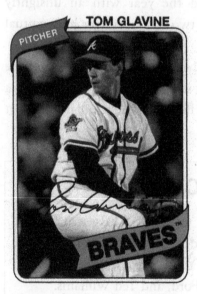

TOM GLAVINE
PITCHER

Courtesy of The Topps Company, Inc.

"All I could think was 'We had a good pitching staff before but now we had a *really* good pitching staff.' There was a little bit of wondering what it was going to be like, how Greg was going to fit in. But it didn't take long during spring training to realize Greg was of the same mold as the rest of us. He loved playing golf and that made for an easy transition."

Maddux might have been No. 1 in theory but Glavine had more 20-win seasons (five), made more

All-Star teams (ten), and won more World Series MVP trophies (one) than the free agent signee. The best right-left tandem of the postwar era, they combined for 438 victories during the decade they were teammates.

With John Smoltz also in the rotation for most of those years, it's easy to see why the Braves seldom lost three games in a row

Glavine's personal highlight reel started spinning in 1991.

"We went into spring training thinking we were going to be a better team, a competitive team, but I think our realistic goal was to play .500 baseball," Glavine admitted. "We had lost 100 games three years in a row and coming from where we were, that was a lofty goal.

"So much was centered around the guys we got: Terry Pendleton, Rafael Belliard, Sid Bream, and Otis Nixon. We knew we were going to play much better defense and that was going to help us. The pitchers realized if they made good pitches and put the ball in play, the guys were going to make good plays behind us. Prior to that, there were times when we pitched away from contact because we weren't sure what would happen if the ball was put into play."

Glavine did his part, posting a 6–0 mark in May that made him National League Pitcher of the Month.

At the All-Star break, Atlanta stood third, nine-and-a-half games out of first, but Cox kept encouraging the players, Glavine said. "Bobby's message was 'We're one good week away from getting back into this thing.' Sure enough, we won seven in a row, the Dodgers lost seven in a row, and we started to think, 'Hey, we've got a legitimate shot at this thing.'"

After finishing a game ahead of the Dodgers in the National League West, the Braves beat the Pittsburgh Pirates in the playoffs and took the Minnesota Twins—another worst-to-first team—to the seventh game of the World Series. "So many of the games were decided by one run," Glavine remembered. "I'll never forget the last game, that 1–0, 10-inning victory for Minnesota. Both teams had opportunities to score some runs early but neither could do it. There was a lot of crazy stuff

Tom Glavine yielded only a bloop single in eight scoreless innings during the last game of the1995 World Series. He took two of the six games to win World Series MVP honors.

AP Photo/Tannen Maury

going on: great pitching, timely hitting, a series in which home-field advantage was huge. The '91 Series was exciting, to be sure, but I thought the '95 World Series was better just because of the way it ended."

As in 1991, the score in the final game was 1–0. But, thanks to Glavine, the verdict went Atlanta's way.

After beating the heavy-hitting Cleveland Indians by a 4–3 score in Game Two, Glavine was even better in Game Six. He pitched five hitless innings, yielded a bloop single to Tony Pena in the sixth, and was still on the hill when David Justice connected for a solo home run that produced the only score of the night.

"I knew I had good stuff that night," said Glavine years later. "But with me, you never know. The first inning was always my Achilles' heel. When I got through the first that night, I thought, 'Okay, the stuff's the same I had in the bullpen. Here we go.' As each inning went on, I got more confident. I was in the zone."

After Pena's pop fell safely in the top of the sixth, Glavine's bid for the second no-hitter in World Series history ended. But his energy didn't.

"Losing a no-hitter was probably a relief," he admitted. "I didn't have to worry about it. I came into the dugout after Pena's hit and remember screaming 'Get me one! Just get me one! They're not getting any runs tonight."

Shutting down the Tribe was a tall order; Cleveland came into the World Series after leading the American League with 207 home runs in the strike-shortened season. Six of the men in the Indians batting order finished on the sunny side of .300. But good pitching stops good hitting, or so the baseball adage says.

"That was the most dangerous, best-balanced lineup I ever faced," Glavine said. "Even their seventh hitter, Jim Thome, had 25 home runs. As each inning went on, and I hadn't given up a hit yet, I got more and more confident. But I never envisioned throwing a one-hitter."

Although Glavine didn't duplicate Don Larsen's feat of 1956, he and closer Mark Wohlers, who pitched a perfect ninth, did produce the first combined one-hitter in the history of the World Series. The closer, who

Owner Ted Turner shares the locker room euphoria with 1995 World Series MVP Tom Glavine after a one-hit, 1–0 victory over Cleveland.

AP Photo/Tannen Maury

was in high school when Glavine broke into the big leagues with the Braves, was the man mobbed by his teammates at the end of the game.

Leaving was Glavine's decision. He just wasn't the same when he took the mound in the top of the eighth.

"It was a little tougher to get loose," said the finesse artist, who walked three and fanned eight while throwing 109 pitches that night. "My pitches weren't as crisp or as sharp. Although I had a 1-2-3 inning, two out of the outs came on mistakes I got away with. As much as I wanted to be the guy out there to finish the game, Wohlers was ready. He had a phenomenal year and I felt he was the better option going into the ninth, with the top of their order coming up."

For the six-game series, Glavine posted a 2–0 record, 1.29 earned run average, and 11 strikeouts in 14 innings.

Glavine had big-game experience even before he pitched the '95 Braves to the first world championship in Atlanta sports history.

He manned the rudder of the worst-to-first voyage in 1991, tying for the league lead with 20 wins and nine complete games while compiling a 2.55 ERA, fanning 192 hitters, and posting a .645 winning percentage. That made him the last man to win a Cy Young before Maddux started his streak of four straight.

In 1992, when pundits predicted the worst-to-first Braves would get a quick reality check, Glavine answered with 13 straight wins, tying a franchise record, and a league-best five shutouts. He yielded only six home runs all season, won a career-peak 22 times, and had a winning percentage of .714. Then he became the first left-hander since Mickey Lolich in 1968 to pitch two complete games in the World Series.

After a see-saw NL West title chase with San Francisco in 1993, the race came down to the last day. If Glavine could beat the Colorado Rockies at home, the Giants would have to win their game against the Los Angeles Dodgers.

"It was one of my more nerve-wracking games," said Glavine, who always projected an image of total composure on the mound. "It was a do-or-die Game Seven situation. You still have a chance if you lose, as long as San Francisco would lose too, but you can't think that way.

"As it turned out, we played a good ballgame, had a couple of clutch plays defensively, and were able to muster out a win. And we got some big help from Los Angeles later that afternoon."

The 5–3 win was Glavine's 22nd and gave the Braves a perfect 13–0 record against the expansion Rockies and improved their season's total to a club-record 104. The Giants, defeated by the Dodgers, won 103 and went home for the winter. It was the last pure pennant race, with the wild-card format yet to be adopted.

For Glavine, it was his third straight 20-win season—a baseball rarity during the days of five-man rotations and pitch counts. "A lot of things have to go right," he said of winning 20. "If you get 34 starts a year, it's tough to win 20 of those. In seasons when you do make it, you win all of the games you should win. As a starter, if you go seven or eight innings and give up two earned runs or less, you should win. Even if you win all of those games, you have to win a few you shouldn't win and you have to win a few where you get lucky. Either you aren't pitching well and your offense bails you out or you stay in the game and get a run in the late innings."

Neither Glavine nor the team missed a beat when Atlanta moved to the National League East in 1994. Two years later, he was the winning pitcher in the final game of both the NL Division Series and the NL Championship Series. In the seventh game of the NLCS, he not only won a 15–0 laugher against the St. Louis Cardinals but cleared the bases with a first-inning triple. He earned his second Cy Young Award in 1998 and enjoyed his fifth and last 20-win season two years later.

The 6–0, 175-pound southpaw even threw a pair of complete-game shutouts at Denver's Coors Field, where pitchers usually go to die.

"People always ask me what was the greatest game I ever pitched," he said. "Game Six of the 1995 World Series comes to mind because of what it meant and the timing. But for me, from a technical or execution standpoint, those two shutouts in Denver stand out. It doesn't get much better than that. A shutout in Denver is as rare as a no-hitter."

The first National Leaguer to start consecutive All-Star games (1991–92) since Robin Roberts (1954–55), Glavine was the first Atlanta pitcher to win a Cy Young. Winning more often than any Braves southpaw since Spahn went 23–7 in 1963, Glavine placed second in innings pitched and third in strikeouts, earned run average, and opposing batting average. But it wasn't his best campaign.

"The 1998 season was a more consistent year for me," he said. "I would call 1991 a coming-out year, a season in which both the Braves and I put ourselves on the map. That might have been a more fun year but in terms of consistency, time in and time out, 1998 was better. I was able to go out there and do what I wanted to do every time."

It wasn't always easy for Glavine, who depended upon location rather than velocity. He lived on the outside corner and was so often the benefit of the "wide" strike that Major League Baseball ordered QuesTec machines to monitor umpire performance behind the plate. All of a sudden, the called strikes Glavine had been getting with his sinker, slider, circle-change, and cut fastball (learned from Maddux) became less frequent.

Even before the umpires started squeezing the strike zone from east to west, Glavine often struggled at the start. For him, facing the first inning was like Superman facing kryptonite.

Aided by longtime Atlanta pitching coach Leo Mazzone, the pitcher made adjustments.

"Throwing twice between starts helped me a lot," said Glavine, who avoided the disabled list until his final year as an active player. "There was a point in time when I didn't feel right and my arm didn't feel great. When Leo said we're going to throw more often, I said, 'Are you crazy? I have a hard enough time with one side session and now we're going to have two?'

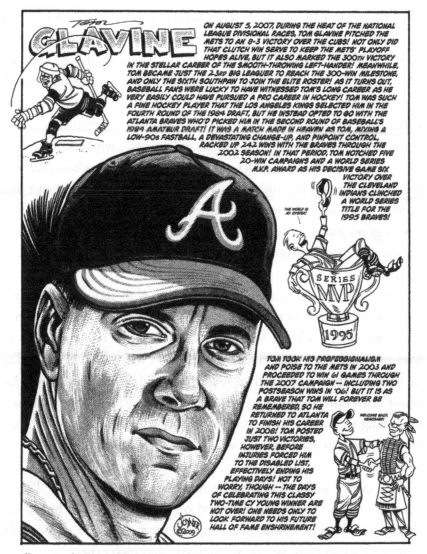

Illustration by Ronnie Joyner.

"But I'm the kind of person that if you tell me something and can back it up with what you're talking about, I'll try and figure out if it's good for me or if it helps me. I tried it and felt better. I felt a little stronger and my recovery between starts got a little better."

Consistency was a Glavine hallmark. "I certainly think luck was part of it," he said of his success. "My pitching style was part of it too. I learned how to pitch when I wasn't 100 percent. I had my share of arm problems, leg issues, and more but there was never anything I couldn't pitch through. Even if I was at 75 or 80 percent, it was my job to pitch every fifth day. I learned how to pitch, be successful, and give my team a chance to win."

The lefty also learned a lot on the golf course, where his partners were usually Maddux, Smoltz, and Steve Avery—or whomever was the fourth man in the rotation. "Pitchers have good games and bad games," Glavine explained. "The time between starts is easy when you have a good game. When you have a bad game, that in-between is a bit tougher. You beat yourself up for four days before you get back out there.

"The ability to get out on the golf course with those guys and get away from the stress of the baseball season was good. It was very thera-peutic for us. I don't care what walk of life you are in—you've got to have an outlet to get away from your job. Golf was it for us. As much as we went out there and just tried to play golf and have a good time, a lot of our conversation centered around pitching. Maybe the other guy saw something we needed to fix. Or maybe we would talk about the team we were going to play next. We would exchange information on how to pitch to a guy.

"The guys I was surrounded by made me a better pitcher. People talked about the competition we had on the pitching staff but it was always in a fun way, a respectful way, and a way in which we honestly drove each other to be better. We learned from each other.

"Greg's greatest influence on me was the way he would have a game plan and either execute it or change it. It was based not only on what he wanted to do but what the hitters were telling him."

Glavine, a member of the National Honor Society in high school, remained a good student: he won 244 games during 17 years with the Braves, missing only the last three years of the 14-year title run.

Spahn's Visit

When Warren Spahn made a clubhouse visit to Bobby Cox in Atlanta, he encountered Greg Maddux and Tom Glavine in the trainer's room. According to his son Greg, who was there, "We walked into the middle of a conversation and dad had a very good exchange with those pitchers. Glavine reminded me of my father with the way he pitched, with the control, although he didn't have the high leg kick. I admired Tom throughout his career but didn't want to see him break dad's victory record. That didn't come into play but Maddux came close, only eight wins short."

When the run was suspended by a 232-day player strike that stretched from 1994 into 1995, Glavine drew the wrath of Atlanta fans because he represented the Players Association in negotiations with the owners. "The first game back, people were throwing money at me in the bullpen," he said. "It lasted into the summer."

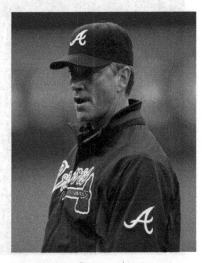

Glavine silenced the fans by hitting a solo home run—the only one of his career —that tied a game against Cincinnati's John Smiley. "I got a curtain call and thought, 'Okay, this is the end of it.' I took a lot of heat."

Two years later, however, with Glavine forgiven by the fans, he was the player the team asked to carry home plate from Atlanta Fulton County Stadium to the new Turner Field.

Tom Glavine's five 20-win seasons helped keep the Braves in first place.

Photo by Bill Menzel.

81

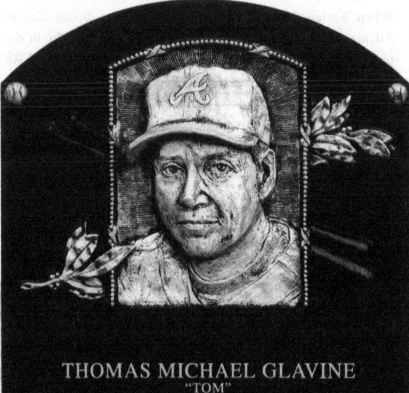

THOMAS MICHAEL GLAVINE
"TOM"
ATLANTA, N.L. 1987-2002, 2008;
NEW YORK, N.L. 2003-07

DURABLE, DOMINANT AND DECEPTIVE STARTING PITCHER, WHOSE CONTROL, CHANGE OF SPEEDS AND PLACEMENT OF PITCHES TRANSLATED INTO 305 WINS. FIFTH LEFTY TO REACH THE 300-WIN PLATEAU. TEN-TIME ALL-STAR, FOUR-TIME SILVER SLUGGER, TWICE A CY YOUNG AWARD WINNER AND 1995 WORLD SERIES MVP, TOSSING THE SERIES-CLINCHING GEM. MEMBER OF FIVE PENNANT-WINNERS, LEADING N.L. IN WINS FIVE TIMES, INCLUDING 20 IN THREE STRAIGHT SEASONS. STARTED AT LEAST 25 GAMES IN 20 STRAIGHT SEASONS, SIX TIMES LEADING THE LEAGUE IN STARTS.

Photo courtesy of the National Baseball Hall of Fame and Museum.

Having the manager in his corner helped. "Bobby gave me every opportunity to go out there and be successful," Glavine said. "He was a positive guy who never said anything negative about anybody in the newspaper or on the radio. I lost 200 games in my career and a lot of them were under Bobby. There were some days when I got up and read the paper and thought, 'Oh, my God, Bobby, were you watching the same game that I was pitching?"

Glavine's tenure included 11 postseason appearances, five pennants, and one world championship. "When I got drafted by the Braves, I didn't know a whole lot about them except for Hank Aaron and Dale Murphy," he said. "From 1984 until I got there, they weren't very good. Then we lost 100 games my first three years in the big leagues.

"To go from that to running off 11 straight division titles while I was there, win a World Series, and play in a few others were things I never could have imagined happening in a million years. We got the right pieces to the puzzle and, being one of those pieces, I was extremely proud of it. I had an opportunity from the ground floor. It was fun being part of that transition."

After spending five years with the New York Mets, who signed him as a free agent after the 2002 season, Glavine returned to the Braves

Tough Choice

Looking back on the 14-year title run, Tom Glavine hesitated when asked to pick a favorite. "It's a toss-up," he said. "You won't find many situations where you ask players what their favorite year was and there's a choice between winning a World Series and another year. "One more win and 1991 would have been my choice. It's second, but not by much. I have to say 1995 was the ultimate. But had we won the World Series in '91, there'd be no way to top that."

as a 300-game winner. By then, the 14-year Atlanta title streak had ended—except as an impressive footnote to baseball history.

"When we were going through it, we didn't think much about it beyond, 'We won last year, let's win again this year.' You live in the moment and try to deal with it," Glavine explained.

"I have more of an appreciation now for what we did and how difficult it was. I don't think it will ever be done again. From the standpoint of today's game, it would be awfully hard to keep those kinds of teams together the way we kept our team together."

6

THE PROFESSOR: GREG MADDUX

HE WALKED TO the beat of a different drummer and answered to different names.

Known variously as Mad Dog, Doggy, or The Professor, Greg Maddux looked more like a librarian than an athlete. His horn-rimmed glasses even suggested Clark Kent, the meek alter ego of Superman. But looks can be deceiving.

Favoring location over velocity, Maddux outpitched the opposition by outsmarting them. He eventually won 355 games, more than any postwar pitcher not named Warren Spahn, and four straight National League Cy Young Awards—an unprecedented feat later duplicated by Randy Johnson.

Maddux joined the Braves as a free agent in 1993 and stayed 11 seasons, most of them teaming with Tom Glavine and John Smoltz in a troika that terrorized all who dared oppose them.

A master of consistency, Maddux never won more than 20 games or less than 15 in any of those seasons. But he won with guile, glove, and an ability to hit and bunt when needed.

The 6–0, 170-pound right-hander not only had the ability to place each pitch precisely where he wanted it but to position his defense properly in advance. He could even predict where the ball would be hit—not only when he was pitching but when he was sitting in the dugout watching somebody else on the mound.

During a game in 2001, Maddux had runners on second and third with one out. Bobby Cox came out to ask whether the pitcher would

Illustration by Ronnie Joyner.

walk the next man, who batted left-handed, to set up a force at any base.

"No," he told the manager, "I'm going to get him to pop up to third base on the second pitch and then get a grounder to get us out of this mess."

Maddux delivered exactly as promised.

A Texas native who moved often as the Air Force transferred his dad from one base to another, Maddux was a control master on and off the mound. His only ailments were a spring training bout with the chicken pox, a case of the flu that caused him to miss a start, and a bruised shin after Philadelphia's Mickey Morandini hit a liner off his leg during a playoff game. Even midseason Lasik eye surgery was nothing more for Maddux than something to do during an All-Star Game to which he was not invited.

It didn't happen often; the man was an NL All-Star eight times and should have gone more. He was overlooked in 1993, for example, even though he was the defending Cy Young Award winner and was in the second season of that four-year streak.

That season, his first with the Braves after he signed a five-year, $28 million pact to pitch for a team that had won consecutive pennants, Maddux would finish with 20 wins—duplicating his 1992 total with the Chicago Cubs. Those would be his only seasons at that plateau but hardly his only years rewriting the record books.

Had they not signed Maddux the previous winter, the Braves would not have won their third consecutive division crown in 1993. The team needed every one of the new pitcher's wins to eke out a one-game victory over the San Francisco Giants in a title chase that went down to the last day. Atlanta finished with 104 wins, one more than the Giants, and advanced into the playoffs.

San Francisco slugger Barry Bonds, a free agent considered by the Braves before they signed Maddux, was the main bane of most pitchers' existence from the minute he arrived on the West Coast.

"Barry was probably the best hitter I faced because he could take you deep and if you walked him, he would steal second and third," Maddux remembered. "He was so good the last 10 years I faced him that he turned into the easiest guy in the world to pitch against. All I had to do was throw four pitches 10 feet outside."

The penultimate control artist, Maddux once went 72 1/3 innings without walking anyone. He worked quickly, mainly because he didn't

<hr>

Marvelous Maddux

The Braves stunned even their own players when they signed Greg Maddux as a free agent. According to Ron Gant, "You start thinking 'How in the world did we pull *that* off?' in getting that caliber pitcher. It didn't surprise me in a way because I knew we were pro-active in the market for putting together a long, extensive run of championships. Nothing the organization did surprised me at that point."

<hr>

believe in wasting pitches, and once needed only 76 pitches to complete a game.

"You pitch to get hitters out," he said. "I was in situations where we usually had leads so I could be a little bit more aggressive in the strike zone.

"It's not how hard you throw but what your ball does in the last 10 feet. I always felt like I threw more balls down the middle of the plate than anybody but was able to have the ball do a little something the last 10 feet that enabled me to get away from that. Because of that, my location looked better."

Although Maddux mixed five pitches into a repertoire that hypnotized rival hitters, he relied most heavily on a sinker and changeup. He had control, command, movement, an ability to change speeds, and a mental book on hitters unmatched by any of his colleagues.

Those skills allowed him to lead National League pitchers in starts seven times, innings and shutouts five times each, wins and complete games three times each, and winning percentage twice.

While others were hyping him for the Hall, Maddux never thought about it. "People would say things from time to time," he said, "but I didn't listen to it. When I was playing, it was all about my next start or what I was doing after the game.

"I never had a goal. I just wanted to pitch. My goal was to find something today that would help me tomorrow."

According to longtime Braves broadcaster Don Sutton, a Hall of Fame pitcher himself, "He didn't have the best fastball, the best curveball, the best slider, or the best changeup. He was just the best pitcher."

A true master of location, Maddux hoped hitters would hit the inside fastball off the handle or turn his changeup into a groundout off the end of the bat. They often did.

Stingy to a fault, Mad Dog made rival hitters feel like they'd

Greg Maddux never pitched a no-hitter but still managed to win more games than any living pitcher.

Photo by the author.

been bitten by a pit bull. In 1994, his earned run average was 1.56, a career best. A year later, it was 1.63.

Not since Walter Johnson in 1918–19 had a pitcher posted such microscopic ERAs in consecutive campaigns.

"He set hitters up," said Leo Mazzone, his pitching coach with the Braves. "He pitched them one way in order to set them up for later. He was like a poker player who never played his hand all at once."

Maddux was great at keeping a poker face; his father Dave was not only a fast-pitch softball player but also a poker dealer at the MGM Grand in Las Vegas.

"Everyone talks about hitting the Lotto but I was lucky enough to hit it for 23 straight years," said Maddux, who was only three when he started playing ball with older brother Mike, later a respected pitching coach for several clubs. The two made baseball history as the first fraternal freshmen to start against each other.

Greg spent his first six seasons in Chicago, winning his first Cy Young before he left, but blossomed into baseball's best pitcher only after his sojourn to the south. During his 11 Atlanta seasons from 1993 to 2003, he posted a .688 winning percentage and 2.63 ERA while winning 194 games. The only time the Braves failed to reach the playoffs during his tenure was the unfinished season of 1994, when a players' strike shut down the game for 232 days starting in August.

Maybe the extended rest helped the veteran pitcher; he was almost unbeatable in 1995. On the road, he went 13–0 with a 1.12 ERA. He finished the regular season with 21 straight scoreless innings, and then beat Colorado in the Division Series and Cincinnati in the Championship Series before winning the World Series opener.

His best game of the season might have been a 1–0 two-hitter against St. Louis that took only an hour and fifty minutes. With better support, Maddux might have had a better record; the team lost by a run in three of his six no-decisions and one of his two losses. In three other games, the Braves won in their last at-bat after Maddux had left the game.

The first National Leaguer to win at least three straight ERA crowns since Sandy Koufax took five in a row from 1962 to 1965, Maddux also became the first pitcher named Associated Press Baseball Player of the Year, an award launched in 1988. He was third in the voting for National League MVP, trailing Barry Larkin and Dante Bichette.

According to Terry Pendleton, who also arrived in Atlanta as a free agent, "He had the heart of a lion. He didn't care who you were, how big you were, what bat you used, or who you played for. He came at you the best way he knew how."

Pendleton, both a teammate and opponent of Maddux, said he liked the fact that the pitcher threw strikes. "I was more comfortable hitting against him than some other pitchers," he said. "You knew he would make you swing the bat. He threw everything with that same motion but kept you off balance with that sinker, slider, and change-up."

A playful pitcher who had a clubhouse reputation as a prankster, Maddux had an uncanny ability to remember what pitch he threw to whom and when but an inability to remember names of non-players he encountered along the way, such as golf caddies. Since he often joined rotation mates Tom Glavine and John Smoltz on the links, that characteristic made the well-liked but mercurial Maddux the target of good-natured teasing.

He hardly cared. He was the kind of guy who once threw Jeff Bagwell a fastball as an experiment in the eighth inning *during a no-hitter*. Maddux never came that close again. But he had a big lead that day and was thinking about how he might pitch the slugger when they met again.

"He was really big on throwing a pitch and seeing the hitter's reaction," said Ryne Sandberg, a fellow Hall of Famer who played with and against Maddux. "If he threw it on the outside corner and the batter leaned over, he was asking for the next pitch to be inside. I tried to think along with him.

"His command was excellent and he was very good at locating his pitches. If he wanted to pitch on the inside corner, the ball ended up there. If he wanted to pitch on the outside, it was there. He also had off-speed stuff that he used very well."

When it came to the World Series, Maddux made the right moves. He throttled the powerful Cleveland Indians with a two-hitter to start the 1995 Fall Classic with a 3–2 victory. The Tribe hit only four balls out of the infield against the sinkerballer.

Maddux collected his fourth and final Cy Young trophy that year but also got his only World Series ring. "When you win a Cy Young," he said, "you go home and you're the only one who's happy. In 1995, it was much more special because everyone in the clubhouse, the front office, and the city of Atlanta got to share it."

WHEN THE BRAVES RULED THE DIAMOND

Although he did not win any personal awards from 1997 to 2000, Maddux remained magnificent. He went 75–31 with a 2.73 ERA and 24 complete games, including a 76-pitch complete game at Wrigley Field in which he threw 63 strikes. He needed only 84 pitches to blank the Yankees in New York, 2–0, while yielding three hits and no walks on July 2, 1997. Since Maddux faced just 28 batters, the game took a crisp two hours and nine minutes.

After going 19–2 in '95, he went 19–4 two years later. During that '97 campaign, when he was runner-up for the Cy Young, Maddux faced 893 hitters in 232 2/3 innings and issued just 14 walks that were not intentional. He did not throw a single wild pitch.

"You only have to do two things to pitch," he explained. "You have to locate the fastball and you have to change speeds. It doesn't matter if you're pitching 75 miles per hour or 100 miles per hour. If you can locate your fastball for strikes on both sides of the plate and change speeds, you've got a good chance to win. Hitting is all timing. You've just got to do something to disrupt a hitter's timing."

The Professor didn't need to keep written notes. A pitching savant, he remembered everything.

"If you throw certain pitches in certain locations, you know that hitters are likely to hit the ball to certain places on the field," he explained. "It's pretty much common sense. If hitters did one thing against five other pitchers, they're probably going to do the same thing against you."

A Michael Jordan fan who also favored cheeseburgers, country music, and Nintendo, Maddux won more games during the '90s than any other pitcher. "When I charted a right-handed pitcher," said the left-handed Glavine, who finished second in victories for the decade, "I usually didn't pay a whole lot of attention. But watching Greg helped because our styles were similar.

"We weren't exactly the same but we both changed speeds and located our pitches. It was good for me to watch him the night before I pitched because I could see the location, how he was getting guys out. I learned a lot from watching Greg."

2

Happy Birthday

Greg Maddux and Tom Glavine were born twenty days apart.

Mad Dog devoured grounders and line drives so well that he proved to be a virtual fifth infielder. He was so adept at fielding his position that he won Gold Gloves in all but five of his 23 seasons.

At the peak of his game, no one could touch Greg Maddux. It hardly mattered that he moved from the Chicago Cubs, then in the National League East, to the Atlanta Braves, then the best in the West.

He met key figures in his career in both cities. Before he fell under the tutelage of Leo Mazzone, Cubs pitching coach Dick Pole made a difference by suggesting that Maddux concentrate on making good pitches rather than getting outs.

"I'd rather make a good pitch and give up a bloop single than make a bad pitch and get an out," the pitcher said. "I only know one way to pitch. I can't get caught up in artificial turf, grass, or short fences."

The fast-working Maddux didn't need pep talks during a game. "We were three months into the season and I hadn't been out to the mound to talk to him all year," Mazzone wrote in his book. "Before one game, he asked me about that. He said, 'It gets kind of lonely out there. I'll look in during the sixth inning so come out and pay me a visit.'

"Sure enough, in the sixth inning, he looked into the dugout and Bobby said, 'Hey, Leo, Mad Dog is looking in. Something must be wrong. Go check it out. I ran out and said, 'Mad Dog, you're pitching a great game.' He said, 'Yeah, I feel good. Everything's going fine.' We shot the bull for a minute and he said, 'Okay, we've got our TV time now. Thanks for coming out.'"

Maddux mentioned that the men who influenced him most were Cox, Mazzone, Bud Black (his manager in San Diego late in his career), and Ralph Medar. Who?

GREGORY ALAN MADDUX
"GREG" "MAD DOG"
CHICAGO, N.L. 1986-92, 2004-06; ATLANTA, N.L. 1993-2003;
LOS ANGELES, N.L. 2006, 2008; SAN DIEGO, N.L. 2007-08
ONE OF GAME'S MOST CONSISTENT, COMPOSED AND
CELEBRATED STARTING PITCHERS. FIRST TO WIN AT
LEAST 15 GAMES IN 17 STRAIGHT SEASONS, EN ROUTE
TO 355 CAREER VICTORIES, EIGHTH-MOST ALL-TIME
AND THE SECOND-HIGHEST TOTAL SINCE THE 1920S.
ONLY HURLER WITH 300 WINS, 3,000 STRIKEOUTS AND
LESS THAN 1,000 WALKS. PREPARATION, COMMAND
AND STUDY OF BATTERS MADE HIM PART-SCIENTIST,
PART-ARTIST, WINNING FOUR STRAIGHT CY YOUNG
AWARDS. ALSO CAPTURED 18 GOLD GLOVE AWARDS.

Photo courtesy of the National Baseball Hall of Fame and Museum.

"When I was 15 or 16, he taught me the importance of making each pitch do something for the last 10 feet," he revealed. "He was a retired guy who knew a lot about the movement of the baseball as opposed to velocity. I bought into it. He changed my arm angle and showed me how to make the ball sink."

Only once, in 1998, did Maddux strike out more than 200 men in a season. Batters, knowing his pitches would be around the plate, jumped on his sinker early in the count but kept pounding it into the ground. Working with a personal catcher helped (he preferred the defense of Charlie O'Brien or Eddie Perez over the offense of Javy Lopez in Atlanta).

Both the Cubs and Braves retired the right-hander's No. 31, a number also worn in Chicago by Hall of Famer Ferguson Jenkins. He reciprocated by keeping his plaque free of any logo.

The Hall of Fame hat flap was hardly surprising for Maddux, who preferred the serenity of the golf course to the commotion of the card show. Not comfortable talking about himself, he conducted interviews in a whisper and never learned to sign a legible autograph.

Even though he had his best years in Atlanta, Maddux made the majors with the Cubs and returned there in 2004 after the Braves found his $15 million salary too stiff for an aging arm.

But Greg Maddux was not just *any* aging arm; he lasted five more seasons, winning his 300th game in Cubs livery, before both he and Glavine hung up their spikes after the 2008 campaign.

His Atlanta achievements alone could have qualified Maddux for Cooperstown: four ERA crowns, three Cy Youngs, three pennants, and a world championship.

"That was my best season," he said of the 1995 campaign. "When you are the last team standing and you have that ring, it's really hard to beat that feeling."

7

THE MVPs: TERRY AND CHIPPER

B OOKENDS. THAT'S WHAT Terry Pendleton and Chipper Jones represent in the history of Atlanta's 14-year string of championships. Both were switch-hitting third basemen who not only won batting titles but MVP awards. In fact, they remain the only Braves players named National League Most Valuable Player since Hank Aaron won his only MVP after the franchise, then based in Milwaukee, won the 1957 World Series.

Pendleton won the trophy in 1991, edging Pittsburgh slugger Barry Bonds, for his part in the worst-to-first season. No Pendleton, no pennant.

Jones, originally a shortstop, brought the trophy back to Dixie eight years later with a September display of timely power that pushed his team to their fifth pennant of the '90s—more than any other club.

Wildly different, they were often the same. They led by example but in different ways.

Pendleton was short, squat, and black; a rah-rah guy who could pick it at the hot corner. More likely to hit a single or double than a home run, he was still a formidable force when he faced opposing pitchers in pressure situations.

Jones, on the other hand, was a white matinee idol who seemed a foot taller than Pendleton. More comparable to Dale Murphy, a quiet slugger who won consecutive MVP awards in 1982–83, he held his own on defense when his knees allowed but struck terror into the hearts of rival managers, who couldn't decide whether he was weaker from the right side or the left.

They came to the team in different ways: Pendleton was plucked off the free-agent market in 1990 after hitting a career-worst .230 with six home runs for the St. Louis Cardinals. That very same year, the Braves made Jones the top choice in the amateur free agent draft.

Pendleton, 30 when he signed, prevailed for four solid seasons before the younger but more brittle Jones replaced him—giving the Braves unbroken continuity at a position that had already been played by Hall of Famer Eddie Mathews and fellow sluggers Darrell Evans and Bob Horner.

Jones, who spent his entire 19-year career in Atlanta, was the third baseman in 2005, the last year of the team's record streak.

That streak would not have started without Terry Pendleton.

He had hit a career-low .230 with the 1990 St. Louis Cardinals, limiting his potential suitors to the Braves and Yankees. Atlanta, primarily looking to bolster its defense at the hot corner, got much more than it expected.

"Going from the Grand Canyon [Busch Stadium] to a regular ballpark absolutely helped," said Pendleton, whose home run total rose from six with the Cardinals to 22 with the Braves. "I joke with people and tell them I led the league in sacrifice flies in St. Louis with nobody on third.

"I knew Atlanta had good young pitching. I also knew Bobby Cox and John Schuerholz had made some changes and wanted good defense. They felt if they could get some defense behind that good young pitching, they could turn the team around."

Pendleton prospered after changing his winter workout regimen. "I went home that winter and started working out a different way with a buddy of mine to gain strength," he revealed. "The other thing that helped me was knowing I was going to be in Atlanta for four years. I didn't have to come in and impress anybody but I wanted to come in and play well. It just seemed everything was so much more relaxed for me in Atlanta when I got there."

Simply put, there were no expectations. The manager and general manager, like Pendleton, were also in their first full season together.

"I thought we could win when I got to spring training and saw what we had," he said. "I even made a comment about it and some reporters said, 'Hey, this is the not the St. Louis Cardinals. This is the Atlanta Braves.' I said, 'You guys can think what you want but what I see here and what I think we're capable of doing is another story.'"

Some of his new teammates were skeptical. "Here's a guy St. Louis was throwing away," said Mark Lemke, "and I'm thinking 'We're signing this guy for four years? What are we doing?'"

Years later, he changed his tune. "Terry was probably the greatest baseball player I ever played with," said Lemke after he became a Braves broadcaster. "I always tell Chipper he was the most talented player I ever played with. But on and off the field, in the clubhouse, as a mentor, a leader, Terry was the greatest."

A big reason the Braves went from worst to first in 1991 was the signing of Terry Pendleton.

Photo courtesy of the Atlanta Braves.

Pendleton started slowly, hitting .234 in April, but then heated up as the weather warmed. He hit .410 in May, .360 in July, and .336 in September, helping the Braves win 29 more games than they had the year before. He played in pain half the time, starting every game after June 15 despite a cartilage tear in his left knee.

When the Braves sat in third place, nine-and-a-half games behind the Dodgers at the All-Star break, Pendleton piped up while some of his teammates seemed gripped by complacency—glad to be out of last place but not expecting to reach first. "This isn't over, this isn't over," he said, mostly to himself but loudly enough to be heard, as he paced the dugout before a game in Los Angeles.

The team went on a tear, coupled with a Dodgers slump, and moved into contention. Pendleton powered the way. His .353 average in the last 28 games featured a solo home run on September 11 that was the only Atlanta tally in a 1–0 combined no-hitter by Kent Mercker, Mark Wohlers, and Alejandro Pena.

"He showed the rest of the team how to act in a pennant race," said Jeff Treadway, who shared second base with Lemke that year.

By the time the season was over, the California native had a .319 batting average—best ever by a Braves third baseman not named Chipper Jones—and 187 hits. He also tied for the league lead with 303 total bases and 52 multi-hit games.

The batting chase, like the division race, went down to the last day. Cincinnati first baseman Hal Morris gave him a run, going 3-for-3 against the Padres before hitting a ball into the gap that was caught by Darrin Jackson.

Terry Terrific

Terry Pendleton paid instant dividends to the Braves after they signed him. "Terry certainly did better than what was expected of him," said Bobby Cox. "We never thought we were signing the MVP or batting champion but he won the award in '91 and was runner-up the following year. That was pretty darn good for a guy who was considered to be washed up. We didn't think he was through at all. He hit a lot of balls to the track in St. Louis and we kept track of those. There were 22 of those in one year that would have been home runs in Atlanta. We obviously thought he had some hitting skills left."

"If he'd have come out and gone 4-for-4, I would've tipped my cap to him," said the gracious Pendleton, noting that Morris was on deck when Reds game ended. "I may not get this opportunity again. To be the top hitter in the National League is an honor. They don't vote on the batting title. I earned that all by myself."

The first Atlanta batting champion since Ralph Garr in 1974, Pendleton pounded Minnesota pitching at a .367 clip in the World Series, homering twice, but just missed winning a ring when the Braves lost Game Seven, 1–0 in 10 innings.

He did win a trophy, however: the Baseball Writers Association of America named Pendleton the Most Valuable Player in the National League. He narrowly outpolled Barry Bonds, the 1990 winner, by 274–259.

"I was shocked," said Pendleton, who was somehow bypassed for the All-Star Game by National League manager Lou Piniella. "I never looked at myself as an MVP. To this day, I don't. When people ask me to sign stuff and put that on it, I say, 'Are you kidding me?'

"When I grew up, I looked at Willie Mays and Hank Aaron as MVPs. Guys you want to watch.

When my phone rang, I looked at my wife and she said, 'You probably ought to pick that up.'

"I actually rode downtown in a helicopter (sent by Atlanta's Channel 5) because I couldn't make it downtown in time for the press conference with all the Atlanta traffic.

"First of all, I didn't want to be in that helicopter. Secondly, I was seriously stunned about the whole thing. But it wouldn't have happened without my teammates. I was the MVP because of everyone around me."

Pendleton might have won the World Series MVP, too, if not for a base-running gaffe by Lonnie Smith. He was on first base with nobody out in the eighth inning of the seventh game when Pendleton lifted a long drive to left field. Not sure whether it could be caught, Smith stopped at second base as the ball fell in. Although Pendleton made it to second base, Smith could not advance beyond third. Neither of them scored as the scoreless duel continued between John Smoltz and Jack Morris.

"I was glad to be playing in it, not watching it," Pendleton said of a Fall Classic many consider the best of all time. "I think I would have had a heart attack watching it but playing in it was relaxing. For me, it was like any other baseball game.

"You knew you were the only two teams still playing—everybody else was done. All we had to do was go play. They were exciting games. The greatest thing for me was that any time something happened, I could have something to do with the outcome."

After a winter of wondering why their worst-to-first season ended by the narrowest possible margin, the Braves regrouped in '92 with Pendleton still leading the charge.

In fact, he was even better than he was the year before.

Barry Bonds, the MVP in 1990, won the award again in '92 as Pendleton dropped to second in the voting. "He said I shouldn't have won it in '91 but that's Barry," the infielder said.

Helping the Braves to their second straight division title, Pendleton hit .311 with 21 home runs and career highs in hits (199) and runs batted in (105). He tied for the league lead in base hits, ranked second in RBI, and tied for sixth in runs (98). Pendleton even pounded his first walk-off homer, teeing off on a low Mitch Williams fastball.

The first Braves third baseman to hit .300 in consecutive seasons (and only the third Brave), he was voted to the starting lineup of the National League All-Star team by the fans—the first Atlanta player so honored since Dale Murphy in 1986. The compact Californian also won his third Gold Glove.

Pendleton was up to his usual tricks in '93, leading the Braves as they engaged in a grueling title chase that went down to the last day. In a reversal of 1991, however, it was the Dodgers who knocked out the Giants rather than the other way around.

Pendleton wasn't always perfect, however. In a late May game, he stalked off the field in the middle of the seventh inning as a protest against the Braves for failing to retaliate against Reds pitcher Tim Belcher for hitting Deion Sanders with a pitch. Belcher was nursing a 4–0 lead and had yielded only one hit: a double by Deion.

"It was very unusual that Terry would do anything like that," said Bobby Cox, who had no choice but to fine the veteran infielder. "He's a first-class person. But everybody snaps once in awhile. I guess that was his time."

Both Cox and Sanders said later they didn't think Belcher was trying to hit anyone. Pendleton apparently disagreed.

At least he produced when needed most, pounding eight home runs in one 25-game stretch en route to a season's total of 17. After hitting .272 with 81 runs scored and 84 RBIs, he hit .346 and knocked in five runs against Philadelphia in a Championship Series that seemed anticlimactic. The Braves fell in six games.

Back problems in '94 landed Pendleton on the disabled list, ending his streak of 187 consecutive games, and a players' strike ended the season early. It also appeared to end Pendleton's playing career with the Braves, as the team decided against extending his four-year contract. They had a younger, more powerful replacement.

Pendleton's Perspective

According to player-turned-coach Terry Pendleton, the 14-year title streak cannot be copied. "Most people who have never played at this level would never understand how unbelievable it is," he said. "There are teams that may have runs of six or seven years and wonder how anybody can do it twice as long. That says a lot about the Atlanta Braves, a lot about John Schuerholz, Bobby Cox, our scouts, and our minor league system—the coaches and managers and how well they did their job. Getting those prospects and guys who could play in the majors and developing them to the point where when they get to the major-league level, they are ready to go, not just learning."

Pendleton signed with the Florida Marlins, homered in his first at-bat, and finished the strike-shortened '95 season with a .290 average. When the Braves needed a hitter for the 1996 stretch drive, however, they brought him back. As a result, he played in his fifth World Series—but again failed to win a ring.

The popular and polite Fresno State product played for the Reds and Royals before rejoining the Braves in 2002 as a batting coach—ironically, one who would help Chipper Jones.

Playing big league baseball was a breeze for Pendleton, who recalled hearing the gunfire from the Watts riots when he was five years old. He even counseled younger players, dealing with Brian Hunter and Keith Mitchell after they had separate alcohol-related automobile accidents.

Although he only spent four years as an Atlanta regular, Terry Pendleton made a profound impact. Team president Stan Kasten, not normally given to hyperbole, called him "the greatest free-agent signing in history." Greg Maddux, who arrived before Pendleton left, might argue.

Certainly the main man who reversed the course of the club, Pendleton had a short tenure as a player when compared with Chipper Jones.

Jones joined the Braves organization in 1990, the same year Pendleton signed, but didn't reach the varsity until the end of the 1993 campaign. With the team embroiled in a grueling divisional title chase, the 21-year-old rookie infielder mostly watched. Given only three at-bats, he had two hits and scored two runs—a harbinger of bigger things to come.

Although Cal Ripken Jr., one of his boyhood heroes, didn't let size hamper his ability to play shortstop, the Braves decided the 6'4" rookie would be a better bet at third. With Pendleton still going strong in '94, Chipper was ticketed for left field, but that was before he tore his ACL while running out a ground ball during an exhibition game against the Yankees.

After replacing Terry Pendleton at third base, Chipper Jones provided power from both sides of the plate.

Photo by Bill Menzel.

Lost for the season, Jones returned in 1995—just in time to win a regular job on a world championship team. "Spring training was shortened to 11 exhibition games because of the player strike," Tom Glavine recalled. "We needed a third baseman so they moved him there. Because he was accustomed to shortstop, playing another position on the infield was a little easier transition than if he had come from the outfield to third base.

"Everybody felt moving him to third would eliminate a lot of his errors but he'd have to make more reaction plays than he did at shortstop. It's a little more difficult to play short than it is to play third but there was no question he had to learn a new position at the big league level. That wasn't an easy thing to do."

Jones not only made the move easily but picked up right where Pendleton left off.

Although he waited until May 9 to hit his first major-league home run, the DeLand, Florida, native hit 22 more home runs, knocked in 86 runs, and had a solid .353 on-base percentage. *The Sporting News* named him National League Rookie of the Year even though the baseball writers curiously preferred pitcher Hideo Nomo of the Dodgers.

He made a dazzling debut, leading all freshmen in runs scored (87) and runs batted in while placing second in both home runs, hits (139), and walks (73).

At his best in the clutch, Jones won three games with ninth-inning home runs and hit .389 with two homers in the Division Series, .438 with one homer in the Championship Series, and .286 with three doubles in his first World Series.

Chipper was off and running. Starting in 1996, he reached triple digits in runs batted in for eight consecutive years—the first third baseman ever to produce such a streak. He also became a consistent .300 hitter with such a sharp batting eye that he collected more walks than strikeouts. In fact, he never fanned 100 times at any time in his 19-year career.

"When you walk to the plate, you need to be the toughest out possible," Jones once said. "In order to do that, you have to draw walks. You have to yield to the guy behind you in the lineup from time to time. The fact of the matter is that there are certain points during the season, or during a game, that teams aren't going to let you beat them. And if you're smart enough to realize when those situations are, you're going to draw a bunch of walks."

Jones challenged for MVP honors in 1996, when he became the first Braves third baseman since Eddie Mathews in 1953 to produce

Chipper Jones was not only the nation's top amateur draft choice but a superstar who spent his entire career with the Braves.

Photo by Bill Menzel.

30 doubles and 30 homers in the same season. He hit in 18 straight games, reached base in 34 straight, and topped the century mark in both runs scored and runs batted in. An All-Star in just his second full season, Jones homered in the Division Series, hit .440 in the Championship Series, and batted .286 with three doubles in the World Series.

A year later, he set his career high (which he would tie in 2000) with 111 RBIs—12 of them coming in a 13-game span when he hit three grand slams. He had 21 home runs during the regular season, then three more in postseason play.

By that time, the Braves knew they got a bargain when they signed Chipper for $275,000 after making him the nation's top choice in the amateur draft. He had been Florida's High School Player of the Year after producing a .448 batting average at The Bolles School in Jacksonville and was such a hot prospect that Atlanta scouting chief Paul Snyder threatened to resign if the team didn't draft him first.

There were only two problems: several front office figures focused on pitcher Todd Van Poppel and Chipper's dad was convinced he could get more money from other clubs.

But Van Poppel dissed the Braves, showing no interest in a club he considered a non-contender, and the senior Jones—his son's agent as well as his mentor—relented when Chipper insisted he wanted to be the nation's top draft choice.

"I'll make plenty of money later," he correctly predicted at the time.

A switch-hitter since the age of five, when he swung a metal pipe at a tennis ball thrown by his father from forty feet away, Larry Wayne Jones Jr. rose rapidly toward the pros. He pitched and played right field in American Legion ball because his team already had a good shortstop. But he could always hit.

A natural right-handed batter who learned to hit left-handed by mimicking such major leaguers as Reggie Smith, a switch-hitter who played for the Dodgers, Chipper followed in the footsteps of his dad, a college shortstop at Stetson University. He even picked his famous No. 10 jersey to emulate his dad, who wore the same digits.

"I never coached him officially," his dad said, "but when we worked out on our own, I was a fundamentals guy. I had him take ground balls and work on some other things."

Chipper paid attention. In fact, he repeatedly called his dad for suggestions whenever he ran into a slump. He always maintained that his dad knew his swing better than anyone else.

Baseball America named Jones the top prospect in the Southern League in 1992 and the No. 2 prospect in the International League a year later, when he set Richmond team records for hits and total bases. Not surprisingly, he was named Atlanta's Minor League Player of the Year.

Many more honors and awards would follow, including the only batting crown of his career in 2008, when he hit .364 with a .470 on-base percentage—both career highs—at the age of 36.

Chipper's best year came in 1999 after new Braves batting coach Don Baylor practically shamed the star into producing more power as a right-handed hitter. By then, Jones was well-established as the face of the franchise, the on-field leader who played every day and was often the trigger man for Atlanta rallies.

Although Jones had hit for a high average from both sides of the plate, he was hitting most of his home runs left-handed—thereby encouraging opposing managers to insert left-handed relievers whenever he came to bat in crucial situations.

After Jones followed Baylor's advice to put more weight on his back foot and move his hands back and away from his chest, the right-handed power followed. That year, he hit 15 right-handed home runs—three more than he had hit in his first four seasons—in 142 at-bats and finished with a career-best 45. No National League switch-hitter had ever hit so many in one season, though Lance Berkman later duplicated Jones's feat.

Hank Aaron, who then held the Atlanta club record of 47 home runs in a season, was a keen observer. "He could have broken my record if he'd had Andres Galarraga [out for the year while undergoing chemotherapy] batting behind him," said Aaron, then a club executive. "There's no doubt in my mind that Chipper had a good shot at Mickey Mantle's record for home runs by a switch-hitter [54 in 1961]."

Bobby Cox, the chief beneficiary of Chipper's power production, also appreciated his infielder. "I don't know that I would have projected him to become a 45-homer man," he said, "but you never know. A lot of guys, including Brooks Robinson and Alan Trammell, didn't hit more than four or five their first couple of years.

"It's hard to judge sometimes. Swings change and kids get stronger. I always thought Chipper had All-Star written all over him. I didn't know what his numbers would be but he had that All-Star look about him. We just didn't know what his position would be."

After his outburst of '99, Jones never scaled the 40 mark again though he did continue knocking in runs at a resounding clip. That he finished with 468 lifetime home runs showed how consistent he was as a slugger.

Following in the footsteps of Dale Murphy, Chipper Jones grew into the face of the Braves franchise.

Photo by Bill Menzel.

To the New York Mets, it seemed that most of his home runs came against them. In a crucial three-game series in September, Jones connected four times—two right-handed and two left-handed—to lead a Braves sweep. One broke a 1–1 tie in the eighth and another, a three-run shot, erased a 2–1 New York lead.

"We had a one-game lead over the Mets with two weeks left," Bobby Cox recalled, "but had to play them in two three-game series, home and away. We were looking to score a run any way we could, to jump out in front, just to win the series. We were hoping for somebody to get hot and hoping that nobody cooled off. Chipper came through for us and helped himself become the Most Valuable Player in the National League. I think MVPs are clutch players and certainly he was a clutch player for us."

The rivals later met in a memorable NL Championship Series, with the Braves winning in six games.

"I knew each time I stepped onto the field at Shea Stadium, I was going to be challenged and pushed so I better be ready," he said in retrospect. "Those fans and those teams pushed me to be the very best I could. I truly respected the New York fans and their knowledge and passion for the game. It was a great rivalry and a pleasure to be part of it."

Although Shea was always considered a pitchers' park, Jones played so well there that he even named his son after the stadium. The park has been replaced by Citi Field but the memories of the Braves-Mets races, especially in 1999, will never disintegrate.

During that season, Jones homered from both sides of the plate three times—something he had never done before 1999—and won four different games with extra-inning home runs.

A model of consistency all year long, he reached base in a club-record 39 consecutive games, tied a National League mark with walks in 16 straight, hit .367 from the seventh inning on, and .349 over the last three months.

Elite Company

Chipper Jones is the only switch-hitter in baseball history to hit at least .300 with 300 home runs.

Like Baylor, Jones parlayed his power production into an MVP award. He got 432 votes in a landslide of Lyndon Johnson proportions. Jeff Bagwell was a distant second at 276.

"Winning the MVP was extremely gratifying and personally fulfilling for me," Jones said years later, "but winning the World Series was still the crowning achievement in my career. To be part of that '95 team that won the World Series meant we were the best team in the best league in the world. I will never forget sharing that moment with all of my teammates."

Chipper had a chance at another World Series ring in 1999 after his power propelled the club to the final round again. "That was one of those seasons where it all came together: the pennant chase, not making mistakes, having a wonderful cast around me, and having a hitting coach I really clicked with," he recalled. "You don't get many of those seasons."

"I always think I demanded my best when it came to being a complete player, but hitting 45 home runs was more unexpected than hitting .364 [and winning the 2008 batting title]. That was satisfying but not that surprising because I tried to be a complete player."

Quiet by nature, Jones led by example. He never hesitated to offer advice to younger players or even to reprimand them behind closed doors. For the Braves, he was an unofficial assistant manager—respected by rivals as well as teammates.

"There's a definite parallel between Chipper and Dale Murphy," said Cox, who managed both MVPs. "Every once in awhile, a player with the looks of a Dale Murphy or a Chipper Jones comes up and gets the fans excited. They become the big star, the franchise player, for your team or your town. Dale and Chipper both had that All-American type of appearance and image."

Always a team player, he willingly shifted to left field for two years after Atlanta signed free agent Vinny Castilla, a better defensive third baseman, in 2002. Two years later, he offered to defer part of his salary so that the team could sign veteran starting pitcher Tim Hudson.

A team player, Chipper Jones offered to shift from third base to left field so that the Braves could sign Colorado third baseman Vinny Castilla before the 2002 season.

Photo by Bill Menzel.

"I was going to do whatever the Atlanta Braves wanted me to do to win games," he explained. "That was my only goal."

Like Ripken and Tony Gwynn, who spent their entire careers with one club, Jones never left the Braves.

"It was much like a successful relationship," he said of his lifelong tenure in Atlanta. "There was give-and-take along the way that was necessary for the long-standing relationship to last. I give all the credit to Bobby Cox, John Schuerholz, and every member of the Atlanta Braves who made the marriage work for so long.

"I never wanted to play anywhere else. Atlanta fit my style and my speed. I'm a Southern kid, born and bred in the Braves organization. I could never see myself playing against an Atlanta team. I saw guys like Glavine and Smoltz do it and know it was hard for them."

By the time Jones concluded his 19-year career in 2012, he had chiseled his name into the team and league record book multiple times.

111

Consider these Chipper achievements:

- Only switch-hitter to hit .300 with 400 home runs
- Trails only Mickey Mantle (536) and Eddie Murray (504) in home runs by switch-hitter
- Oldest switch-hitter to win a batting title at age 36 (2008), he hit .399 at Turner Field, had a .470 on-base percentage, and was just one point behind Mickey Mantle's .365 record average for switchers
- First player to hit .300 with 100 runs, 100 RBIs, 100 walks, 40 doubles, 40 homers, and 20 stolen bases (1999)
- Set Atlanta club record with 87 extra-base hits (1999)
- Tied Joe DiMaggio as the only players to bat .300 with 100 RBIs for a first-place team in seven straight seasons
- Tied Paul Waner with extra-base hits in 14 consecutive games
- Joined Frankie Frisch as the only switch-hitters to top .300 from both sides of plate
- First third baseman since Pie Traynor (1927–31) with five straight 100-RBI years
- More career walks (1,512) than strikeouts (1,409)
- Most home runs for the team that drafted him than any other No. 1 amateur draft pick
- Most runs batted in (1,623) than any player whose primary position was third base
- Most runs scored (123) by a third baseman in a season (1998)
- Eight-time All-Star who homered in his own ballpark during an All-Star Game (2000)
- Had .401 lifetime on-base percentage and .529 slugging percentage
- Hit .315 in Championship Series

"It takes twice as much work to be a switch-hitter as it does to be one-sided," Jones said after hanging up his famous No. 10 jersey. "I can't imagine walking up to the plate and facing Pedro Martinez righty-on-righty or Randy Johnson lefty-on-lefty. I thank God every day that my dad made me turn around in our backyard."

Because the senior Jones idolized Mantle, his son did, too. "The big thing for me was passing Mickey in RBI," he told *Baseball America* columnist and author Jayson Stark. "Mickey was put on such a high pedestal when I was a kid, from my dad, that it's hard for me to believe I could pass him in anything."

Unlike most of his colleagues, Jones was aware of the legends he was chasing. "I knew what the standard was," he said. "I knew that Mickey Mantle and Eddie Murray were the two best switch-hitters of all time. While I never expected to hit 300 or 400 home runs, I wanted to be mentioned with those two guys, if not right behind them. I finally got to the point where every homer and every RBI passed a Hall of Famer. It was a lot of fun."

What wasn't fun for Chipper were the assorted ailments that ate into his playing time as he aged. He played fewer than 140 games in all but one of his last nine seasons.

He still compiled quite a legacy; Chipper's team won 428 more games than it lost while he was an active player. Only Derek Jeter, whose Yankees had 554 more wins than losses during his tenure, made such an impact.

"The 1996 season is the only one I looked back on with any regrets," said Jones, the owner of a nine thousand-acre South Texas spread called the Double Dime Ranch. "I thought we had the best team. We showed it during the first two games of the World

JONES-ATLANTA-NL™

Courtesy of The Topps Company, Inc.

Series but not after that. Every other year, we were beaten by a better team, at least at that particular time in the season.

"As for 14 straight, it took a true commitment to scouting, player development, and the Braves Way. Oh, and those three Hall of Fame pitchers and a Hall of Fame manager didn't hurt things. Just a really special group of guys on the field, in the clubhouse, in the front office and in the scouting and player development systems. I can't fathom that [the streak] will ever happen again in today's game."

Hall of Fame electors have already paid tribute to the key cogs in that run by electing Bobby Cox, Greg Maddux, and Tom Glavine in 2014; John Smoltz in 2015; John Schuerholz in 2017; and Chipper Jones in 2018.

SEASONS

SEASONS

8
1991: WORST TO FIRST

Opening Day

Sanders, lf

Treadway, 2b

Gant, cf

Justice, rf

Bream, 1b

Pendleton, 3b

Heath, c

Belliard, ss

Smoltz, p

Best Hitter: Terry Pendleton

Best Pitcher: Tom Glavine

Best Newcomer: Terry Pendleton

The Season

BEFORE THE 1991 season, they could have been called The Bad News Braves. With three straight last-place finishes and not a single season on the sunny side of .500 since 1983, Fulton County Stadium resembled a morgue that General Sherman should have torched.

Sure, there were a few diamonds in the coal mine—Ron Gant made a successful conversion from infield to outfield while pulling off a rare 30/30 season, fellow slugger David Justice won Rookie of the Year honors after replacing longtime Atlanta icon Dale Murphy, catcher Greg Olson made the NL All-Star team in his first full season, and John Smoltz led the pitching staff with 14 wins despite a defense that led the major leagues in errors.

Determined to stop giving games away, new general manager John Schuerholz studied the free-agent list with his eye on players who knew what to do with a glove.

With the blessing of owner Ted Turner, who supplied the checkbook, and team president Stan Kasten, who wisely kept Bobby Cox as manager, Schuerholz scoured the market like a savvy shopper searching for dinner party ingredients.

His major acquisition was Terry Pendleton, a switch-hitting third baseman coming off a dismal season in St. Louis (.230 with six home runs). He also added Rafael Belliard, a shortstop whose pedigree precluded any help from his bat, and Sid Bream, a first baseman with strong defensive skills but hardly the type of hitter typically found at the gateway.

A veteran player on a young club, Pendleton relished the chance to be a team leader. He also appreciated the fresh start in Atlanta, where

"The Chop"

When Deion Sanders came to the Braves in 1991, fans who had followed him as a football star for the Florida State Seminoles started saluting him with the same chopping motion they had used during his college days. The chop, which began when Sanders batted during spring training in West Palm Beach, soon became standard for all Braves players. Fans added an Indian war chant and Atlanta Stadium organist Carolyn King accompanied them. Not only did owner Ted Turner and former president Jimmy Carter participate but the Braves began selling foam rubber tomahawks—conceived by Paul Braddy—that fans could wave in support of their team.

Fulton County Stadium would prove more friendly to his power—a factor that figured into his signing.

Pendleton not only supplied Gold Glove defense but hit for both power and average—silencing critics who claimed he was over the hill. He played hurt, starting every game after June 15 until the team clinched despite a cartilage tear in his left knee. In addition, Pendleton took it upon himself to counsel teammates with personal problems, including Brian Hunter and Keith Mitchell after both had alcohol-related automobile accidents that summer.

Although Bream came with surgically-repaired knees and a reputation as the slowest runner in the league, John Schuerholz found dazzling speed in two more new acquisitions: outfielders Otis Nixon and Deion Sanders. Both Nixon, acquired from Montreal in a spring training trade, and Sanders, a minor league free agent who also played pro football, had never distinguished themselves at the plate. But the GM saw potential in both.

He also knew the defense would be vastly improved. Bouyed by the knowledge that their infielders would turn grounders into outs, the young pitching staff Bobby Cox developed during his tenure as general manager blossomed like the cherry trees in Washington. The team went from 65–97 in 1990 to 94–68 in 1991—from 26 games behind to one game ahead.

It was the first time in the history of modern baseball that a team had finished with the worst record in the majors one year but finished first the next.

After lulling their followers to sleep with a slow start in April, the Braves hit their stride in May, winning 17 of 26. Justice was National League Player of the Month while Tom Glavine, a left-hander just two years removed from a 7–17 campaign, was the NL Pitcher of the Month. En route to the first of five 20-win seasons, he went 6–0 with a 1.76 earned run average to earn the honor.

A June swoon, coupled with injuries to Justice (back) and Bream (knee), burst the Braves balloon as they limped into the All-Star Game

Changes That Worked

Atlanta's defense was decidedly different in 1991. Terry Pendleton replaced Jim Presley at third, Rafael Belliard supplanted Andres Thomas at short, and Sid Bream succeeded a first-base rotation that included Tommy Gregg, Francisco Cabrera, Mike Bell, Jody Davis, Presley, and David Justice. With Otis Nixon in center, Ron Gant moved to left, sending Lonnie Smith to the bench.

one game below .500 and nine-and-a-half games from the NL West lead. Since the players were still getting to know each other, the Braves may have needed the three-day break. Either that or they ate their spinach—*something* triggered a second-half explosion that started with a 9–2 mark after the break. Led by Nixon, Pendleton, and 21-year-old lefthander Steve Avery, Atlanta gained seven games on the front-running Los Angeles Dodgers in a 12-day span.

They never let up, going 55–28 after the All-Star break for a .663 winning percentage. Taking 21 of their last 29 (.724) helped.

Along the way, the Braves even got a combined no-hitter from Kent Mercker, Mark Wohlers, and Alejandro Pena, acquired in a waiver trade in August to replace the injured Berenguer (stress fracture of the forearm). Pendleton hit a home run for the Atlanta run but backed away from an infield chopper with two outs in the ninth. When it bounced off Rafael Belliard's glove, the crowd groaned, assuming it would be ruled an infield hit. But the official scorer, who doubled as a local sportswriter, charged an error instead. All Pena had to do was retire Tony Gwynn, the toughest out in the league. He did, coaxing a fly ball, and the National League's first combined no-hitter was official.

That September 11 masterpiece was not the only surprise of the second half.

The Chop Shop

As the 1991 season progressed and the Braves looked more like winners, fans responded with a frenzy that rivaled the Beanie Baby craze. They beat tom-toms, waved tomahawks, and wore Indian garb. The Chant started almost by spontaneous combustion, while David Justice was batting against the Dodgers in a big September series. Even though the organ was silent, the chanting could be heard at Morehouse College, two miles away.

On August 21, Atlanta was one out away from a 9–6 defeat against Cincinnati when third-string catcher Francisco Cabrera turned a Rob Dibble fastball into a three-run homer with two outs in the last of the ninth. The Braves eventually won the game on a Justice double in the 13th.

Just five days later, the Braves parlayed a Justice homer and Jeff Blauser grand slam into a 14–9 win over Montreal—after trailing early by a 7–1 margin.

Bream's grand slam on September 15 contributed to a big win over the Dodgers, giving the Braves a game-and-a-half lead, but the lead changed hands seven times in the final month.

Perhaps the biggest game of the nail-biting campaign came on October 1. The Reds led early, 6–0, but the lead had dwindled to 6–5 by the ninth. Enter Dibble, the fearsome fireballer who had been victimized by Cabrera six weeks earlier.

Strange Coincidence

David Justice was born on April 14, 1966—two days after the debut of major league baseball in Atlanta.

Though Justice would play only 109 games that season, his flair for the dramatic seemed almost routine by that point. An impatient hitter who often tinkered with his stance, he had all the moving parts going in the right direction that night. He connected with a man on to win the game, 7–6, and put the Braves one game back with four to play. A day later, a Braves win and Dodgers loss left the clubs tied. Avery's win over the Houston Astros on October 4, coupled with a Dodgers defeat in San Francisco, put the Braves up by one with two left.

Then John Smoltz, capping a 12–2 second half after a 2–11 start, pitched the Braves to their eighth win in a row, clinching a tie. If the Giants could beat the Dodgers again, the title chase would be over. They did—as a packed house at Atlanta Fulton County Stadium watched the broadcast on the scoreboard.

Down the stretch, potent pitching plus timely hitting pushed Atlanta over the top.

One year after finishing with the worst earned run average in the majors (4.58), Braves pitchers posted a 3.49 mark, fanned a club-record 969 hitters, and held rivals to a league-best .240 batting average. Atlanta also proved stingy, yielding the fewest hits of any National League staff.

The front four starters all had fine seasons. Glavine tied for the NL lead in wins and complete games while finishing second in innings pitched and third in strikeouts. The first Braves pitcher to win 20 since Phil Niekro in 1979, Glavine capped his campaign by winning the Cy Young Award.

Southpaw Stars

The 1991 Braves were the first team since the 1917 New York Giants to have three left-handed pitchers with at least 15 wins: Tom Glavine, Steve Avery, and Charlie Leibrandt.

The stoic southpaw refused to admit he was superstitious but acted otherwise. He always took the same number of warmup pitches, sat in the same spot in the dugout, hung his jacket on the same hook, and took off his cap and put it back on his head three times when on the mound. During one game, he lost the gum he was chewing, grabbed it off the dugout floor, washed it off, and put it back in his mouth. Glavine was merely following the advice of Ralph Kiner, the Hall of Fame outfielder who always stepped over the white lines when running to his position. "I'm not superstitious," he said, "but I didn't want to take any chances."

Fellow left-handers Avery, third in the league in wins, and Charlie Leibrandt, the stablizier of an inexperienced staff, started 69 games and won 33 of them. Avery won his final five to become the youngest 18-game winner in Braves history. Smoltz also finished strong, winning eight of his last nine.

In the bullpen, Berenguer and Pena blew only one of a combined 28 save opportunities while the left-handed Mike Stanton proved a durable and dependable setup man. Mark Wohlers, who would blossom into a quality closer later, even worked in 17 games after making his major league debut in 1991.

The team's biggest surprise was the 30-year-old Pendleton, whose availability through free agency did not convince many suitors. He not only led the league with a .319 batting average but finished first in hits and total bases and third in slugging. He was rewarded after the season with the National League's Most Valuable Player Award, Comeback

---

Stealing Pays

One of the reasons the 1991 Braves outlasted their opposition was good team speed. "We started adding speed right away," said Ron Gant en route to his second straight 30–30 year. "We knew we were going to be able to steal bases with guys like Otis Nixon, Deion Sanders, and myself. Speed never goes into a slump. So getting speed was kind of conventional thinking by the organization."

Gant's Move

Ron Gant's power and speed were the calling cards that brought him to the big leagues. His glove? Not so much. Tried at both second and third, he finally became a regular only after moving to the outfield in 1990. He played both left field and center during his seven years with the Braves.

Player of the Year honors, and a Gold Glove for fielding excellence. That made him the first Brave to win MVP honors since Dale Murphy won back-to-back trophies in 1982–83 and the first to win a batting title since Ralph Garr in 1974.

Bream and rookie Brian Hunter formed a left-right platoon at first base, contributing a combined 23 home runs, while Jeff Treadway hit .320 while sharing second with Mark Lemke and the versatile Blauser. Niether Belliard nor Olson managed to hit .250 but compensated with strong glovework.

Gant was third in home runs (32) and runs batted in (105), both tops on the club, and led the majors with 21 game-winning hits. In completing his second straight 30–30 season, he joined Willie Mays and Bobby Bonds as the only players at that time to turn the trick two years in a row.

Nixon, like Gant and Sanders, added considerable speed to the lineup. Thanks to a career-best .297 average that allowed him to reach base often, he swiped a club-record 72 bases, second in the circuit, before he was suspended September 16 for substance abuse. He had failed a drug test in July but was allowed to continue playing after he and agent Joe Sroba contested the results. Nixon's absence was felt most keenly in the postseason—especially since Lonnie Smith served as his primary replacement.

The Braves began their domination of the National League with a worst-to-first season in 1991 and played in two World Series in three seasons.

Photo courtesy of the Braves Museum and Hall of Fame.

The Postseason

To reach the World Series for the first time since 1958, the Braves had to beat the power-packed Pittsburgh Pirates in a best-of-seven playoff. Although the more experienced Pirates were favored, pundits hadn't factored in the enormous potential of Atlanta's young pitching.

Pittsburgh had led the league in batting and runs scored during the season but that didn't matter to Atlanta pitchers.

Steve Avery took the second and sixth games by 1–0 scores, working 16 1/3 straight scoreless innings, a National League Championship Series record, to win Most Valuable Player honors. John Smoltz clinched the flag with a 4–0 shutout in the seventh game.

125

No Justice

When ex-Brave Zane Smith beat the Braves, 1–0, for the Pittsburgh Pirates in the 1991 NL Championship Series, he had some unforeseen help from David Justice. In the fourth inning, the Atlanta right fielder crossed the plate but was then called out for missing third base.

Atlanta pitching was impregnable. It posted a composite 1.57 earned run average while holding the heavy-hitting Pirates scoreless for the last 22 innings of the entire series. Nor did Pittsburgh score a run in its last 27 innings at home.

Pittsburgh won the opener at home, 5–1, but Avery combined with Alejandro Pena for a 1–0 shutout in the second game. After the series moved to Atlanta, the Braves won Game Three behind Smoltz, 10–3, before the Pirates won consecutive squeakers, 3–2 in 10 innings and 1–0. That meant the Braves had to win both games in Pittsburgh to win the pennant.

They not only won but held the heavy-hitting Pirates scoreless. Avery and Pena combined for another 1–0 win on October 16 and Smoltz, buoyed by a three-run first, blanked the Bucs with a six-hit complete game the next night. Pena, who had converted all 11 of his save chances after his August arrival from the Mets, saved both of Avery's wins and added another save as well.

The Braves had lots of other heroes, including a few surprises.

One year after becoming the first Braves rookie to make the All-Star squad, 30-year-old catcher Greg Olson became a surprise hitting hero when it counted most. His .333 NLCS batting average tied Brian Hunter for best on the Braves and he even hit a rare two-run homer in the third game. Hunter, Sid Bream, Ron Gant, and David Justice also homered in the seven-game series while Gant and Justice shared the team lead with four runs scored (Gant's seven stolen bases, an NLCS record, helped).

Southpaw Steve Avery, all of 21, wiped off champagne after winning MVP honors in the 1991 NLCS against Pittsburgh.

AP Photo/Chaz Palla

MVP honors went to Avery, a 21-year-old left-hander who had won 18 regular season games, two of them during the pressure-packed final month. Nicknamed "Poison" Avery by Pirates outfielder Andy Van Slyke, he became the youngest pitcher ever to win a playoff game. He fanned 17 men in 16 1/3 innings while posting a perfect 2–0 mark and 0.00 ERA against Pittsburgh.

The 1991 NLCS was the first postseason series to feature three 1–0 games. That score would resurface in the next round.

Some Lift

Even an owner isn't immune to mechanical problems. Ted Turner and Jane Fonda were among fourteen people stuck on a ballpark elevator for ten minutes before the fifth game of the 1991 NLCS.

The World Series pitted two worst-to-first teams with the Braves against the Minnesota Twins.

Each team won all of its home games, thanks in part to partisan crowds whose decibel levels were amplified by the Hubert H. Humphrey Metrodome.

As John Schuerholz said later, the Braves were the champions of the outdoors while the Twins were the indoor champions.

In one of the most exciting Fall Classics in baseball history, five of the seven games were one-run affairs, four were decided on the final pitch, and three of those four extended into extra innings—a Fall Classic first. The series remained deadlocked through nine innings of the seventh game, eventually won by the Twins, 1–0.

Playing at home, Minnesota won the first game, 5–2, and led the second, 2–1, in the top of the third when controversy raised its ugly head. After Lonnie Smith was safe on an error by third baseman Scott

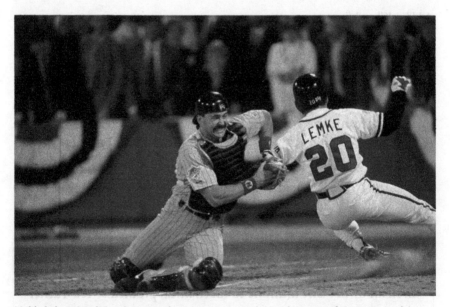

Unlikely hero Mark Lemke scores the winning run in the ninth inning of Game Four of the 1991 World Series.

AP Photo/Jim Mone

Leius, Ron Gant singled to left. Seeing Dan Gladden's throw get by Leius, Gant rounded first with second base in his sights. But pitcher Kevin Tapani retrieved the ball and fired a strike to first baseman Kent Hrbek. As the 170-pound Gant lunged for the bag, the 250-pound Hrbek appeared to lift his leg off the bag. Although Gant claimed interference, umpire Drew Coble called him out, ending the inning and killing a rally in a game the Twins eventually won by one run, 3–2, when Leius redeemed himself with a solo home run in the eighth inning against Tom Glavine.

Atlanta needed six pitchers and home runs from Justice and Smith to win a 12-inning duel in Game Three, a 5–4 affair played in Atlanta on October 22. Smith and Pendleton pounded solo homers the next night but the biggest hit was a ninth-inning triple by Mark Lemke, who came home with the winning run in a 3–2 game.

Smith, Justice, and Brian Hunter cleared the Fulton County fences in the fifth game, a 14–5 blowout in which the Braves scored a combined nine runs in the seventh and eighth innings.

Back in Minnesota, the Twins tallied two in the first against Avery and never trailed. It took 11 innings but the home team prevailed on a Kirby Puckett poke against veteran lefthander Charlie Leibrandt, making a rare relief appearance. Puckett, whose circus catch above the wall in the third nullified two Atlanta runs, was the only man Leibrandt faced.

That set the stage for a Game Seven showdown that pitted Smoltz against Morris.

Stop the Chop

Native Americans, upset with the chants and chops of Braves fans as well as the team's nickname, picketed Atlanta Fulton County Stadium during the 1991 World Series.

After becoming the first National Leaguer to homer in three straight World Series games, Smith made a baserunning gaffe in the eighth inning of the last game that denied the Braves their best chance to score.

Smith, who played for three different world championship teams, was quick on the bases and in the outfield. But he lacked good judgment, both on the bases and in the field, where he acquired the unflattering nickname of "Skates" for the way he glided after balls hit his way.

Smith's shortcomings were evident even earlier than the 1991 finale. Smith had been thrown out at home in the fifth inning of Game Four, keeping the score tied at 1–1, when he couldn't score from second on a double by Terry Pendleton. Only when the ball got past centerfielder Kirby Puckett did Smith start his run from second base to home. Puckett threw a strike to second baseman Chuck Knoblauch, who relayed to catcher Brian Harper, and Smith was out. Fortunately for him, the Braves rallied to win.

He wasn't so lucky in the seventh game, however.

On first base with a leadoff single, he headed for second as Jack Morris threw the next pitch. Pendleton belted it to left-center but Smith, running with his head down, saw neither the ball nor the third-base coach. Noticing the runner's confusion, Knoblauch deked the runner by pretending to feed the ball to shortstop Greg Gagne as if he were making a double play. The ruse worked as Smith, who could have scored easily, stopped at second.

By the time he realized the Twins were still tracking down the ball, he could only advance to third. With runners on second and third and nobody out, the scoreless tie seemed to be on life support. By bringing in their infield, Minnesota needed a grounder to hold the runner at third and erase the batter at first. Fleet Ron Gant, coming off his second straight 30–30 season, obliged, with Smith holding at third.

David Justice, a dangerous left-handed hitter, drew an intentional walk, setting up a double play possibility that could end the inning. Sid Bream, a lumbering runner easy to double on any grounder, provided just that—preserving the deadlock. The play went first-to-catcher-to-first.

"I made the mistake of not looking in," said the 35-year-old Smith. "I heard the crack of the bat and saw Knoblauch make a fake. Then I saw Dan Gladden move. By the time I got to second, I had to slow down to see if Gladden or Kirby (Puckett) could catch the ball. By the time I saw they weren't going to catch it, I started running toward third but (third base coach) Jimy Williams held me up."

Things could have been different if Otis Nixon had not been suspended for substance abuse in September. He had stolen a club-record 72 bases in the first five months and made a habit (double meaning intended) of driving rival pitchers to distraction. The Braves also missed the speed of Deion Sanders, who was spending the team's unexpected postseason playing football for the Atlanta Falcons.

Nixon never got a chance to veto the Twins, allowing Lonnie Smith to fill his position. As a result, the Braves got more power but also more problems.

As a reward for escaping the eighth-inning jam, Minnesota manager Tom Kelly allowed Morris to stay in the game. In a Twins uniform for the last time, Morris meandered on into overtime.

John Smoltz worked into the eighth for the Braves but yielded to Mike Stanton in the eighth and Alejandro Pena in the ninth. Pena, who had converted all 11 save chances for Atlanta after arriving from the New York Mets, finally proved mortal after the game remained scoreless in regulation time. In the Minnesota tenth, a Dan Gladden double, Knoblauch bunt, and two intentional walks loaded the bases with one out. Hoping for a double play from Gene Larkin, Pena instead

Costly Habit

Otis Nixon's 1991 drug suspension cost him $103,168.60 of his $850,000 salary.

allowed a single over the drawn-in outfield that scored the only run. It was only the second time that the seventh game required extra innings to produce a winner.

The hero for the Braves in the 1991 World Series turned out to be little second baseman Mark Lemke, not known for his speed or his bat. A .234 hitter during the regular season, he singled in the winning run in Game Three, scored the game-winner in Game Four, and wound up with a .417 batting average that included three triples, tying a World Series record. His slugging percentage was .708. Not bad for a guy who couldn't run.

Morris won the MVP honors that otherwise would have gone to Lemke. To compound the felony, the right-handed workhorse also positioned himself to haunt the Braves again a year later when he joined the Toronto Blue Jays as a free agent.

The young Braves missed stepping on the summit by only a step. Owner Ted Turner, taking the podium in the clubhouse after the last game, had a message for his team. "I told them I was real proud of them, no matter how the game came out, and I looked forward to seeing them next spring."

He wouldn't have to wait that long: the city saluted their heroes with a ticker-tape parade that snaked down Peachtree Street on October 29, 1991. Police estimated the frenzied crowd at 750,000—almost as many people as the Bad News Braves of the '70s and '80s would draw in a season.

MARTA, the city's sleek subway system, reported triple its normal weekday ridership. The procession stretched for twelve blocks in a virtual sea of fans waving tomahawks and chanting. "I could hardly

Historic Finish

The last game of the 1991 World Series was the first extra inning Game Seven since 1924 and the first to end in a 1–0 score since 1962.

imagine what would happen if we'd *won* the World Series," mused batting coach Clarence Jones.

Braves mania went viral. A woman wearing a Braves shirt in the New York Marathon was greeted by chants and cheers in all five boroughs. As far away as Japan, sporting goods stores were besieged by requests for foam-rubber tomahawks.

Although Atlanta missed a world championship by a whisker, the winter awards season was sweet. In addition to Pendleton's MVP trophy and Glavine's Cy Young, Bobby Cox was named Manager of the Year and John Schuerholz Executive of the Year. The team they built was young, talented, and capable of winning many more accolades in the years to come.

9

1992: BACK-TO-BACK

Opening Day
Sanders, cf
Pendleton, 3b
Gant, lf
Justice, rf
Bream, 1b
Blauser, 2b
Olson, c
Belliard, ss
Glavine, p
Best Hitter: Terry Pendleton
Best Pitcher: Tom Glavine
Best Newcomer: Jeff Reardon

The Season

AFTER THEIR WORST-TO-FIRST season of 1991, the Braves were worried that they might just be a one-year wonder. That theory gained some credibility when the team started slowly losing 27 of their first 47 and sitting seven games behind on May 26.

Then, all of a sudden, the ballclub warmed with the weather.

Terry Pendleton came close to winning his second straight MVP award while Tom Glavine made a valiant effort to keep Greg Maddux, still with the Cubs, from claiming permanent ownership of the Cy Young Award.

The Braves led the league in home runs, slugging percentage, shut-outs, and earned run average. The team not only won 98 games, the most by the franchise since the Boston Beaneaters of 1898, but led the league in ERA for the first time since the Milwaukee Braves won the National League pennant in 1958.

Winning four more games than they did in 1991, the Braves had some breathing room at season's end, finishing eight games ahead of the runner-up Reds.

Once the Atlanta express gathered a full head of steam, no one could stop it. Between May 27 and August 19, it played at a .746 pace (53–18) to open a comfortable lead over the favored Reds.

It was a team effort from start to finish.

Even the broadcasters made headlines: when father-and-son broad-casters Skip and Chip Caray of the Braves worked at the same game as patriarch Harry Caray, voice of the Chicago Cubs, they became the first three-generation family to announce the same game.

On their own team, Braves broadcasters had plenty to talk about.

Slow Start

The momentum of the 1991 worst-to-first season didn't carry over into 1992. The Braves struggled from the gate and stood dead last, seven games behind San Francisco, with a 20–27 mark on May 27. Culprits ranged from World Series hero Mark Lemke barely hitting above the Mendoza Line, to David Justice, whose April batting average of .037 would have made a great earned run average. The bullpen was unsettled, too, with erstwhile ace Alejandro Pena battling elbow issues that cut five miles per hour off his previous 90 mph velocity. Despite the team's struggles, Bobby Cox and coach Ned Yost took a trolley from San Diego to Tijuana to buy saddles for the manager's horses.

Deion Sanders, who had hit .191 the year before, hit .407 with six triples during a torrid two-week stretch in April. Jeff Blauser, of all people, hit three home runs in a midsummer game. Otis Nixon, back from his drug suspension, made a ninth-inning, game-saving catch of an Andy Van Slyke drive on July 25 that would have cleared the fence with a man on.

Dubbed "The Catch" by broadcaster Pete van Wieren, Nixon's perfectly-timed leap allowed the Braves to bag their 13th straight win, tying the 1982 club record.

Glavine had his own 13-game winning streak while becoming the first Brave since Warren Spahn with consecutive 20-win campaigns. Five of his 20 wins were shutouts, allowing him to finish tied for tops in both categories.

Smoltz led the league in strikeouts—the first time an Atlanta pitcher did that since Phil Niekro in 1977—and completed a club-high nine of his 15 victories. He tied a club record with 15 whiffs in a 2–1 win over Montreal May 24.

Leibrandt, the wily veteran, also won 15, giving Bobby Cox a terrific troika at the top of his rotation. Steve Avery and Pete Smith combined for 18 more victories.

The best of the eight relievers who recorded saves for the '92 Braves turned out to be 36-year-old Jeff Reardon, acquired from Boston in an

Blauser's Blasts

Before he hit three home runs in a game against the Cubs at Wrigley Field on July 12, 1992, Jeff Blauser had been hitting .154 in his previous 23 games. Blauser, who had hit four home runs in 85 games before his big day, connected in the second and sixth innings before hitting a three-run shot in the 10th against Paul Assenmacher.

August waiver deal. In 14 games, he went 3–0 with a 1.15 ERA. Before his arrival, Alejandro Pena, Juan Berenguer, and Mark Wohlers were among those who served as closers-by-committee.

Because Pena, the late-summer sensation of 1991, was hobbled by injuries and illness, the 1992 bullpen workhorses were the right-handed Marvin Freeman and lefties Kent Mercker and Mike Stanton. Over one stretch of 22 appearances, Mercker managed 25 straight scoreless innings.

Seeking more flexibility, Mercker, Stanton, and Smoltz chipped in to hire their own physical therapist. Smoltz said those stretching exercises with Chris Verna helped add velocity to his fastball.

For the second straight year, Pendleton was the prime producer of the offense. He hit career peaks with 199 hits and 105 runs batted in without sacrificing his batting average (a club-best .311). He tied for the NL lead in hits, finished second in RBIs, and ranked fourth in total bases. The defending Most Valuable Player could have won the award again but the writers chose Barry Bonds, who had won the award in 1990, instead.

Pendleton and Justice shared the club lead with 21 homers—the former golfed a low Mitch Williams serving for his first walk off—but five other players also finished in double digits.

First baseman Sid Bream and platoon partner Brian Hunter combined for 24 homers, more than any Brave managed alone in 1992, but both chafed at their platoon status.

Nixon, though unhappy at sharing outfield time with Sanders and Lonnie Smith, still managed to steal a team-high 41 times in 120

Whitewash Wonders

The 1992 Atlanta pitching staff threw three straight shutouts in late April, duplicating a franchise record shared by the 1959 and 1963 Milwaukee Braves.

Lonnie's Night

When the 1992 Braves opened a seven-game road trip in Pittsburgh, Bobby Cox decided to give David Justice a night off. Lonnie Smith, who started in right field instead, responded with his best night as a Brave: five hits and six runs batted in, four of them coming on a second-inning grand slam.

games. Sanders played just 97 games but had a league-best 14 triples to go with 26 stolen bases and a .304 batting average that was a 113-point improvement over his 1991 mark. For the second year in a row, Nixon, a .228 lifetime hitter before coming to Atlanta in 1991, just missed hitting .300.

Justice and Gant both had off-years but found time to market posters called "Justice Prevails" and "Pumping Gant," respectively. The former depicted a judge with a black robe, law books, and gavel, while the latter showed the muscular Gant about to delve into a weightlifting workout.

Maybe the posters were a jinx: Gant's bid for a third straight 30–30 season fell short though he did steal 32 times while Justice slumped, prompting fans to throw peanuts at him when he was in the on-deck circle. He did hit a home run off the field, however, meeting and betrothing Hollywood star Halle Berry.

Although the Braves were strong up the middle defensively with Greg Olson catching, Rafael Belliard at short, Mark Lemke at second, and Nixon in center, none of them provided much power. In fact, they combined for just 11 homers—three less than the versatile Blauser hit by himself. Jeff Treadway, back from hand surgery, saw some action at second base, as did Blauser, but Cox eventually settled on Lemke because of the defense he provided.

Nixon's the One

Although he missed the 1991 postseason after he was suspended for substance abuse in September, Otis Nixon returned in 1992 after the Braves gave him a new $2.7 million contract. Fans and writers who panned the deal relented when Nixon made a game-saving, ninth-inning catch against Pittsburgh during the season and then tied the last game of the '92 World Series with a hit in the ninth.

Unfortunately for the Braves, Olson was knocked out of the play-offs—literally—when Houston's Ken Caminiti made a hard slide into the plate on September 18. Idled with a broken leg and dislocated ankle, Olson watched as Damon Berryhill, a switch-hitter who finished with 10 home runs in 307 at-bats, took over behind the plate.

Eleven days after the mishap, Atlanta clinched its second straight divisional crown.

The Postseason

As Yogi Berra might have put it, the 1992 NL Championship Series was deja vu all over again. In fact, it ended the exact same way: with the Braves needing a full seven games to beat the Pittsburgh Pirates four times.

Pittsburgh was a powerhouse, coming off a season in which it led the majors with 693 runs scored. The Pirates, who finished nine games ahead of Montreal in the NL East, won 37 one-run games and 14 extra-inning games en route to a final record of 96–66, just two games off Atlanta's pace. But they had lost the season's series to the Braves, dropping seven of 12.

John Smoltz won the opener, 5–1, with eight strong innings while Ron Gant was the Game Two hero with a grand slam that sparked a 13–5 Atlanta rout.

Gant homered again in the third game, along with Sid Bream, but the Braves managed only three other hits against the dizzying knuckleball of Pittsburgh rookie Tim Wakefield, who pitched a complete game to win, 3–2. Smoltz beat Pittsburgh ace Doug Drabek for the second time to take the fourth game, 6–4, on October 10.

So close to a pennant that they could smell it, the Braves faced one of their former mainstays, Bob Walk, in Game Five. An 11-game winner for Joe Torre's Atlanta team that won the 1982 NL West crown, Walk made maximum mileage out of a four-run first that knocked out Steve Avery. His 7–1 win meant Atlanta had to again face Wakefield, who had been unhittable since his July 31 promotion from Triple-A Buffalo.

Wakefield, who had gone 8–1 with a 2.15 ERA during his short stint with the Bucs, banked heavily on his pet pitch. He was almost as good the second time as he was the first.

Even in Fulton County Stadium, Atlanta did only marginally better against the rookie right-hander's dancing deliveries and lost a one-sided game, 13–4. Just as Avery was two days earlier, Atlanta starter Tom Glavine was kayoed early—during Pittsburgh's eight-run second. Two David Justice home runs caused just small blips on the radar of a losing cause.

There were no home runs in the finale but fans who stayed till the end saw one of the most dramatic finishes in baseball history.

Twilight Zone

Early in Game Seven of the 1992 NL Championship Series, home plate umpire John McSherry took ill and was replaced by first-base ump Randy Marsh. According to Pittsburgh catcher Mike "Spanky" LaValliere, that altered the strike zone before the ninth inning, when Pirate pitchers were charged with two critical walks during Atlanta's pennant-winning rally.

The Game Seven pitching matchup was Smoltz against Pittsburgh ace Doug Drabek, whom the Braves had already beaten twice.

With Pittsburgh nursing a 2–0 lead in the sixth, Atlanta loaded the bases with nobody out. But Jeff Blauser hit a liner to third baseman Jeff King, who stepped on the bag to retire Mark Lemke for the second out. When Terry Pendleton lined to left, the threat was over.

Drabek, determined to get even with Smoltz and pitch his team into the World Series for the first time since 1979, held Atlanta score- less heading into the home ninth inning. The Pirates had scored on a sacrifice fly in the first and an Andy Van Slyke single in the sixth. But David Justice prevented a third Pittsburgh run when he nailed Orlando Merced at the plate in the eighth.

Entering the bottom of the ninth, Pittsburgh needed only three outs to take the pennant. They never got them.

Pendleton, hitless against Drabek in three previous trips that night, led off with a double into the right-field corner. Justice, the next hitter, sent a routine grounder to sure-handed second baseman Jose (Chico) Lind. But the infielder booted it, placing Atlanta runners on the cor- ners with none out. When Drabek walked Bream, a former Pirate, his night was done.

Pittsburgh manager Jim Leyland may have made a fatal mistake when he lifted the durable and determined Drabek, who had thrown 129 pitches, for the fresh arm of the less dependable Stan Belinda.

Ron Gant ripped a deep drive to left, exciting fans who thought it would clear the fence and clinch the pennant. But the ball became a sacrifice fly when it dropped into the glove of Barry Bonds for the first out. Pittsburgh still led, 2–1.

After a walk to Damon Berryhill reloaded the bases, Brian Hunter popped up for the second out.

Then, with the season on the line, Bobby Cox sent third-string catcher Francisco Cabrera to the plate as a pinch-hitter.

A Dominican who had spent most of the year in the minors, Cabrera had three hits in 10 at-bats during the 1992 season.

Belinda threw two balls, forcing him to feed a fastball to the right-handed fastball hitter. Cabrera ripped it hard to left but couldn't keep it fair. Still ahead on the count, however, he expected another heater. He didn't miss it.

Cabrera ripped a single to left, scoring Justice with the tying run. Right behind him was Bream, one of the slowest men in the league. A two-time recipient of knee surgery, he rounded third, running with his heart rather than his legs.

Pittsburgh catcher Mike "Spanky" LaValliere blocked the plate as he prepared to receive the throw from Bonds. A perfect throw from an outfielder with a better arm would have had him.

But the 6'4", 220-pound Bream evaded the desperate lunge of the 5'8" catcher and touched the plate before the tag. Atlanta Fulton County Stadium exploded as Skip Caray screamed, "Braves win! Braves win! Braves win! Braves win!"

Bonds, who would leave Pittsburgh for San Francisco via free agency, and centerfielder Andy Van Slyke, another solid performer, just sat on their gloves, seemingly in a state of stupor, as the Braves cavorted in a home-plate pile in front of their frenzied fans.

Only Jane Fonda refrained from joining the on-field pandemonium. The actress, engaged to marry Braves owner Ted Turner, told a lone reporter in the clubhouse that she was waiting for Ted to join her. Apparently, she had no interest in being part of the home-plate pileup.

Cabrera vs. Belinda

Before delivering the pennant-winning single that gave the Braves the 1992 NL title, Francisco Cabrera had one career at-bat against Stan Belinda. He hit a home run against him on July 29, 1991.

The Francisco Cabrera Game
1992 NL Championship Series Game 7
At Atlanta Fulton County Stadium
October 14, 1992

Pittsburgh Pirates	AB	R	H	RBI	Atlanta Braves	AB	R	H	RBI
Alex Cole, rf	2	1	0	0	Otis Nixon, cf	4	0	1	0
Lloyd McClendon, ph-rf (b)	0	0	0	0	Jeff Blauser, ss	4	0	0	0
Cecil Espy, pr-rf (c)	0	0	0	0	Terry Pendleton, 3b	4	1	1	0
Jay Bell, ss	4	1	1	0	David Justice, rf	4	1	0	0
Andy Van Slyke, cf	4	0	2	1	Sid Bream, 1b	3	1	1	0
Barry Bonds, lf	3	0	1	0	Ron Gant, lf	2	0	0	1
Orlando Merced, 1b	3	0	0	1	Damon Berryhill, c	3	0	1	0
Jeff King, 3b	4	0	1	0	Mark Lemke, 2b	2	0	1	0
Mike LaValliere, c	4	0	1	0	Lonnie Smith, ph (d)	1	0	0	0
Jose Lind, 2b	4	0	1	0	Rafael Belliard, 2b	0	0	0	0
Doug Drabek, p	3	0	0	0	Brian Hunter, ph (f)	1	0	0	0
					John Smoltz, p	1	0	0	0
					Jeff Treadway, ph (a)	1	0	1	0
					Deion Sanders, ph (e)	1	0	0	0
					Francisco Cabrera, ph (g)	1	0	1	2
Total	**31**	**2**	**7**	**2**		**32**	**3**	**7**	**3**

(a) Singled for Smoltz in the sixth inning; (b) Intentionally walked for Cole in the seventh inning; (c) Pinch-ran for McClendon in the seventh inning; (d) Flied out for Lemke in the seventh inning; (e) Struck out for Avery in the eighth inning; (f) Popped out for Belliard in the ninth inning; (g) Singled for Jeff Reardon in the ninth inning.

Pittsburgh	1	0	0	0	0	1	0	0	0	—	2
Atlanta	0	0	0	0	0	0	0	0	3	—	3

Pittsburgh Pirates	IP	H	R	ER	SO	BB
Doug Drabek (L) +	8.0	6	3	1	5	2
Stan Belinda	0.2	1	0	0	0	1

Atlanta Braves	IP	H	R	ER	SO	BB
John Smoltz	6.0	4	2	2	4	2
Mike Stanton	0.2	1	0	0	0	1
Pete Smith	0.0	0	0	0	0	1
Steve Avery	1.1	2	0	0	0	0
Jeff Reardon (W)	1.0	0	0	0	1	1

+ Pitched to three batters in the ninth inning

E—Lind. DP—Pittsburgh 1. LOB—Pittsburgh 9, Atlanta 7. 2B—Bell, Van Slyke, King, Lind, Pendleton, Bream, Berryhill. SB—Nixon. SH—Drabek. SF—Merced, Gant.
Umpires—John McSherry, Randy Marsh, Steve Rippley, Gary Darling, Gerry Davis, Ed Montague. (Note: McSherry left game after the first inning due to illness and was replaced by Marsh behind the plate)
Time—3:22. Attendance—51,975.

Source: Baseball-almanac.com

Horsing Around

When Atlanta mounted police were stationed in the bullpen prior to the end of 1992 NLCS Game Seven, prescient Braves reliever Marvin Freeman objected. "Get those horses out of here," he said. "We're gonna make a comeback." The horses were moved and the Braves fulfilled the forecast.

John Smoltz, who went 2–0 with a 2.66 ERA and a no-decision in the Cabrera game, was named Most Valuable Player of the Championship Series. The writers almost named Cabrera, who became such an instant folk hero in Atlanta that he could have been elected mayor.

After that climactic finish, which rivaled the previous year's pennant race and postseason for high drama, the World Series almost seemed like an afterthought.

Facing the Toronto Blue Jays in the first international Fall Classic, Atlanta drew first blood when Tom Glavine beat Jack Morris, 3–1, on the strength of a three-run Damon Berryhill home run. Glavine yielded just four hits in a complete game effort.

The Braves had the second game won, too, before little-known Ed Sprague ripped a two-run pinch-homer in the ninth against Jeff Reardon for a 5–4 win.

Toronto, powered by that unexpected head of steam, won the next two games to come within one of the World Championship.

In Game Five, however, Justice hit a solo shot and Lonnie Smith connected with the bases loaded to lead a 7–2 win and send the series back to Atlanta.

Toronto nursed a 2–1 lead until the bottom of the ninth of Game Six, when the Braves rallied against Toronto closer Tom Henke. Blauser singled, Berryhill bunted him to second, Lonnie Smith walked, and playoff hero Francisco Cabrera lined out to left, with Candy Maldonado

Francisco Cabrera became a footnote to history when he stroked a pennant-winning hit with two outs in the home ninth inning of 1992 NLCS Game Seven.

Courtesy of Jason Hyman collection.

Postseason Pop

The six players who hit postseason grand slams in Braves franchise history were Ron Gant and Lonnie Smith (both in 1992); Ryan Klesko, Eddie Perez, and Andres Galarraga (all in 1998); and Adam LaRoche (2005). Klesko, Perez, and LaRoche connected in the Division Series, Gant and Galarraga in the Championship Series, and Smith in the World Series.

making a leaping grab. Nixon then tied the game with a seeing-eye single to left but Gant, benched for much of the Series, flew out to center.

Then history repeated itself: for the second straight year, the left-handed Leibrandt lost the sixth game of the World Series when he gave up an extra-base hit to a right-handed hitter. The culprit in 1992 was Dave Winfield, whose two-out double with men on first and second provided the margin of victory.

The game and the series ended when Otis Nixon tried to bunt the tying run home from third with two outs in the bottom of the 11th. Nixon, who had 17 bunt hits during the season, dropped a drag bunt toward first base but failed to place it between the pitcher and the charging first baseman.

Both he and the rest of the Braves were out by an eyelash.

Toronto won, 4–3, in 11 innings. Making the score even more frustrating was the fact that it was Atlanta's seventh straight one-run loss in World Series play.

Deion Sanders, who hit .533 with five stolen bases, was the surprise hitting hero for the Braves.

Although the Braves had won their second straight NL flag after a decade of futility, Cox knew big-time cast changes would follow the disappointment of another losing World Series.

Free agency claimed Alejandro Pena, Lonnie Smith, Jeff Reardon, and Mike Bielecki; Jeff Treadway and Tommy Gregg were released;

Double Duty

Deion Sanders, who played in the 1992 World Series with the Braves, was the first athlete to appear in both the World Series and the Super Bowl.

David Nied, Armando Reynoso, and Vinny Castilla went to Colorado in the expansion draft; and Charlie Leibrandt was traded to Texas to clear salary for a young stud named Greg Maddux.

10
1993: THE GREAT RACE

Opening Day

Nixon, cf
Blauser, ss
Gant, lf
Pendleton, 3b
Justice, rf
Bream, 1b
Berryhill, c
Lemke, 2b
Maddux, p
Best Hitter: David Justice
Best Pitcher: Greg Maddux
Best Newcomer: Fred McGriff

The Season

ADD GREG MADDUX and Fred McGriff to the roster of the 1992 National League champions, mix, and serve.

For the third straight year, the Braves increased their win total—from 94 in 1991 to 98 in 1992 to 104 in 1993—but needed every game to clinch their third straight NL West crown.

The club got off to its usual slow start, losing more than it won in April, and finishing the first month in third place. The chief culprit, oddly enough, was Terry Pendleton, who had just polished his resume by finishing first and second in the voting for Most Valuable Player in the National League the past two years.

Although the switch-hitting third baseman rebounded with a strong second half, the team struggled to score before the July acquisition of McGriff, a first baseman whose 191 home runs over the previous six seasons led both leagues. In fact, McGriff had hit at least 31 home runs every year since 1989.

Acquired from San Diego for three prospects who never prospered, McGriff hit a home run in his first game, added 18 more in his 68 games as a Brave, and became the reliable cleanup man the lineup lacked. He also became the first big leaguer to hit at least 15 home runs for two teams in one season.

"McGriff brought something to this team," said Deion Sanders. "He sat in the batter's box and you knew every pitch could be gone. You didn't want to sit around and watch; you wanted to join him."

Unknown to the Braves, McGriff arrived in Atlanta on July 20 with sore ribs—the result of a brawl between the Padres and Giants a week earlier. Hoping to nurse his wounds with a day of rest, the left-handed slugger saw his name listed in the lineup against St. Louis that night. While introducing himself inside the

Crime Dog's Deal

According to Fred McGriff, traded from San Diego to Atlanta on July 18, 1993, a midseason deal is tough to take. "When you get traded in the middle of the year," he said, "you walk into a situation where you know some of the guys. But it's better to get traded in the offseason because you have all of spring training to get to know your teammates, going out to dinner or whatever. When you get traded during the year, you have to get right in there and start playing. I was lucky to play first base because I had a chance to meet people every night."

clubhouse, McGriff heard a commotion that contained the word "fire!" Emerging onto the field, he and his teammates looked up to see the press box engulfed in flames. Since it took time to restore order, the game was delayed—giving the slugger two extra hours in the trainer's room.

Courtesy of The Topps Company, Inc.

McGriff's bat immediately became the hot story. Powered by their new cleanup man, the Braves rebounded from a 10-game deficit on July 22 to the top of the division by season's end. They went 51–17, playing .750 ball, after the acquisition of The Crime Dog (nicknamed for a canine cartoon character called McGruff).

Thanks mainly to McGriff, the Braves had a second-half mark of 54–19, the best for any team.

Atlanta needed every one of McGriff's 55 runs batted in—not to mention the 117 contributed by Ron Gant and the team-best 120 by David Justice. With two-team totals of 37 home runs and 101 RBIs, McGriff gave the Braves three 100-RBI men for the first time since the 1970 lineup featured Hank Aaron, Orlando Cepeda, and Rico Carty.

Justice had a career-best 40 homers, four more than Gant, and became the fourth Brave with at least 40 homers and 100 RBIs in a season (joining Hank Aaron, Jeff Burroughs, and Dale Murphy). The late-starting Pendleton powered 17 long balls of his own, while Jeff Blauser not only became the first Braves shortstop to hit .300 since Alvin Dark in 1948 but also scored 110 runs, a franchise record for his position.

The potent troika of Ron Gant, David Justice, and Fred McGriff powered the 1993 Atlanta Braves to the best record in the big leagues over the second half of the season.
Courtesy of The Topps Company, Inc.

With 40 home runs and 120 RBIs, David Justice was the primary power producer for the Braves as they endured a grueling NL West title chase with the Giants in 1993.

Artwork by Gene Locklear.

MVP Contender

After hitting 40 home runs with 120 RBIs in 1993, David Justice finished third in the voting for National League Most Valuable Player. Only Barry Bonds and Lenny Dykstra got more votes.

The team also had speed and defense. Otis Nixon stole 47 bases, Deion Sanders swiped 19, and Gant came within four steals of his third 30–30 season in four years. Blauser played in a club-high 161 games and formed a fine double-play tandem with Mark Lemke, while Rafael Belliard backed both positions. Sid Bream, still a superb defender at first base, eventually lost his spot to McGriff while Nixon and Sanders sparred for playing time in center between Justice and Gant. Damon Berryhill did most of the catching and combined with Greg Olson for 12 home runs. Javy Lopez also surfaced just long enough to hit the first of many home runs. The team's .983 fielding percentage placed second in the senior circuit.

The Braves led the league in homers (169) and earned run average (3.14) for the second year in a row and won the most games in the majors. During their three-year tenure as NL West champions, they won 14 more games than anyone else.

Twenty-two years before they reunited in Cooperstown, Tom Glavine, John Smoltz, and Greg Maddux showed they were something special.

AP Photo/Doug Mills

153

Greg Maddux made a huge difference. The veteran control artist, signed as a free agent after winning the Cy Young Award with the Chicago Cubs in 1992, was even better with the Braves. He led the league in starts, complete games, innings, and earned run average while tying a career high with 20 wins.

Tom Glavine, who had been the staff ace before Maddux arrived, responded with his own peak in wins. He tied Maddux and Cincinnati's Jose Rijo for the league lead with 36 starts and won 22, most in the majors. It was his third straight 20-win season—the best by any pitcher since Ferguson Jenkins reeled off his sixth straight in 1972. En route to a third-place showing in the Cy Young Award voting, the classy left-hander also tossed two of Atlanta's five complete-game shutouts.

Steve Avery won 18 and John Smoltz 15, giving the franchise four 15-game winners for the first time in the modern era that began in 1901.

Atlanta's strong bullpen featured Steve Bedrosian, Marvin Freeman, Jay Howell, and Mark Wohlers as setup men for closers Mike Stanton, a left-hander who started strong, and rookie right-hander Greg McMichael, a changeup artist who picked up the slack when Stanton faded.

His streak of 15 straight saves convinced Rookie of the Year voters to place McMichael second only to Dodgers catcher Mike Piazza.

Bedrosian, originally a Brave who once won a Cy Young Award as a closer for the Phillies, made a strong comeback after rejoining the club in 1993. Out for a year with a circulatory problem, the fireballing

Pair of Aces

In 1993, Greg Maddux and Tom Glavine gave the Braves their first pair of 20-game winners since Warren Spahn and Lew Burdette in 1959.

right-hander posted a 5–2 mark with a microscopic 1.63 earned run average in 49 games as a setup man.

Persistence paid off for the pesky Braves, who refused to roll over after going 19–9 in July and 19–7 in August. Even a nine-game winning streak from August 8 to 18 wasn't enough to topple the Giants from their beanstalk.

On August 23, Atlanta arrived in San Francisco for a three-game showdown. Backed by timely long balls, Avery, Glavine, and Maddux all won their starts, cutting the deficit to four-and-a-half games. Atlanta went 19–7 in August and maintained the pace into September, winning eight of their first ten. With momentum and McGriff a marriage made in baseball heaven, the Braves finally tied San Francisco for first place on September 10. Six days later, the Braves led by four. But the Giants would not relent.

Like a schoolyard seesaw, the NL West race kept going back and forth. It was still deadlocked on October 3, the last day of the season. Knowing the Braves game on that final Sunday would start three hours before the Giants game, McGriff stated the obvious: "We've got to throw up a win early so that they see it."

Completing a 13–0 season sweep of the expansion Colorado Rockies, Glavine parlayed a Justice homer into his 22nd win. After winning that 5–3 game on the East Coast, the team had to wait for word from the West—just as it had in 1991.

That season, the Giants had knocked out the archrival Dodgers on the final day. Now it was time for payback.

Los Angeles won, handing the title to Atlanta without requiring a playoff before the playoffs. The Giants had won 14 of their last 17 but it wasn't enough.

Swinging Turnstiles

The 1993 Braves drew a franchise-record 3,884,720 fans.

Like The Great Race that involved vintage automobiles racing across the country, the Braves crossed the finish line first, collecting all the marbles in a winner-take-all treasure trove. They won 104 games, allowing them to move on, while the Giants, with 103, went home for the winter. Had a wild-card format been in place that year, the day-to-day drama of a truly gripping title chase would have been negligible. It was the first time since 1954 that a team had won that many games without reaching the postseason.

"The only good thing about it," said Giants outfielder Barry Bonds, who watched as the Braves beat his Pirates twice, "was that I didn't have to see them celebrate on the field like I did the last two years."

Although the Braves thus became the first team to win three consecutive National League West crowns, that streak would end; they were part of a massive realignment that created three divisions per league in 1994. But the team's title streak would continue right through the first half of the next decade.

The Postseason

In their last season in the National League West, the Braves advanced to the playoffs against the Philadelphia Phillies, champions of the East. Like the Braves of 1991, the Phils were a worst-to-first team, rebounding from a last-place finish the year before.

With 104 victories, most in the major leagues, Atlanta should have been favored. But the intensity of the grueling NL West race, which went down to the final day, made the Championship Series seem almost anticlimactic.

In addition, some of the Braves considered the series a mere stepping stone to a World Series berth that they had claimed in the two previous seasons.

Not so fast: although the Braves had a better batting average (.274 to .227) and earned run average (3.15 to 4.75) than their opponents, the Phillies hit more home runs and pitched better in relief, taking three

---

Deion's Demise

The Braves were so disappointed that Deion Sanders left the team to play football during the 1993 playoffs that they traded him to Cincinnati the following year.

---

one-run decisions. The main reason Atlanta outscored the Phils in the series (33–23) was a blowout in the second game.

More than 62,000 fans witnessed each of the three games at Philadephia's Veterans Stadium.

In the opener on October 6, they watched a pitching duel between Steve Avery and Curt Schilling. The Phils took a 3–2 lead into the ninth, yielded the tying run on an error by Kim Batiste, and then rallied against Greg McMichael in the bottom of the 10th. After John Kruk doubled, the little-known Batiste redeemed himself with an RBI single, ending the game, 4–3.

Atlanta's offense ignited the next night, when four home runs backed Greg Maddux in a 14–3 romp. The Braves built an early 8–0 lead and never looked back, getting long balls from Fred McGriff, Terry Pendleton, Jeff Blauser, and Damon Berryhill.

Moving to Fulton County Stadium on October 9, Atlanta spotted the Phils a 2–0 lead, then erupted for nine runs in the sixth and seventh innings. Braves starter Tom Glavine yielded two runs in seven innings.

Perhaps the Braves should have distributed their hits and runs more efficiently. They scored just a lone second-inning run in Game Four against Danny Jackson, who also singled in the go-ahead run in the fourth against John Smoltz after an error set up two unearned runs. That was the extent of the scoring in a 2–1 Philadelphia win.

With the series tied, Curt Schilling took a 3–0 shutout into the bottom of the ninth in the pivotal Game Five. But after a walk and an error, Phillies manager Jim Fregosi brought in closer Mitch Williams,

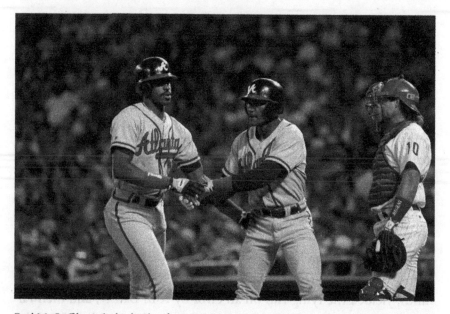

Fred McGriff brought his big bat from San Diego in July and kept it fine-tuned right into the 1993 playoffs.

AP Photo/Amy Sancetta

a wild but hard-throwing left-hander who was effective in three other NLCS outings.

That afternoon, however, he allowed both inherited runners to score, plus another of his own, and the momentum of the series seemed to have shifted—at least for the moment.

With Mark Wohlers working the 10th, the Braves hoped to keep the Phillies off the board. But Lenny Dykstra had other ideas; the fleet leadoff man, who had hit 19 home runs during the regular season, hit his second of the playoffs at a perfect time for the Phils. Larry Andersen, normally the setup man for Williams, held the Braves at bay in the bottom of the inning to wrap up a 4–3 game—matching the score of the opener.

Needing one more win for the National League pennant, the Phils went with Tommy Greene, formerly with the Braves, in Game Six at Veterans Stadium. He pitched seven innings, besting an ineffective

---

The Last Pennant Race

The 1993 NL West title chase between Atlanta and San Francisco was so grueling that the Braves players compared the daily pressure to the postseason pressure they had experienced in 1991 and 1992. "We felt like we were in the playoffs before the season ended," said slugger Ron Gant. "It was so tight that we pretty much had to win every game. We almost did. We put pressure on the Giants but still needed a little help from the Dodgers, which we got. By the time we got to the playoffs, though, we were running on fumes. We used up so much energy in catching the Giants."

Greg Maddux in a 6–3 game. One of Atlanta's five hits was Blauser's second homer of the series. The Phils had seven—the only time they had more hits than the Braves in any of the six games.

It was not the way Maddux wanted to finish his first season in an Atlanta uniform. But his problems probably resulted from a Mickey Morandini liner that banged off his right shin in the first inning. Maddux, who would go on to win more Gold Gloves (18) than any National League pitcher, couldn't react quickly enough. The incident created an interruption while Bobby Cox and Leo Mazzone conferred with their ace on the mound but Maddux—realizing the importance of the game—maintained his ability to continue. Given the chance to do it again, the pitcher might have decided differently.

"Could I have pitched better?" Maddux asked the media throng afterward. "I can't tell you that. All I can tell you is that I felt it."

It was the first time in the NLCS that Philadelphia scored more than four runs and the first time their margin of victory was greater than one. As a result, they became the first team from the NL East to reach the World Series since 1987.

That would soon change, with the Braves ticketed to switch divisions the following year.

11
1995: NIRVANA

Opening Day
Grissom, cf
Blauser, ss
Jones, 3b
McGriff, 1b
Justice, rf
Lopez, c
Kelly, lf
Lemke, 2b
Maddux, p
Best Hitter: Fred McGriff
Best Pitcher: Greg Maddux
Best Newcomer: Chipper Jones

The Season

LIKE BEETHOVEN'S UNFINISHED Symphony, the 1994 season had no ending. A players' strike started on August 12 and stretched for 232 days—until a federal judge named Sonia Sotomayor, later a Supreme Court Justice, delivered a ruling against the owners that led to the players returning to work.

After an abbreviated spring training, the clubs returned to play a 144-game schedule—10 less than the format that governed baseball before the advent of expansion in 1961.

Atlanta's powerful pitching staff, well-rested after the long layoff, proved potent again. The club went 90–54, a pace that left them 21 games ahead of the Philadelphia Phillies and New York Mets, who tied for second in the National League East. It was the biggest victory margin during the Braves' 14-year title run.

Although first place was familiar territory for the Braves, the National League East was not. They moved there in 1994, when the leagues split into three divisions each and a wild-card winner (the second-place team with the best record) was added to the postseason tournament.

Geographically, Atlanta should have been a no-brainer for the NL East but wound up in the West when divisional play was introduced in 1969. The New York Mets refused to sign off on the new alignment unless they could have the St. Louis Cardinals, then defending NL champions, in their division. Since the Chicago Cubs were natural rivals of the Cards, the league placed both Chicago and St. Louis in the East but Atlanta and Cincinnati in the West.

That bogus arrangement was fixed when the Central Division was added in 1994. The Cubs, Cards, and Reds all joined the Central while the Braves went East—albeit with some concern about how they could compete against the big-spending Mets.

If not for the strike, Atlanta might have had another champion in 1994. Although a blue-chip rookie named Chipper Jones was lost for the year after he tore up his knee while running the bases in Grapefruit League play, the Braves won 13 of their first 14 games. They also set a modern National League record by winning their first seven road games at the start of a season.

Hitless Wonder

Greg Maddux, Tom Glavine, and John Smoltz never threw a no-hitter but teammate Kent Mercker was involved in two. He started the first combined no-hit game in National League history on September 11, 1991, working the first six innings and teaming with Mark Wohlers (two innings) and Alejandro Pena (one). Three years later, the lefty pitched a complete-game no-hitter against the Los Angeles Dodgers on April 8.

Two fellow freshmen, catcher Javy Lopez and outfielder Ryan Klesko, provided pop behind first baseman Fred McGriff, who became the ninth man with seven straight 30-homer seasons. He also turned a Lee Smith pitch into a game-tying, two-run homer in the ninth inning of the All-Star Game, thus becoming the first Brave to win the game's MVP trophy.

Greg Maddux, in his second year with the team, led the league with 202 innings, 10 complete games, a 1.56 earned run average, and 16 wins. The starting pitcher in the All-Star Game, he later received his third straight Cy Young Award.

Overcoming the season-long sidelining of Chipper Jones, the loss of Ron Gant after a February dirt-bike accident, and the free agent departures of Sid Bream, Damon Berryhill, Francisco Cabrera, and Otis Nixon ultimately proved too much.

On the day the strike began, the Braves were actually closer to the top of the division than they had been on the same date the year before. Officially, they were six games off the pace of the front-running Montreal Expos. Unofficially, they had made a habit of playing the tortoise to everyone else's hare. Slow but steady usually wins the race unless a strike stops it.

Gant's Last Stand

Ron Gant's career with the Braves came to a crashing halt in 1994 when he broke his leg in a preseason dirt bike accident. "It was one of those things I tried for fun that I shouldn't have," Gant said long after he left the game. "I ended up wiping out and breaking my leg right before spring training. I missed all of that year. The Braves did the right thing: they had the option to void my contract and pay a percentage of it or keep me and pay the entire $5.5 million. It was a business decision and I don't blame them for making it."

In 1995, there was no stopping the determined Braves.

By the time the team clinched the division, the clubhouse looked like it had been cast by Disney:

- Golf-loving pitcher John Smoltz kept his clubs in his locker
- Nintendo-loving Greg Maddux liked to play poker but hated to organize his unsightly stall
- Left-handed starter Tom Glavine stopped thinking about the professional hockey career he could have had
- American-born Mark Lemke spoke fluent Spanish but fellow infielder Fred McGriff hardly spoke in any language
- Slugger David Justice, who had the look and swagger of a matinee idol, was married to actress Halle Berry
- Owner Ted Turner, who looked like Rhett Butler of *Gone With the Wind*, was married to actress Jane Fonda
- The locker of backup catcher Charlie O'Brien looked like a hunting store
- Marquis Grissom, a local product, had huge phone bills, thanks to 14 brothers and sisters
- Ryan Klesko, a regular outfielder, was once a top high school pitching prospect
- Luis Polonia, the shortest man on the team, was also the snappiest dresser

The clubhouse had everything except Jerry Seinfeld and George Costanza. It even had, for the very first time, a Chipper off the old block.

Maddux provided the only real scare of the season when he came down with a rare adult case of chicken pox that threatened to knock him out of his Opening Day start. After a few anxious days, however, he was able to put the "fowl" spring training experience behind him and concentrate on activity between the foul lines.

The only NL East team to win more than they lost, Atlanta started the season on April 26 by beating San Francisco, 12–5, and won four of its first five to sit at the top of the division before the calendar turned to May.

Chipper Jones started his path to Cooperstown with a ninth-inning home run—his first—against Josias Manzanillo of the Mets at Shea Stadium on May 9. The switch-hitting third baseman also went 13-for-30 (.433) with runners in scoring position.

Maddux, another Brave with a Hall of Fame future, proved the hardest pitcher to hit for the second month in a row, holding hitters to a .174 batting average. His best game came May 28, when he held the Houston Astros hitless before deciding to see whether Jeff Bagwell could hit his fastball. He could, so Maddux had to settle for a one-hit complete game that was not a shutout. It would be the only one-hitter of his career.

Although the Braves went 16–12 in May and 15–12 in June, they finished both months four games behind Philadelphia in the standings. That trend would prove short-lived.

Buoyed by a stingy staff that yielded just 2.8 runs per game in July, Atlanta parlayed a nine-game winning streak into a 20–7 mark for the month. Ten wins in their last at-bat helped.

The Braves rode the arms of Maddux (4–0, 1.27) and closer Mark Wohlers (0.66 earned run average) to vault eight-and-a-half games ahead of Philadelphia by the July 31 trade deadline.

They maintained the momentum in August, going 19–10, with Tom Glavine the main hero on the hill. The wily left-hander not only went 4–0 with a 1.45 ERA but hit his first major league home run against Cincinnati southpaw John Smiley. It tied up a game that the Braves went on to win 2–1.

There was plenty of justice in Atlanta, too: David Justice hit .311 with nine homers while Chipper chipped away at a .317 pace while knocking in 21 runs. As a result, the Atlanta lead expanded to 15 games before Labor Day.

On August 25, singer Elton John visited the batting cage at Wrigley Field. "I've always been a big Braves fan," said John, who sent telegrams to Bobby Cox whenever the Braves played well or went on a streak. "Even during the dog days, I watched on television all the time. I used to watch Phil Niekro and Dale Murphy. I really like baseball—no sport is more romantic."

In 1995, many Braves fans felt that way.

Finishing with a flourish, the Braves clinched first place on September 13 when they beat the Rockies, 9–7, in Denver and the Phillies lost, 5–4, in Montreal. Roaring down the stretch at a 47–29 clip, the Braves stretched their second-half winning percentage since 1991 to .655 (220–116).

Lopez led the team with a September average of .348 while Klesko hit .306 with nine home runs. Maddux managed a 4–0 mark and 0.29 ERA, giving him a season's record of 19–2 with a 1.63 ERA. He also became the first pitcher ever to win 18 straight games on the road.

In addition, the 6-foot, 175-pound right-hander was the first pitcher since Walter Johnston to have consecutive earned run averages below 1.80. And Johnson did it in 1918 and 1919, when the rest of the planet was still recuperating from World War I.

Everybody chipped in. Glavine (16–7, 3.08) and John Smoltz (12–7, 3.18) teamed with Maddux at the top of a rotation that also included left-handers Steve Avery, a 1991 postseason star, and Kent Mercker, who had pitched a no-hitter against the Dodgers in 1994. Maddux, Glavine, and Smoltz all ranked among the league's Top 10 in earned run average as the Atlanta staff produced a 3.44 mark that led the majors for the third time in four seasons. Braves pitchers also had the most strikeouts (1,087) and fewest home runs allowed (107) in either league.

Stingy Star

During Atlanta's championship run in 1995, Greg Maddux held opposing hitters to 6.31 hits per nine innings.

165

Bullpen workhorses Greg McMichael and Brad Clontz combined for a 15–4 mark and Pedro Borbon Jr. also appeared more than 40 times. Wohlers, who became the closer in June, fanned 90 hitters in 64 2/3 innings while crafting a 2.09 ERA in 65 outings. He converted 21 consecutive save chances from June 5 to September 3.

The pitchers got plenty of support: the Braves had four 20-homer men for the first time since 1973. McGriff led with 27, followed by Justice (24), Jones and Klesko (23 each). Lopez, Grissom, and Jeff Blauser also reached double digits in long balls, giving the Braves seven men at that level for the first time in franchise history.

Lopez and Klesko had the best batting averages on the ballclub but McGriff knocked in the most runs. Chipper Jones would usurp leadership in both departments for years to come.

Although injuries idled regulars Klesko (thumb), Justice (shoulder), and Mark Lemke (hamstring) at various times, Atlanta stayed afloat because of a strong bench and good scouting system.

Key bench players ranged from Charlie O'Brien, often the designated catcher for Maddux, to infielders Mike Mordecai and Rafael Belliard and outfielder Dwight Smith, a free agent who signed in April. Eddie Perez, a catcher whose defensive skills superseded a lackluster bat, also surfaced for the first time—after nine years in the minor leagues. His first big league hit was a home run at Cincinnati on September 15.

John Schuerholz, the astute and respected general manager, made his major move just before the opener when he added smooth-fielding Marquis Grissom, who had been playing center field for Montreal. The cost was steep: Roberto Kelly, Tony Tarasco, Esteban Yan, and cash.

The GM also acquired three key players in August: outfielders Luis Polonia, plucked from the Yankees, and Mike Devereaux, who was with the White Sox, plus returning relief pitcher Alejandro Pena, hooked from the Marlins, all proved pivotal down the stretch and beyond.

The Postseason

For the first time, the Braves had to win two playoff rounds to reach the World Series.

With two hitter-friendly ballparks in play, the first Division Series was a slugfest from the start.

Opening in Denver, where the alpine air of the Mile High City doesn't deter baseballs in flight, the Braves and Colorado Rockies combined for 25 hits, including four home runs. Chipper Jones hit a pair, including a solo shot in the ninth that gave the Braves a 5–4 win at the new Coors Field.

Marquis Grissom, who also homered for Atlanta in the opener, smacked a pair of long balls in Game Two. A four-spot in the ninth tipped the game to Atlanta, 7–4, and sent the best-of-five series to Fulton County Stadium.

For the third straight game, the Braves scored in the ninth inning to take the lead or forge a tie.

But Mark Wohlers, who had saved the first two games, quickly turned the 5–5 score into a 7–5 Colorado win.

The Rockies jumped on Greg Maddux for three runs in the third inning of Game Four but didn't get much more. The Atlanta ace worked seven innings, with seven strikeouts and no walks, of a 10–4 win that clinched the series. He got all the support he needed from Fred McGriff, the third Brave to enjoy a two-homer game in the NLDS.

Pitching took a back seat to hitting throughout the series; Braves batters combined for a .331 average while the Rockies hit a composite .285—not too shabby against the vaunted Atlanta pitching staff.

The next round would be radically different, although the rival Cincinnati Reds had already advanced by beating the Los Angeles Dodgers in the other initial Division Series.

Both of the first two games went into extra innings. The Reds nursed a 1–0 lead into the ninth inning of Game One behind Pete Schourek but allowed the Braves to score solo runs in the ninth and 11th for a

2–1 victory at Riverfront Stadium. The winner crossed on a single by Mike Devereaux, acquired in an August waiver deal.

Game Two, played on October 11, was a 2–2 tie until the 10th. That's when the Braves posted a four-spot, primarily because Javy Lopez homered with two men on following a run-scoring wild pitch.

Fulton County Stadium lived up to its "Launching Pad" nickname when Atlanta scored all of its runs on long balls in Game Three. Charlie O'Brien, hardly the biggest threat in the Braves lineup, broke up a scoreless tie in the sixth with a three-run homer. An inning later, Chipper Jones connected with a man on. That was enough for Greg Maddux, with ninth-inning help from Mark Wohlers, to win, 5–2.

The big blow of the fourth game was a three-run Devereaux home run that highlighted a five-run seventh and gave the Braves a 6–0 win behind Steve Avery, who had been equally stingy against Pittsburgh sluggers in the 1991 NLCS. With his help, Atlanta posted a 1.15 ERA against Cincinnati hitters. Though not quite The Big Red Machine of the '70s, the Reds were red-faced at their total power vacuum. None of their big hitters was able to hit a home run.

The Braves knew they had a tougher task in beating the Cleveland Indians, whom they met in the World Series for the first time since 1948. They knew that having the home-field advantage would help. And they knew that good pitching stops good hitting.

Surprise MVP

Mike Devereaux, a waiver wire acquisition from the White Sox late in the 1995 campaign, proved his value in the NLCS against Cincinnati. He singled in the winning run in the 11th inning of the opener, then homered with two men on in the seventh inning of Game Four while filling in for David Justice (bad knee). The Braves won the game, 6–0, and the series, 4–0, while Devereaux won MVP honors.

Maddux and Glavine won the first two games, 3–2 and 4–3, before the series shifted to Cleveland. In the opener, the teams combined for five hits but one of them was a Fred McGriff home run. Maddux, who went the route, allowed only three base-runners: opposite-field singles by Kenny Lofton and Jim Thome coupled with an error by shortstop Rafael Belliard.

Javy Lopez hammered a two-run homer in the sixth inning of the second game to provide the margin of victory.

In Game Three, however, Cleveland scored in the eighth and 11th to wrap up a 7–6 victory. Home runs by McGriff and Klesko couldn't compensate for an off-night by John Smoltz, knocked out in the third inning.

Klesko homered again in Game Four on October 25 as Steve Avery and three relievers won on the Tribe's home turf, 5–2. A three-run burst in the seventh broke up a 1–1 tie.

Yet another Klesko home run—his third in as many games—was one of four hit in the fifth game. But Maddux, so masterful in the opener, yielded four runs in seven innings as the Braves lost, 5–4. Little-used Luis Polonia powered another Atlanta homer in a losing cause.

The Braves needed only one more win to clinch the first world championship by any Atlanta team. Tom Glavine, a study in determination, wanted to make that happen.

He held the Indians hitless for the first five innings. Then Tony Pena popped a bloop single to right. It turned out to be the only Cleveland hit.

McGriff's Momentum

Fred McGriff was a red-hot hitter right through the 1995 World Series. In 14 postseason games that fall, he hit .333 with four home runs. His lifetime average in postseason play for the Braves was .323 (nine series).

A solo homer by David Justice was the only run scored in the final game of the 1995 World Series.

AP Photo/Tannen Maury

When David Justice answered with a long home run against left-handed reliever Jim Poole, he gave the Braves a 1–0 lead that neither Glavine nor Mark Wohlers, who relieved in the ninth, would surrender. The outspoken outfielder had irritated Braves fans by telling Atlanta newspapers he thought they lacked spirit and enthusiasm. The fans retaliated by booing the slugger—until he silenced them with a single swing of his bat.

Glavine had been almost flawless through eight scoreless innings but started tiring in the top of the eighth. With Wohlers available to save the game, he had no qualms telling Bobby Cox he'd had enough—even though he wanted to be on the field for the postgame celebration.

Wohlers, who became the last man on the mound when the 1995 campaign ended, worked in 11 of the 14 postseason games. "I wanted to be there," the pitcher said. "After a loss, any relief pitcher wants to

170

get right back out there and redeem himself. I was able to get out there a lot because of our position in the standings."

After winning world championships in Boston (1914) and Milwaukee (1957), the Braves had finally brought a title to Atlanta. A long time coming, it created memories that would last a lifetime.

It also created expectations of more.

12
1996: POWER PLUS PITCHING

Opening Day
Grissom, cf
Blauser, ss
Justice, rf
McGriff, 1b
Klesko, lf
Lopez, c
Lemke, 2b
Mordecai, 3b
Maddux, p
Best Hitter: Chipper Jones
Best Pitcher: John Smoltz
Best Newcomer: Jermaine Dye

The Season

BUOYED BY THE euphoria of Atlanta's first world championship, the Braves began their title defense with the same formula: powerful pitching supported by potent hitting.

The minute the gate opened, the team started a confident trot toward the finish line. With a 16–11 April and 19–6 May, Atlanta had a five-game lead through the first two months.

Led again by the talented troika of Greg Maddux, Tom Glavine, and John Smoltz, the pitching staff posted more strikeouts (1,245) and less walks (451) than any other team in the majors.

Smoltz lost his first start, and then followed with a 14–0 record and 1.91 earned run average over his next 15 appearances. By season's end, he had 24 wins, an Atlanta record; 276 strikeouts, a Braves franchise record; and the Cy Young Award. Since he was also the winning pitcher in the All-Star Game and a four-time winner in the postseason, Smoltz ended the year with a 29–9 mark and 293 2/3 innings pitched.

That stopped a streak of four straight Cy Young Awards for Maddux, who joined Glavine as 15-game winners. Bobby Cox worked all three aces heavily, with Glavine's 36 starts lead-

Fun-loving John Smoltz won 29 games, including the All-Star Game and four postseason contests in 1996.

Photo by Bill Menzel.

ing the league. Considered the Three Horsemen of the Apocalypse by opponents, they were among the six big league starters who compiled earned run averages of less than 3.00 in 1996.

Steve Avery, hobbled by an injury to his oblique, won seven times in 23 starts but the Braves filled out their rotation at various times with Terrell Wade, Mike Bielecki, Jason Schmidt, and Brad Woodall. Only after the late-summer arrival of Denny Neagle from Pittsburgh did the Braves have a reliable fourth starter. Wade went 5–0 with a 2.97 ERA but Neagle, a more experienced left-hander, proved to be a better long-range investment.

A potent pen helped the Braves survive the sweltering summer despite the depleted rotation. Mark Wohlers converted 39 of 44 saves chances while striking out 100 in 77 1/3 innings. Greg McMichael,

What, Me Worry?

Mark Wohlers was converted to closing in the minors because he worried too much between starts.

who mastered a changeup that looked like it was falling off a table, worked 73 times, four less than Wohlers, but sidearmer Brad Clontz was the busiest bullpen arm with 81 outings. When his elbow allowed him to pitch, Pedro Borbon Jr. also helped, as did Joe Borowski. The pitchers posted a composite 3.52 earned run average, helping the Braves win 96 times, but needed considerable support. Thanks to 100-RBI men Chipper Jones and Fred McGriff, they got it.

Chipper led the Braves in two of the three Triple Crown categories: batting (.309) and runs batted in (110), but his 30 home runs were four behind Ryan Klesko's team-high total.

With David Justice limited to just 40 games by shoulder problems, Jermaine Dye got a shot in right field and immediately made the most of it by homering in his first at-bat, against Cincinnati on May 17. No Braves rookie had done that since Chuck Tanner in 1955, when the team was based in Milwaukee.

Both Dye and shortstop Jeff Blauser, limited to 83 games by a broken bone in his hand, reached double digits in home runs. Looking to boost their run production, the Braves struck oil in some unexpected places.

Painful Swing

David Justice separated his shoulder with a swing-and-miss in his last at-bat for the Braves. The season-ending mishap occurred in May 1996, ten months before the slugging outfielder was traded to Cleveland.

Late-season arrival Luis Polonia, a skilled left-handed pinch-hitter, batted .419 in 22 games. Other late-season add-ons included Danny Bautista and switch-hitters Terry Pendleton, leader of the 1991 worst-to-first team, and Mark Whiten, who once hit four home runs in a game. Season-long bench players were Mike Mordecai, who played all four infield positions; Dwight Smith, an outfielder with left-handed power in the pinch; and Eddie Perez, primarily the "designated catcher" for Maddux. Even Rafael Belliard, a .169 hitter clinging to a big league berth by the fingertips of his glove, got into 87 games on either side of second base.

The most underrated aspect of the team was its strength up the middle, with Javy Lopez the regular catcher, steady Mark Lemke at second, Blauser at short, and Marquis Grissom in center field. Both Lopez and Grissom contributed 23 home runs to the cause but Blauser had the biggest day: a two-homer, seven-RBI outburst at Philadelphia on May 11.

Grissom, best-known for his speed and defense, was a key cog in the offense, delivering a career-best 207 hits (65 of them for extra bases). That made him the first Brave to reach the 200-hit plateau since Ralph Garr in 1974. Grissom's 28-game hitting streak from July 25 to August 24 was the longest since Rowland Office had a hit in 29 straight games during the 1976 campaign. Among Grissom's team-best 28 stolen bases was a theft of home against the Reds on June 2.

End of an Era

In the last regular season game at Atlanta-Fulton County Stadium, on September 23, 1996, the Braves beat the Expos, 3–1, before 49,083 spectators. Greg Maddux was the winning pitcher, Ryan Klesko had the last hit by a Brave, and Luis Polonia had the last stolen base. The last Braves home run was hit the night before by Marquis Grissom.

Atlanta Stadium's altitude and dimensions made it so conducive to home runs that pitcher Pat Jarvis dubbed it "the Launching Pad" but Tom Glavine held the Cleveland Indians to just one hit over eight innings to clinch the 1995 World Series there.

Illustration by Thomas Kolendra, © Bill Goff, Inc./goodsportsart.com.

Even with all that success, the 29-year-old Grissom started to realize his tenure was temporary after the August arrival of Andruw Jones. The fourth-youngest player in Atlanta history, Jones was only 19 years, three months, and 23 days old when he homered in his second big league game, a 5–4 win over Pittsburgh on August 16. He was the youngest NL player to clear the fences since Houston pitcher Larry Dierker in 1965.

Jones, who had started the year at the Class A level, capped his meteoric rise though the farm system with four more home runs, giving him five home runs and 13 RBIs in his first 31 games, along with a .217 batting average that seemed innocuous at the time. But Jones had hit 39 home runs while playing at four different levels and bigger things were just over the horizon. A two-time Minor League Player of the Year, Jones was preceded to the majors by his own reputation. None other than Paul Snyder, Atlanta's astute player development chief, called him "the best prospect the Braves have ever signed."

Although Andruw played the outfield corners because Grissom was still a productive center fielder, it wasn't long before the Curacao native claimed the position for himself. His combination of light-tower power plus high-light-film defense later inspired Bobby Cox to compare him with Hall of Famer Willie Mays.

Jones wasn't the only young stud primed to keep The Streak

ANDRUW JONES
outfield ATLANTA BRAVES™

Courtesy of The Topps Company, Inc.

intact; the Braves were named Organization of the Year by *Baseball America* for the first time since 1991.

The Postseason

After winning the NL East by eight games over the Montreal Expos, the Braves moved into the playoffs high on pitching, power, and confidence. They had won 96 games, most in the National League, and knew they could add to that total.

Their first obstacle was beating the Los Angeles Dodgers, a wild-card winner who opened at home because the Division Series schedule then awarded the last three games of the best-of-five series to the team with the better record.

The three-hour time difference didn't bother the three horsemen of the Atlanta rotation. John Smoltz, with a one-inning save from Mark Wohlers, beat Ramon Martinez in the October 2 opener, 2–1. The winner crossed on a solo home run by Javy Lopez in the top of the 10th.

The Braves won the second game when Greg Maddux, Greg McMichael, and Wohlers combined on a three-hitter that yielded a 3–2 victory. The Dodgers held a 2–1 lead when Fred McGriff tied it with a leadoff home run in the seventh. Two batters later, Jermaine Dye connected to put the Braves ahead to stay.

Back in Atlanta, Tom Glavine parlayed a four-run Atlanta fourth against Hideo Nomo into a 5–2 clincher. Nomo left in the fourth after surrendering a two-run double to Mark Lemke, a postseason hero before, and a two-run homer to Chipper Jones.

The Dodgers managed just 14 hits and five runs, none on home runs, while the Braves got home runs from five different players: Dye, McGriff, Chipper, Lopez, and Ryan Klesko. Atlanta hit only .180 against Dodger pitching and scored only 10 runs but didn't need more.

"When you're facing a staff like Atlanta's," said Dodgers first baseman Eric Karros, "you're going to get two or three pitches to hit all day. You've got to hit them. If you don't, you're in big trouble."

St. Louis was to be Atlanta's next victim—or so the Braves thought. But it wouldn't be easy.

In their fifth consecutive Championship Series, Atlanta drew first blood, winning the opener, 4–2, on a two-run, eighth-inning Javy Lopez single. Chipper went 4-for-4, Smoltz got the win, and Wohlers picked up his fourth straight save of the 1996 postseason.

The pennant express, seemingly clicking on all cylinders, suffered a sudden return to reality one night later. Already trailing, 4–3, the Braves winced when Gary Gaetti hit a grand slam against Maddux in the seventh inning. The Cards won it, 8–3, tying the best-of-seven series.

Glavine was only marginally more successful in Game Three, played October 12 at Busch Memorial Stadium. Former teammate Ron Gant reached him for two home runs to pace a 3–2 Cardinals victory.

When St. Louis won by a 4–3 score the next night, beating Greg McMichael on a Brian Jordan homer in the eighth, the Braves looked finished. Denny Neagle had held a 3–0 lead with two outs and nobody on base in the seventh before the Cards rallied to tie.

No National League team had ever rebounded from a deficit of three games to one in the Championship Series—but the Braves were determined to end that hex. They were also determined to do it in a big way.

With five in the first and two in the second behind Smoltz in Game Five, Atlanta made an early statement. The Braves crushed an LCS-record 22 hits, four of them by Mark Lemke, in a 14–0 rout that also featured home runs from Fred McGriff and Javy Lopez (who also had two doubles and a single).

Back home, the Braves banked on their usual formula of winning with quality pitching.

Maddux and Wohlers held the Cards to six hits in a 3–1 win that knotted the series. The only Cardinal run crossed on a wild pitch by the reliever.

The bats were back in the finale, with the Braves jumping on Donovan Osborne for a six-run first highlighted by Glavine's opposite-field triple with the bases loaded. Glavine and two relievers limited St. Louis to four hits as Atlanta waltzed, 15–0—topping the record for runs in a game they set just three days earlier.

During the seventh-inning stretch, the team dispensed with the customary playing of "Take Me Out to the Ballgame" and substituted Frank Sinatra's version of "New York, New York." More than 52,000 fans, already looking ahead to the World Series, sang along. Broadcaster Pete Van Wieren called it "one of the greatest sights and sounds I've ever experienced."

Javy Lopez won NLCS MVP honors with a .542 average (13-for-24) that included five doubles, two home runs, and six runs batted in. Smoltz could have also won it with his 2–0 record, 1.20 earned run average, and 12 strikeouts in 15 innings. Other candidates were McGriff, who homered twice, and Lemke, whose .444 average also included a rare four-bagger. All three Atlanta outfielders—Grissom, Ryan Klesko, and Andruw Jones—also homered.

Andruw, quickly making a name for himself, would maintain that hot hand even after the Cards were off the table.

The Braves advanced to their second straight World Series and fourth out of the last five played (the first NL club to do that since the 1952–56 Brooklyn Dodgers).

The defending World Champions, whose pitching had stymied the heavy-hitting Cleveland Indians the previous fall, believed they would be just as successful against the free-spending New York Yankees. At the outset, that theory seemed justified.

Carrying the momentum of their last three playoff victories, the Braves knocked out Yankee starter Andy Pettitte in the third inning of the first game. Smoltz and four relievers held the powerful Yankees to four hits in a 12–1 laugher that contained a giant Andruw Jones footprint.

The 19-year-old outfielder, recalled only two months earlier, homered in his first two World Series at-bats, duplicating the 1972 feat of Gene Tenace, and became the youngest player ever to hit a home run on that grand stage. Jones, who once kept in shape for baseball by swinging a sledgehammer in his native Curacao, knocked in five runs in the first game. With a two-run homer in the second and a three-run homer in the third, Jones toppled Mickey Mantle's mark as the youngest slugger to connect in the Fall Classic. Jones was only 19 years and 180 days old at the time, while Mantle was 20 years and 362 days old when he hit a World Series home run.

"I never thought this could happen that fast," said Jones, who had only 106 at-bats before exploding onto the national stage. "I just want to have fun."

Counting his home run in the sixth inning of the final game of the NLCS, the affable outfielder had actually hit three in a row.

Maddux was the main man for the Braves in Game Two, played at Yankee Stadium on October 21. He worked eight scoreless innings as Atlanta won, 4–0. All but five of the 24 outs he got came on ground balls.

The veteran right-hander got all the support he needed from McGriff, who followed a two-RBI performance in the opener with a three-RBI night in the second game. His postseason total of 16 would be a major-league record.

After watching Atlanta reverse Sherman's March with their victories in New York, practically every baseball pundit predicted a Braves victory if not a sweep. After all, the team was headed to friendly turf where twirling tomahawks often intimidated visiting teams. In addition, the Braves had outscored their opponents, 48–2, in their last five games.

Pitching prevailed in Game Three, however, with David Cone beating Glavine, 5–2. A two-run, eighth-inning Bernie Williams home run expanded New York's 2–1 lead.

Atlanta tried another southpaw, Denny Neagle, in the fourth game. He took a 6–0 lead into the sixth but left when the Yankees cut it in half. New York struck for another three-spot in the eighth when Jim Leyritz turned a Mark Wohlers slider into a home run with two men on base. Second-guessers suggested later that the closer should have used his super-heated fastball rather than his third-best pitch. Leyritz had fouled off a couple of Wohlers heaters before the closer countered with a hanging slider. The slugger didn't miss it.

Wohlers, used exclusively in the ninth inning until that night, didn't get much help from his defense. After allowing two singles, he coaxed a ground ball to sure-handed shortstop Rafael Belliard, who bobbled the ball, blowing a likely double play and placing two men on for Leyritz, a powerful pinch-hitter with a penchant for producing under pressure.

The deadlock ended when the Yankees pushed across two 10th-inning runs, thanks in part to a bases-loaded walk to Wade Boggs, the American League's most disciplined hitter, by erstwhile starter Steve Avery.

Smoltz was on his game a night later but so was Pettitte. The Braves lost, 1–0, when Marquis Grissom—who commited just one error during the regular season—made a rare miscue in the fourth. He dropped a ball after rookie right fielder Jermaine Dye crossed in front of him and obscured his vision. The two teams combined for only nine hits.

In the same game, played on October 24, the Braves came within a whisker of beating Yankees closer John Wetteland with two outs in the bottom of the ninth. Joe Torre ordered his closer to issue an intentional walk to left-handed slugger Ryan Klesko—an unconventional strategy that put the winning run on base—and pitch to Dye. Bobby Cox countered by sending little Luis Polonia to the plate as a pinch-hitter.

At 5-foot-8, Polonia had a small strike zone. He was also a great fastball hitter, coming in to face a pitcher with a great fastball.

He fouled off three straight heaters, lacing line drives straight back or over the third-base dugout. That told Yankees coach Jose Cardenal, a former outfielder, that Polonia probably couldn't pull a pitch to right field. He jumped to the top step of the dugout and motioned Paul O'Neill to move eight steps toward right-center.

Three more pitches, three more foul drives. And then Polonia connected, sending a screaming liner toward the gap in right-center field. O'Neill, slowed by a severely strained left hamstring, took off and lunged. He just barely snagged the ball in his outstretched glove.

"That at-bat sent me to Mexico," said Polonia, who spent the next two seasons south of the border. Had O'Neill not moved, he never could have caught up with it.

Instead of a 2–1 victory and 3–2 lead in the World Series, the Braves found themselves behind the eight ball, forced to return to New York needing to win both games to defend their world title.

After the stunning NLCS comeback against the Cardinals, the club had hope. But it didn't last long.

Maddux yielded all three Yankee runs in the third inning and the Braves never caught up. The 3–2 win in Game Six gave New York a world championship it did not expect to win.

Atlanta's Big Three were impressive: Smoltz had a 0.64 ERA, Glavine was at 1.29, and Maddux finished at 1.72. Grissom, who hit .444, and Andruw Jones, who hit .400 as a teenager, did well, as did McGriff (two home runs). The Braves actually outhit the Yankees, .254 to .216, outhomered them (4–2), and outpitched them (2.33 ERA to 3.93).

The team had a long winter to reflect on what might have been. Were they overconfident? Or were they careless?

With contract and roster decisions to make, the offseason would be a busy one—and a good time to look ahead rather than look back.

One major change would be the ballpark itself. When Atlanta Fulton County Stadium hosted its first Braves game in 1966, the Atlanta battery consisted of pitcher Tony Cloninger and catcher Joe Torre. In its last contest, Game Five of the 1996 World Series, Torre and Cloninger were there again—as the manager and pitching coach, respectively, of the visiting New York Yankees.

13
1997: FRIGGIN' FLORIDA

Opening Day
Lofton, cf
Lemke, 2b
C. Jones, 3b
McGriff, 1b
Klesko, lf
Tucker, rf
Lopez, c
Blauser, ss
Smoltz, p
Best Hitter: Chipper Jones
Best Pitcher: Greg Maddux
Best Newcomer: Kenny Lofton

The Season

NEW SEASON, NEW ballpark, same old results.

The Braves switched to Turner Field, which had been built for the 1996 Summer Olympics, without missing a beat.

After owner and namesake Ted Turner threw out the first pitch, Atlanta beat Chicago, 5–4, in an opener witnessed by 45,044 fans. Chipper Jones got the first hit, first walk, first stolen base, and first game-winning RBI for the Braves, who won with a two-run burst in the bottom of the eighth. Mark Wohlers then got the first Turner Field save.

Michael Tucker hit the first home run in the new stadium, while Javy Lopez hit the first grand slam—10 days after the April 4 opener.

Atlanta started well, winning more April games (19) than any previous major league team. The Braves won 12 of their first 13 at home, enabling them to stay atop the NL East from April 13 through the end of the 162-game schedule.

The fans responded, flocking to Turner Field in record numbers. The 81 home games had 33 sellouts and a total attendance of 3,464,488.

Attendance would have been higher had the stadium kept its original dimensions. Its seating capacity was reduced from 85,000 to 50,000 when the field was converted into a baseball park. Dubbed "the Ted," Turner Field had an official capacity of 49,743. It stood right across the street from the old Atlanta Fulton County Stadium for four months— until the old place was demolished on the morning of August 2. The old circular ballpark, built for the mere pittance of $18 million, was gone even though its reputation lived on.

The Braves shifted from Atlanta Fulton County Stadium to Turner Field (above) in 1997.
Illustration by Bill Purdom, © Bill Goff, Inc./goodsportsart.com.

From 1970 to 1977, more home runs were hit at "the Launching Pad" than were hit in any other ballpark.

Not surprisingly, Turner Field instantly proved more favorable to pitchers. Janet Marie Smith, vice president of planning and development for the Braves, designed both Olympic Stadium and Turner Field. She had also been involved in the design of Oriole Park at Camden Yards, the first new ballpark to feature an old look.

The fans liked the look of both the park and the team, especially since it was trying for its third straight pennant despite a radically revamped roster.

David Justice and Marquis Grissom were gone, traded to Cleveland for fleet leadoff man Kenny Lofton, and smooth-fielding shortstop Walt Weiss signed on as a free agent. Others added since the '96 team went to the World Series were infielder Keith Lockhart, a premier pinch-hitter, and outfielders Michael Tucker and Gerald Williams, who all arrived in trades.

Denny Neagle was also relatively new. Acquired from Pittsburgh the previous August, the left-handed starter celebrated his first full season in Atlanta by topping the 1997 team and the league with 20 wins. He reached the charmed circle for the first time in his career when he and the bullpen blanked San Diego, 4–0, on September 7.

Neagle, solid all season, posted a 2.97 earned run average, made the All-Star team for the second time, and finished third in the Cy Young Award voting.

The youthful pitching staff—average age 26—produced almost every night. How could they not with future Hall of Famers Greg Maddux, Tom Glavine, and John Smoltz joining Neagle in a formidable

Pricey Park

Turner Field cost $235 million to build, more than 10 times the construction price of Atlanta Fulton County Stadium ($18 million).

rotation? En route to 101 wins, most in the majors, Atlanta pitchers posted a 3.18 earned run average and spun 17 shutouts—both best in the big leagues that season.

All of the Big Four starters worked at least 230 innings and kept their ERAs right around three earned runs per game. Because Maddux was considerably better at 2.20 (second in the league), he went 19–4 for a league-leading .826 winning percentage. Since six of his 20 walks were intentional, the crafty control artist could have had more wins than walks.

Glavine was NL Pitcher of the Month in April, when he went 4–0 with a 1.64 earned run mark, and became the first man to pitch two shutouts at Denver's Coors Field, normally a shooting gallery for hitters. He was one of four Braves starters to crack the league's Top 10 in ERA.

After blanking the Rockies in a 14–0 romp on April 18, Glavine said of Coors Field, "I love this place. I knew I pitched a shutout here before so I knew it could be done in this ballpark." The eight-hitter was his 14th career shutout but first since he also whitewashed the Rockies in the same ballpark two years earlier.

Though bothered by elbow problems, Smoltz led NL pitchers in innings pitched (256) and fanned 200 for the fourth time.

The team never really settled on a fifth starter, with Kevin Millwood the best of a group that also included Terrell Wade, Paul Byrd, and Chris Brock. Millwood, later a key cog in the rotation, moved up from the minors after Jason Schmidt was sent to Pittsburgh in the Neagle deal.

In the pen, closer Mark Wohlers, obviously recovered from the devastating Jim Leyritz home run that reversed the momentum of the 1996 World Series, saved 33 of the 71 games he worked. He struck out 92 hitters in 69 1/3 innings en route to his second straight 30-save season. No previous Braves closer had achieved that feat.

Brad Clontz, Mike Bielecki, and lefty Alan Embree were busy, too, with all working at least 50 times. Elbow and knee issues sidelined

Pedro Borbon Jr. for the year but Kerry Ligtenberg surfaced for the first time and showed that his side-winding delivery might just be too deceptive for big league hitters.

Atlanta not only had durable arms but productive bats in 1997. They did their best work with the bases loaded, producing a dozen grand slams. In addition to that major league mark, Chipper Jones hit three in a 13-game stretch, a league record for most slams in the shortest time.

Four Braves vaulted over the 20-homer plateau. Ryan Klesko led the club with 24, followed by Javy Lopez at 23, Fred McGriff at 22, and Chipper at 21. Right behind them were Andruw Jones, Jeff Blauser, and Michael Tucker.

Chipper was chipper all year, a rarity for the injury-plagued third baseman. He led the club in games, at-bats, runs, hits, walks, doubles, total bases, and runs batted in. Lopez led in slugging and intentional walks.

Andruw Jones, still considered a rookie despite his World Series heroics of the previous fall, was only 20 when the season started. A year removed from the Class A level, the powerful center fielder showed he was still learning the ropes but managed to hit two home runs that won games in Atlanta's last at-bat. The Braves won 22 games in that situation, and Andruw and Blauser accounted for eight of them (four apiece).

McGriff, in his final Atlanta season at age 33, knocked in 97 runs, second only to Chipper's 111 among the Braves, before bringing his left-handed bat to his native Tampa Bay via a cash transaction.

Blauser, whose bat was better than his glove, provided unusual power for a shortstop, once hitting three home runs in one game. But the Braves, seeking better defense, let Blauser jump to the Chicago Cubs after the 1997 campaign.

His double-play partner, Mark Lemke, also concluded his Braves career that season. A .248 hitter in 10 years with the team, his moment in the sun came in the 1991 World Series, when he somehow legged out three triples. Known for his defensive skills and willingness to take a dive into the dirt if it would help his team win, the Lemmer was only 33 when he completed his playing career with the Red Sox—the only time he did not wear a Braves uniform—a year later.

Lofton also would leave that winter. Though ranked fourth in the league batting derby (.333) and eighth in on-base percentage (.409), his base-stealing skills seemed to evaporate overnight. He stole 27 bases but was caught a league-high 20 times.

The fleet center fielder had two five-hit games in the same week early in the season but was unable to stay healthy. Limited by injury to 122 games, Lofton looked lackadaisical at times, made five errors in center field, and never fit well into the usually-cohesive Atlanta clubhouse. Bobby Cox didn't make an effort to prevent Lofton from returning to Cleveland as a free agent after the season ended.

Cox got a lot out of his bench, including infielders Tony Graffanino, Mike Mordecai, and Rafael Belliard; backup catcher Eddie Perez; and pinch-hitting specialists Greg Colbrunn, a late-season addition, and Lockhart. The diminutive Belliard, like Lemke a hero of the 1991 worst-to-first season, even managed to hit his first home run in 10 years—a game-tying drive into the left-field stands at Shea Stadium, probably the league's most difficult home-run target, on September 26.

"It just goes to prove that his first one wasn't a fluke," said Blauser of Belliard, who had not connected for 10 years, 4 months, 21 days, and 1,869 at-bats. Guys who stand 5-foot-6 and weigh 160 pounds dripping wet don't connect very often.

Timely Power

The 1997 Braves hit a club-record 12 home runs with the bases loaded. Chipper Jones had three of them.

For the second year in a row Braves batters hit at least .270, a feat not accomplished in franchise history since the NL champion Boston Braves did it in 1948. That mark was superseded by all the slugging records. The team had nine-run innings twice within 12 games, on June 22 and July 3, and had two grand slams in a game (by Ryan Klesko and Tim Spehr on July 14) for the fifth time in the history of the three-city franchise. Maintaining that pop during the chill of October would be another matter entirely.

The Postseason

Although winning the 162-game season was a breeze for the Braves, winning their third straight NL pennant proved as formidable as a Florida hurricane.

In their third Division Series, the Braves faced what would become a familiar postseason opponent in the Houston Astros. Powered by the Killer B's of Jeff Bagwell, Craig Biggio, and Derek Bell, the 'stros struggled to take the NL Central title. They finished just six games over .500 but were the only one of the five NL Central teams to win more than they lost.

They would not win another game.

Atlanta's vaunted Big Three of Greg Maddux, Tom Glavine, and John Smoltz allowed five earned runs in 24 innings for a microscopic 1.88 ERA while the offense parlayed 20 hits into 19 runs. Houston scored a grand total of five.

Maddux was a master in the September 30 opener, the first postseason game ever played at Turner Field. He went the route in a 2–1 triumph and yielded seven hits, five more than the Braves managed. Maddux needed no further help from his hitters after Ryan Klesko hit a solo home run against Darryl Kile in the second inning. He walked just one while fanning six.

Then it was Glavine's turn. The offense, apparently rested from its Game One snooze, tallied 10 hits and 10 walks, taking advantage of a wild Mike Hampton. Atlanta scored runs in bunches, with three in the third, three more in the fifth, and five in the sixth. Glavine and two relievers rolled to a 13–3 win that sent the series back the Astrodome.

Two days later, Atlanta clinched on a complete game by John Smoltz. The right-hander fanned 11 and walked one in his three-hit performance.

The Braves hit only .217 in the series but made the most of their opportunities. Jeff Blauser and Chipper Jones joined Klesko as the only Braves who cleared the fences, while the Astros homered just once—a solo shot by Chuck Carr for Houston's only run off Smoltz in Game Three.

With their pitchers operating on full throttle and the clubhouse oozing confidence, the Braves went into the next round with one eye on the National League pennant. They had won two in a row and were facing an opponent many didn't believe deserved to be there.

The Florida Marlins, nine games behind Atlanta's 101-win pace during the season, had other ideas, however.

Like a marlin ensnared by a fisherman's hook, they suddenly roared to life—with the assistance of an Eric Gregg strike zone wider than the Gulf of Mexico.

Poor defense doomed the Braves in the opener, the first postseason game ever played at Turner Field. Greg Maddux gave up all five Florida runs in a 5–3 loss but all of them were unearned after Atlanta committed two errors. A sinkerball specialist who thrived by coaxing opposing batters to hit the ball on the ground, he had given up only *one* unearned run during the entire regular season.

Backed by the long-ball power of Chipper Jones and Ryan Klesko, both of whom homered, Tom Glavine won Game Two with bullpen support from Mike Cather and Mark Wohlers. Atlanta pitching held Florida to just three hits.

Moving to Miami for Game Three, the Marlins hooked John Smoltz, normally one of the most reliable pitchers in postseason action. Charles Johnson, the Florida catcher, was the chief culprit; his sixth-inning double with the bases full erased a 2–1 Atlanta lead and sparked a 5–2 victory that put the Braves in a 2–1 hole.

Like his fellow left-hander, Denny Neagle befuddled the Fish in his first postseason start. The former Pittsburgh ace blanked the Marlins, 4–0, in a route-going effort that was the only complete game by an Atlanta pitcher in the Championship Series that year. He yielded just four hits.

Coupled with his three scoreless innings of relief in the opener, Neagle worked 12 scoreless frames against Florida.

Maddux hoped to emulate that effort but ran into an unexpected obstacle in Game Five: an overweight home-plate umpire whose strike zone seemed to extend from Tampa to Miami.

From the first inning on, Braves hitters found themselves called out on strikes more than a foot off the plate. Forced to swing at balls they couldn't reach, they ended up on the wrong end of a 15-strikeout "performance" by Livan Hernandez, a 22-year-old Cuban refugee who had gone 9–3 with a 3.18 ERA while making 17 regular-season starts. He had started the pivotal playoff game because Kevin Brown came down with the flu.

Two starts later against the Cleveland Indians in the 1997 World Series, Hernandez fanned only two but walked eight—the result of more accurate umpiring by Randy Marsh. In the pennant playoff, however, Hernandez had good luck on his side in the person of portly Eric Gregg.

The result was a 2–1 Florida win that put the wild-card Marlins on the cusp of a championship.

They got it on October 14 when they tagged Tom Glavine for four first-inning runs and coasted to a 7–4 win. The Braves had narrowed the score to 4–3 against Kevin Brown, a 16-game winner, but couldn't do more—even with the Turner Field faithful engulfed in a red sea of tomahawks.

Atlanta's hitting heroes were Chipper Jones and Ryan Klesko, with two homers each, and Keith Lockhart, who went 8-for-16 in five games for a team-high .500 average. Blauser and Michael Tucker also went deep, but it wasn't enough.

The whole affair left a bittersweet taste in the mouths of players, coaches, and fans. Atlanta had outhit the Marlins, .253 to .199, and outhomered them, six to one. The Braves also outpitched their southern rivals (2.60 ERA to 3.57). But the Marlins, after sweeping the favored San Francisco Giants in their half of the NL Division Series, somehow stole a pennant that seemed certain to stay in Atlanta for the third straight year.

14
1998: JUGGERNAUT

Opening Day
Weiss, ss
Graffanino, 2b
C. Jones, 3b
Galarraga, 1b
Klesko, lf
Tucker, rf
E. Perez, c
A. Jones, cf
Maddux, p
Best Hitter: Andres Galarraga
Best Pitcher: Tom Glavine
Best Newcomer: Andres Galarraga

The Season

STILL **SMARTING FROM** their debacle against the Marlins in the previous fall's Championship Series, the Atlanta Braves opened the 1998 campaign with four new players in their starting lineup.

The biggest addition—literally as well as figurately—was Andres Galarraga, a 6' 3", 235-pound Venezuelan who signed as a free agent after producing 88 home runs and 290 runs batted in during his last two seasons with the Colorado Rockies.

Although he was a beneficiary of the rarefied air in mile-high Denver, Galarraga brought consecutive RBI titles in tow to Atlanta. The Braves were intrigued by his 75 extra-base hits, 120 runs scored, and Gold Glove defense during the '97 campaign.

Called "The Big Cat" because of his agility around the first base bag, Galarraga also fit smoothly into the cleanup slot in the lineup—giving Chipper Jones protection in the No. 3 spot.

Even at age 37, Galarraga produced gargantuan numbers: 44 home runs, 103 runs scored, and 121 knocked in on the strength of a .305 batting average. The newcomer led the team in both home runs and runs batted in.

Chipper Jones and Javy Lopez both reached triple digits in RBIs, homering 34 times each, while Andruw Jones added 31 more. It was the first time in franchise history that four players had topped 30 home runs in the same season.

En route to a team total of 215 home runs, second only to the Cardinals among National League clubs, the Braves hit at least one in a league-record 25 straight games. St. Louis stopped that streak on May 14.

Walt Weiss, who had shared the infield with Galarraga in Colorado, preceded the first baseman to Atlanta by four days. A switch-hitting shortstop best known for his fielding and bunting, Weiss worked out so perfectly as a catalyst at the top of the order that he made his only appearance in the All-Star Game. He not only hit 22 points above his career average of .258 but finished fifth in the league with a .403 on-base mark. In games he started, the Braves went 68–27 for a robust .716 winning percentage.

Weiss shared shortstop with Ozzie Guillen, who started 58 games there, while Keith Lockhart, a left-handed hitter, and Tony Graffanino shared the other side of the second base bag. Shoulder issues dogged Lockhart all year but he still had two four-hit games and the second two-homer game of his career at Tampa Bay on July 2.

The only other regulars were Lopez, the starting catcher in 123 games, and Andruw Jones, who started all but six games in center field.

Bobby Cox, given the chance to form left-right platoons at several spots, used seven men in left field and five in right. Ryan Klesko, the best of the bunch, contributed 18 home runs to the cause.

Ex-Yankee Gerald Williams, who played both outfield corners, reached double digits in home runs, leading a bench that also included Danny Bautista, Curtis Pride, Greg Colbrunn, and backup catcher Eddie Perez.

With more than enough support from the hitters, the Braves rolled to a club-record 106 victories, good for an 18-game bulge over the second-place New York Mets.

All five starting pitchers won at least 16 games, another franchise mark.

Tom Glavine (20–6) led the league in wins, Greg Maddux (18–9) in shutouts and earned run average, and John Smoltz (17–3) in winning percentage. Kevin Millwood (17–8) and Denny Neagle (16–11) completed a rotation with no soft spots.

Glavine, who had a career-best 2.47 earned run average, won his second Cy Young Award, beating his golf buddies in their annual quest for a trophy that rarely left Atlanta during the decade. He clinched the award by going 8–2 with a 1.98 ERA from July 17 on. The first Atlanta pitcher to produce four 20-win seasons, Glavine went 11–2 after a Braves loss.

Thanks to a career-best five shutouts, Maddux crafted a 2.22 ERA, best in the league for the fourth time (1993–1995 and 1998). He finished with 204 strikeouts, a personal peak, and won his ninth consecutive Gold Glove for fielding excellence.

Smoltz, on the disabled list twice with lingering elbow woes after offseason surgery, still managed to make 26 starts. After posting perfect 4–0 marks in July and September, he finished third in the league with 9.3 strikeouts per nine innings. His .850 winning percentage made pretty good dressing on an impressive resume.

Millwood won as many games as Smoltz with far less experience. In fact, the 1998 campaign was his first full season in the majors. Though he finished strong with a 3–0 record and 1.40 ERA in his final four outings, Millwood's best game was a 6–0 one-hitter against the Pirates in Atlanta on April 14.

Neagle, a 29-year-old left-hander, completed five of his 31 starts while joining Glavine and Maddux above the 200-innings plateau. But a strong September showing by Bruce Chen, another southpaw, allowed the Braves to send him to Cincinnati after the season.

Although Atlanta's main starters went 88–37 in 153 starts during the 1988 campaign, the performance of the bullpen was often bleak. Kerry Ligtenberg, obtained from an Independent League team for several truckloads of equipment, led the Atlanta staff in saves (30) and games (75) but his supporting cast didn't always pull a fair share of the load.

Although Mark Wohlers converted all eight of his save chances before succumbing to injury, John Rocker, Rudy Seanez, and Norm Charlton each saved only half of theirs. Mike Cather, Alan Embree, Odalis Perez, Norm Charlton, and Russ Springer were even worse.

The Braves even coaxed 43-year-old Dennis Martinez out of retirement, allowing him to pass Hall of Famer Juan Marichal for the most victories by a Latino. He tied the longtime San Francisco standout with his 243rd win on June 2, then topped him with his 244th in a relief role against the Giants on August 9. Martinez, a rubber-armed Nicaraguan nicknamed El Presidente, went 4–6 before retiring for good with 245 career victories. All but five of his 53 appearances came in relief.

As a group, the Atlanta pen blew a whopping 17 save chances and surrendered 33 home runs. Ligtenberg, the most consistent Atlanta relief man, blew four save chances but had a streak of 18 straight conversions over a three-month span that started May 27. The rookie, who had pitched 15 times the year before, finished with 79 strikeouts in 73 innings.

That sometimes leaky pen—which often seemed more like a playpen than a bullpen—would prove a problem in postseason play.

The Postseason

The sequence really didn't matter: Greg Maddux, Tom Glavine, and John Smoltz were a formidable force for the Braves for more than a decade.

In the 1998 NL Division Series, Smoltz had little trouble dispatching the Chicago Cubs, who were there as a wild-card entry. He worked scoreless ball into the eighth, combining with two relievers for a 7–1 win in the September 30 opener at Turner Field. The big blow was a Ryan Klesko grand slam.

Game Two wasn't so easy; the Cubs, behind Kevin Tapani, nursed a 1–0 lead until the bottom of the ninth. Then, with one out, Javy Lopez hit a bases-empty home run. An RBI single from Chipper Jones in the home 10th gave Atlanta a 2–1 win. Tom Glavine started and pitched well but Odalis Perez, the fifth Braves pitcher, got the win.

Greg Maddux mounted the familiar Wrigley Field mound for Game Three on October 3. He had no trouble with Chicago hitters, yielding two harmless runs in the eighth after his team had built a 6–0 lead. Although Maddux scored the first Atlanta run after doubling to lead off the third, the big hit for the Braves was an eighth-inning grand slam by Eddie Perez, a light-hitting receiver who played primarily when Maddux worked—at the pitcher's request.

Kerry Ligtenberg completed the game with two scoreless innings and was on the mound when the Braves clinched the series with a 6–2 win. In addition to the grand slams by Klesko and Perez, the Braves also got home runs from Javy Lopez and Michael Tucker.

Early returns from the Championship Series, however, suggested the Braves might be running on fumes.

After beating Houston in a four-game Division Series that featured low scores, San Diego proved its pitching prowess was no mirage.

The Padres won the October 7 opener at Turner Field on a 10th-inning solo home run by Ken Caminiti, who would win league MVP honors that season. Overtime was needed after an Andruw Jones sacrifice fly in the ninth tied the game, 2–2.

Kevin Brown's three-hit shutout the next night gave San Diego a 3–0 win and a 2–0 advantage in the best-of-seven set. Glavine yielded only one run in the first six innings.

It was the first time since 1969, when they faced the Miracle Mets, that the Braves had lost the first two games of a Championship Series at home.

The situation became even more dire on October 10, when a soft-tossing southpaw named Sterling Hitchcock mystified Atlanta hitters. Three times in that game, the Braves loaded the bases—but failed to score any of those runners. San Diego's 4–1 victory left the Braves wondering how they scored just three runs in the first 28 innings of the pennant playoff.

Seeking a miracle no team had claimed previously, Atlanta revived in the seventh inning of the next game. Like a phoenix rising from the ashes, the Braves rode an Andres Galarraga grand slam to a six-run inning that led to an 8–3 win. Dennis Martinez, who had relieved Denny Neagle an inning earlier, got the win.

Yet another late-inning outburst—five in the eighth—fueled the fire in the teepee one night later. The Braves used a 14-hit attack to win, 7–6, but needed Greg Maddux to snuff out the flames of a ninth-inning uprising. Making his first relief appearance since 1987, the veteran right-hander retired the Padres to save the win for Ligtenberg in a game Smoltz started.

With the Padres still needing one win to clinch the pennant, the series returned to Atlanta. Needing a miracle finish, the Braves had even more trouble with the mysterious Hitchcock. He directed a two-hit shutout, winning 5–0 with the help of four equally-stingy relievers.

The Padres had won their second pennant but wouldn't win another game that season; they were swept away by the New York Yankees in the World Series.

Atlanta's pennant express, derailed for the second straight year, would get back on track in 1999 only after making multiple cast changes again.

In the biggest deal, the Braves sent Neagle to Cincinnati in a five-player swap that netted left-handed relief pitcher Mike Remlinger and hard-hitting Bret Boone, a much-needed second baseman. The Reds also got Michael Tucker, the Atlanta right fielder, and minor league pitching prospect Robbie Bell.

Boone, coveted for his Gold Glove as well as his bat, was immediately tabbed to replace the unproductive left-right platoon of Keith Lockhart and Tony Graffanino.

15

1999: MR. CLUTCH

Opening Day
Nixon, lf
Boone, 2b
C. Jones, 3b
Jordan, rf
Lopez, c
Klesko, 1b
A. Jones, cf
Weiss, ss
Glavine, p
Best Hitter: Chipper Jones
Best Pitcher: Kevin Millwood
Best Newcomer: Brian Jordan

The Season

IN HIS FIFTH major league season, Chipper finally got off the old block.

Picking up the slack for injured teammates Galarraga (lymphoma) and Javy Lopez (knee), the 27-year-old third baseman produced the best season of his career.

He not only hit a career-best 45 homers—the most ever by a National League switch-hitter—but hit them when it counted, with 31 after June 30 and four of those in a three-game September showdown with the second-place Mets.

His final numbers were staggering: 116 runs scored, 110 runs batted in, 126 bases on balls, .319 batting average, .441 on-base percentage, and .633 slugging percentage. He even stole 25 bases.

Chipper didn't lead in any major category except leadership. Mark McGwire and Sammy Sosa, allegedly aided by banned substances, had more home runs but Chipper was third in homers and walks; fourth in on-base percentage, slugging, and total bases; seventh in runs; and tenth in batting. As a result, the Most

L.W. JONES, ATLANTA · NATIONALS

Courtesy of The Topps Company, Inc.

Valuable Player trophy Terry Pendleton had brought to Atlanta eight years earlier returned to town.

Taking all but three of the 32 first-place votes, Chipper finished with 432 votes, a landslide of Lyndon Johnson proportions.

For the team, it was a fine finish after a slow start. In fact, that year's April showers were more like a steady downpour.

Kerry Ligtenberg submitted to Tommy John surgery on April 14, Mark Wohlers was swapped to Cincinnati a week later, and the introduction of QuesTec technology designed to tighten the strike zone

Good Wood for Chipper

During his MVP season in 1999, Chipper Jones became the first player to hit .300 with 40 doubles, 40 homers, 100 RBIs, 100 runs scored, 100 walks, and 20 stolen bases. He also homered from both sides of the plate in three different games.

caused Greg Maddux and Tom Glavine to alter their previous pitching styles.

As late as April 28, Glavine was 0–3 with a 5.61 earned run average—his worst start since his 1988 rookie season—but Maddux was only slightly better. On May 15, after yielding a career-worst 14 hits to his old Cubs club, his ERA was an uncharacteristic 4.83, with opposing hitters nailing him for a .356 batting average. With a 6–5 record after his first 15 starts, Maddux did not deserve or receive an invitation to the All-Star Game. But the mercurial right-hander used the time off to get LASIK eye surgery without telling the team. When he returned, his sight and his record both improved dramatically.

John Smoltz, just three years removed from his Cy Young season, endured two bouts of elbow woes that landed him on the disabled list, also hampering the club's pitching plans.

But Kevin Millwood rode to the rescue.

A National League All-Star, he won six straight down the stretch en route to a career-best 18–7 record. Maddux, with a second-half rally, finished with one more win to top the team but Millwood was the team's best pitcher. In just his second full season, Millwood held opponents to a .202 average, best among major league starters, and finished third in the voting for the Cy Young Award.

The rotation also got help from veteran left-hander Terry Mulholland, a swingman who won four of his eight starts after arriving from the Cubs at the trade deadline, and southpaw setup man Mike Remlinger, a workhorse who went 10–1. Acquired with Bret Boone in a preseason swap that sent starting pitcher Denny Neagle to the Reds, Remlinger joined Rudy Seanez, Kevin McGlinchy, and controversial closer John Rocker as Atlanta relievers who appeared more than 55 times each. Seanez would have worked even more but was sidelined for the last month with a stress fracture in his right elbow.

Though he often railed at the media, the fans, and even his own teammates, Rocker rolled up impressive numbers: 104 strikeouts in 72 1/3 innings, 38 saves, and a .180 opposing batting average. The lanky left-hander burst into games like a bull into a ring, racing the length of the field to the mound while snorting his contempt for enemy hitters. Adept in holding hitters at bay, he was less successful in holding his tongue, which later caused a clubhouse rift that led to his removal from Atlanta.

Among position players, five Braves reached the 20-homer plateau: Andruw Jones, Ryan Klesko, Brian Jordan, Bret Boone, and Chipper Jones. Shortstop Jose Hernandez and outfielder Gerald Williams, initially ticketed as role players, came close to joining that select circle. Andruw became the third Atlanta Brave to appear in all 162 games, joining Felix Millan and Dale Murphy, and provided daily doses of dynamic defense in center field.

Jordan, signed as a free agent, led the team with 115 runs batted in—five more than Chipper—even though he hit 22 fewer homers and played through a painful hand injury sustained when he was hit by a pitch on June 22. His hang-tough football mentality helped (Jordan played professional football before deciding to concentrate on baseball).

Chipper paced the regulars in hitting but Javy Lopez and backup first baseman Randall Simon were just two points behind him. Klesko, despite a dreadful start, finished at a career-high .297.

He also reached a personal best with 21 home runs, thanks to a cluster of three two-homer games between July 16–21.

The team scored 840 runs, a franchise record that superseded the peak years of the Milwaukee juggernaut led by Hank Aaron and Eddie Mathews.

On the down side, erstwhile hero Otis Nixon was impeached as the starting left fielder when his average shrunk to .173 by Memorial Day. Another slick fielder who started Opening Day, shortstop Walt Weiss, also failed to produce at the plate.

Boone, in his only Atlanta season, proved to be an enigma—brilliant in the spring but a bigger bust in the summer than Dolly Parton. Fortunately for the Braves, his bat revived again down the stretch.

Perhaps the team's unsung hero was Eddie Perez, who filled huge shoes when the slugging Lopez was sidelined for the season with a partially torn ACL on July 24 after catching only 60 games. A superior defensive player, Perez held his own at the plate with a .249 batting average and seven home runs in 104 games. He got even better as the season morphed into the playoffs.

The Postseason

After leading the majors with 103 wins and a .636 winning percentage, the Braves had home-field advantage throughout the playoffs. Until the World Series, that helped.

Atlanta pitching, which posted a league-best 3.63 staff earned run average during the regular season, proved stingy again in October.

In the best-of-five Division Series, the Houston Astros won only the opener, with Shane Reynolds working the first six innings of a 6–1 win. Greg Maddux yielded an uncharacteristic 10 hits in seven innings, putting the Braves in a temporary hole.

Kevin Millwood was almost perfect as the Braves drew even on October 6, yielding just a second-inning home run to Ken Caminiti. He fanned eight and walked none in a complete game one-hitter that took only two hours and 13 minutes. The final score was 5–1.

Game Three, in Houston, belonged to Brian Jordan. He solved Mike Hampton for a three-run homer in the sixth and delivered a two-run double in the top of the 12th as the Braves won, 5–3.

The Astros came within a whisker of winning in the bottom of the 10th when they loaded the bases with nobody out. Desperate for strikeouts, Bobby Cox called closer John Rocker out of the bullpen. He retired the first man but then yielded a Tony Eusebio smash up the middle that seemed certain to break the 3–3 tie. Instead, a lunging Walt Weiss made a miraculous diving stop, scrambled to his feet, and forced the runner at home. Rocker escaped further damage, following with a less-perilous scoreless frame, and watched as Millwood pitched a perfect inning to notch the save just two days after his route-going win.

Neither Tom Glavine, who started, nor Greg Maddux, who walked the only man he faced in a rare relief outing, proved up to the task but the Braves prevailed anyway.

The series seemed over when Atlanta took a 7–0 lead behind John Smoltz in Game Four on October 9. He even collected a single, a double, and a run scored while outlasting Houston starter Shane Reynolds, who won the opener. But the Astros knocked Smoltz out with a four-run eighth, forcing the Braves to use three relievers. Rocker, the best of them, worked an inning-and-a-third, fanning three, for the series-clinching save. He made things exciting, walking Stan Javier to open the inning, but struck out Jeff Bagwell and Carl Everett before getting Ken Caminiti, who had already homered three times in the series, on a long drive to center.

Atlanta had 15 hits, including three by Bret Boone and two each by Gerald Williams and Eddie Perez.

Perez was even hotter in the next round, the NL Championship Series against the New York Mets. Filling in for injured regular receiver Javy Lopez, he went 10-for-20 with two home runs and five runs batted in—totally atypical numbers for a player whose

Pressed into service when Javy Lopez was hurt, Eddie Perez won MVP honors in the 1999 NL Championship Series.

Photo by Bill Menzel.

defensive skills kept him in the big leagues. He homered in the opener, hit a two-run shot in the second game, and had two hits and two RBIs in Game Six.

A .249 batter during the regular season, Perez downed more spinach than Popeye before the playoffs. His numbers against the Mets included a .500 batting average, .524 on-base percentage, and .900 slugging percentage. He was an easy choice as the MVP of the Championship Series.

The last five games were decided by one run with two of them requiring extra innings.

Maddux mystified the Mets in Game One, throwing seven innings of one-run ball en route to a 4–2 triumph. Perez and Weiss combined for five of Atlanta's eight hits.

Millwood pitched into the eighth inning of Game Two, a 4–3 Braves win that featured the first relief outing in the career of John Smoltz. He got the save with a perfect ninth but Rocker had set the stage. With the tying run on second and one out in the eighth, he struck out John Olerud, issued an intentional walk to Mike Piazza, and fanned Robin Ventura.

A pair of two-run homers in the sixth inning, by Brian Jordan and Perez, gave Atlanta all the runs it needed.

That gave the Braves a 2–0 edge as the series moved to Shea Stadium.

Glavine, given an early lead when Atlanta scored an unearned run in the first inning of the third game, fired seven scoreless frames that Remlinger and Rocker protected. A Game Four win would mean a sweep of the Mets and a pennant for the Braves.

Smoltz pitched one-run ball into the eighth but Remlinger and Rocker couldn't repeat their magic of the previous night. Atlanta's 2–1 advantage with two outs in the home eighth turned into a 3–2 New York win when Olerud, a left-handed hitter, turned a Rocker heater into a two-run single.

Remlinger and Rocker combined for three-and-a-third scoreless innings in Game Five but it wasn't enough. By the time the marathon game entered the 15th inning, the Atlanta pitcher was inexperienced rookie Kevin McGlinchy. An RBI triple by Keith Lockhart in the top of the frame had given the Braves a 3–2 lead but McGlinchy, unscored upon in the 14th, came unglued in the save situation.

The rookie yielded a leadoff single followed by three walks in the 15th—including one to Todd Pratt with the bases filled—before Ventura hit what appeared to be a game-winning grand slam over the right field wall.

What should have been a 7–3 win for New York reverted to 4–3 when Ventura, in the euphoria of the moment, failed to complete his circuit of the bases. He received credit for a single but it still was enough to end the game after five hours and forty-six minutes, then the longest by time in postseason history.

Both teams needed the October 18 off-day as the series returned to Atlanta. Initially, it looked like the Braves would be celebrating in short order: a five-run burst in the first sent Mets ace Al Leiter to the showers before he could retire a batter. But Millwood was off his game, too, yielding eight hits and three earned runs in five-and-a-third innings. Smoltz, asked to relieve, only added fuel to the fire.

In just one-third of an inning, he gave up four runs on four hits, including a two-run Piazza blast that tied the score at 7–7 in the seventh. Both teams scored single runs in the eighth and the tenth, with the Braves squaring the score on a pinch-hit RBI from light-hitting Ozzie Guillen against Armando Benitez. The Mets closer had held the Braves to one hit in 30 at-bats all year before their 10th-inning rally that night.

After Russ Springer worked a scoreless top of the 11th, erstwhile starter Kenny Rogers struggled in the home half. A leadoff double by Gerald Williams was followed with a sacrifice, placing the winning run on third with one out. Mets manager Bobby Valentine ordered Rogers to walk Chipper Jones and Brian Jordan. That brought up Andruw Jones, a free swinger who seemed to have an aversion to taking a free pass. But Rogers, anxious to coax a double play that would prolong the game, couldn't find the plate. Jones walked and the Braves won, 10–9, to take their fifth pennant of the decade, more than any other team.

Exhausted after their extra-inning games with the Mets, the Braves were running on fumes by the time they faced the other New York team.

The hitting and pitching that had been so potent during both the season and the playoffs seemed to evaporate simultaneously. The Braves had only one hit—a Chipper Jones homer—until the ninth inning of the opener against Orlando (El Duque) Hernandez and three relievers. They got just five hits in both the second and fourth games.

Coupled with shoddy defense that tacked unearned runs onto the equation, Maddux and Millwood lost the first two games, 4–1 and 7–2, at home. Bret Boone smacked three doubles in the third game at Yankee Stadium, but the locals countered with four home runs. It didn't help that Atlanta starter Tom Glavine was off his game because of a bout with the flu. After taking a 5–1 lead, the Braves were blanked for the final six innings.

Game Three ended with a 6–5 score when Chad Curtis, an unlikely hero, led off the home 10th with a home run against Remlinger.

When Roger Clemens outpitched Smoltz the next night to win, 4–1, it extended Atlanta's World Series losing streak to eight games.

16

2000: CHIPPER, ANDRUW, AND ANDRES

Opening Day
Veras, 2b
Sanders, lf
C. Jones, 3b
Jordan, rf
Galarraga, 1b
A. Jones, cf
Perez, c
Weiss, ss
Maddux, p
Best Hitter: Andruw Jones
Best Pitcher: Tom Glavine
Best Newcomer: Rafael Furcal

The Season

THE RETURN OF Andres Galarraga, coupled with continued production from the Jones boys, allowed the Braves to overpower opponents en route to the league's second-best record.

Idled by cancer all of the previous season, The Big Cat almost claimed Comeback of the Year honors in the first week of the season, with two home runs and five RBIs in his first eight at-bats.

Chipper and Andruw Jones contributed a club-high 36 homers each and joined Galarraga at the 100-RBI plateau. All three hit .300, led by Chipper's .311.

210

Former Colorado first baseman Andres Galarraga added enormous power to the Atlanta lineup after he arrived as a free agent.

Photo courtesy of the National Baseball Hall of Fame and Museum.

Getting Galarraga back was a terrific tonic for the Atlanta attack. An All-Star for the fifth time, he hit his 10th career grand slam on April 8 and finished with both a .300 average and triple digits in RBIs for the fifth consecutive time. Ten of Galarraga's 28 homers either tied the game or gave the team a lead in the fifth inning or later. Not surprisingly, the Braves went 24–3 when Galarraga homered.

The Big Cat hit .359 in day games and .347 against left-handed pitchers. Galarraga's fast start (10 homers in April) coincided with the team's (18–6 in the first month). In no other month did the 2000 Braves win that many games.

With Galarraga hitting so well behind him, Chipper Jones had six multi-homer games, two four-hit games, and a .323 average at Turner Field. He connected twice against Randy Johnson on September 5— exactly one year after performing the same feat at Turner Field. That made Jones the only player to hit two home runs in a game against Johnson twice.

Gold Glove center fielder Andruw Jones, an infielder during his youth, loved to take grounders at shortstop.

Photo by Bill Menzel.

The switch-hitting third baseman reached the 30-homer plateau for the fourth time, fashioned a career-best 19-game hitting streak, and fanned just 64 times, a career low. When Chipper made contact, things happened.

Andruw Jones could make the same statement.

At the ripe old age of 23, the slick center fielder from Curacao played in his first All-Star Game and won his third consecutive Gold Glove. He led the league in at-bats (656) and was third in hits (199), fifth in runs (122), and tied for fifth in total bases (355).

Andruw's Start

Because of his strong throwing arm, Andruw Jones was a catcher and third baseman during his amateur days in Curacao.

A big reason the three sluggers knocked in so many runs was the presence of rookie speed merchant Rafael Furcal, a 20-year-old fleet middle infielder who rocketed to the varsity from Class A at the end of spring training. Even though he started the season as a backup for shortstop Walt Weiss and second baseman Quilvio Veras, injuries to both gave Furcal a chance to play.

Weiss went down in May with hamstring issues while Veras tore the ACL in his right knee two months later. Given a chance, Furcal flourished in the field and at bat. Bobby Cox, the chief beneficiary of his bunting skills, was quick to label Furcal's throwing arm "the best in baseball."

His .295 batting average, 87 runs scored, and 40 stolen bases (including a steal of home against the Giants on April 9) made him an easy choice for National League Rookie of the Year—the first time the trophy went to an Atlanta player since David Justice claimed it in 1990. No other Braves rookie had ever stolen that many bases. In fact, only

RAFAEL FURCAL
shortstop ATLANTA BRAVES™

Courtesy of The Topps Company, Inc.

Otis Nixon and Gerald Perry had ever swiped more bags in a season while playing for Atlanta.

Furcal certainly lived up to his advance billings; one year earlier, *Baseball America* had named him the best batting prospect, best defensive shortstop, fastest runner, owner of the best throwing arm, and the most exciting player in the South Atlantic League.

His rifle arm came as advertised but Furcal spent extra time perfecting his footwork and learning to turn double plays. His hitting, bunting, and baserunning skills were a bonus, along with his more than occasional power. Three years after his electrifying debut, Furcal made the NL All-Star squad for the first time. He was chosen in two later years as well after leaving the Braves.

Furcal hit .295, posted a .394 on-base percentage, and led all rookies in runs, walks, and steals. He was also the hardest man to double up in the majors.

Catcher Javy Lopez also bolstered the attack, hitting .287 with 24 home runs, but injuries neutralized the production of Reggie Sanders, acquired from Cincinnati, and B. J. Surhoff, a trade deadline arrival from Baltimore. Brian Jordan spent time on the disabled list in April but managed to hit 17 home runs.

Eddie Perez, the Most Valuable Player of the 1999 Championship Series against the Mets, returned in a reserve role, serving as understudy to Lopez and personal receiver for Greg Maddux, the maestro who led the pitching staff.

Aside from its aces, that staff took a few lumps. Barking elbows idled stalwart starter John Smoltz for the entire year and reliever Rudy Seanez for most of it. Closer John Rocker clashed with fans, media members, and even teammates after inflammatory comments attributed to him appeared in two magazines, *Sports Illustrated* and *Bill Mazeroski's Baseball Yearbook*.

Among other things, Rocker railed against his manager and teammates, unwed mothers, homosexuals, foreigners, and all things New York—especially fans of the Mets and riders of the No. 7 subway line that linked midtown with Shea Stadium. Perplexed general manager John Schuerholz said Rocker had a cannon for an arm but a cannonball for a head.

The season started without Rocker, who was suspended for 30 days and fined $2,000 by the commissioner's office. Even though the sentence was reduced to 15 days and $500 after an appeal by the Players Association, Rocker was never the same. Neither sensitivity training nor a meeting with Hank Aaron and Andrew Young, a former Atlanta mayor and UN Ambassador,

Controversial closer John Rocker antagonized teammates, opponents, and fans so much that the Braves had to trade him.

AP Photo/Mark Lennihan

helped. Unable to control his mouth or his pitches, Rocker even slipped back to the minors for a week. He finished with 24 saves but shared ninth-inning duties with Mike Remlinger and Kerry Ligtenberg, whose surgically-repaired elbow proved sound again.

Rocker finished the season with the Braves but his days were numbered. He started a field fight with the Toronto Blue Jays, got into a shouting match with a Yankee fan, and made an obscene reference to the New York media. In addition, his outbursts forced the Braves to hire extra security to protect him and his teammates.

Smoltz, the antithesis of Rocker, made a valiant effort to pitch, even trying to work through his elbow pain by throwing knuckleballs, but knew he was through when he couldn't lift a fork. He underwent Tommy John surgery that repaired his torn elbow ligament and spent the season on the sidelines. He even flirted with retirement, a thought that ended after Tommy John reported in a telephone call that he enjoyed 11 solid seasons after returning from the procedure.

Atlanta's rotation again leaned on the left-right tandem of Tom Glavine and Maddux, who won 21 and 19 games, respectively. The only other starters who reached double digits were Kevin Millwood and John Burkett, with 10 wins each. Burkett, once a 22-game winner for San Francisco, would never come close to winning 300 games but bowled more than a dozen in his alter ego as a professional bowler. He freely dispensed bowling tips to teammates.

The Braves also got a few good starts from Terry Mulholland, a left-handed swingman who once pitched a no-hitter, and Andy Ashby, acquired from Philadelphia.

Glavine led the league in wins while Maddux posted the best ratio of walks per nine innings (1.5). The pair combined for five shutouts.

Rival teams complained incessantly about the strike zone widening whenever Maddux and Glavine pitched. Tired of watching umpires call pitches he thought were wide, Milwaukee manager Davey Lopes protested, claiming that the Atlanta grounds crew had made the catcher's box wider than the proscribed forty-three inches. Backup backstop Fernando Lunar was actually called for a rare catcher's balk on a balmy June evening when he set up to receive pitchers with one of his feet outside the box. Bobby Cox argued but television cameras compared the box from one game to the next and did indeed discover a difference.

Such incidents were just a minor distraction for Cox and his club.

The combination of pitching, power, and speed made Atlanta almost invincible in April. A 15-game winning streak, longest in the majors and a franchise record, allowed the Braves to build a big lead in the National League East—a division they eventually won by a single game. The Mets even sneaked into first place by a half-game on August 31 but returned to the runner-up slot to stay two days later.

Atlanta clinched the division in New York on September 26 after winning 10 of 13 games.

When the smoke cleared at the end of the 162-game schedule, the Braves had joined the Yankees (1947–58) and the Cubs (1904–12) as the only clubs in big league annals to win at least 90 games for nine straight completed seasons.

Hosting the All-Star Game at Turner Field didn't help, however. Although the Atlanta contingent included Maddux, Glavine, Galarraga, and the two Joneses, the American League rode to victory on the back of Yankees shortstop Derek Jeter.

The Postseason

The Braves would have preferred playing New York or San Francisco in the NL Division Series but wound up with the St. Louis Cardinals, a team that also went 95–67. Atlanta had won the season's series against both the Mets and Giants but not against St. Louis.

The Cards had swept the Braves in 1982, when they were Championship Series opponents, and had always proven pesky rivals, particularly in postseason play.

Anxious to avenge the 1996 NLCS when the Braves overcame a 3–1 St. Louis lead to win the pennant, the Cardinals made quick work of the 2000 team, sweeping the NLDS. They scored 10 first-inning runs and short-circuited the sluggers from the South. The Braves batted just .189 with a single home run—by Andruw Jones—and their legendary pitchers performed like mere mortals.

Andruw's Deal

Andruw Jones negotiated his own contract, without using an agent. "He received a lucrative, fair deal to play for as long as he wanted to play, without the angst and posturing of free agency and arbitration," John Schuerholz recalled. "I can't remember the last time I dealt directly with a player. Even guys in the minor leagues have agents."

Once pulled in the middle of an inning when Bobby Cox thought he was loafing, Andruw Jones developed into a Gold Glove center fielder who drew comparisons to Willie Mays.

Photo by Bill Menzel.

Atlanta led only once, after scoring two runs in the top of the first in the second game, but Will Clark wasted little time erasing that advantage with a long home run in the home half of the inning.

Aided by five errors, Maddux, Glavine, and Millwood never posed a problem for the Redbirds. The final scores were 7–5, 10–4, and 7–1—ending Atlanta's five-year winning streak in the Division Series.

For the Braves, it was a disappointing end to a solid season.

17
2001: WINNING BY A WHISKER

Opening Day
Furcal, ss
Veras, 2b
A. Jones, cf
C. Jones, 3b
Surhoff, lf
Jordan, rf
Lopez, c
Brogna, 1b
Burkett, p
Best Hitter: Chipper Jones
Best Pitcher: Greg Maddux
Best Newcomer: Marcus Giles

The Season

SURPRISE, SURPRISE: POTENT pitching pushed the Braves across the finish line first in the National League East, which they again won by a whisker. They took just 88 games, a low total for a top-tier team, but that was two more than the second-place Philadelphia Phillies.

From June 22 to the end of the season, the teams were never more than three-and-a-half games apart in the standings. The Braves' pitching made the difference.

Atlanta pitchers compiled the best team earned run average for the fifth year in a row, thanks primarily to Greg Maddux, who led the staff with 17 wins, and Tom Glavine, who was one behind him. Maddux, the ultimate control artist, even pushed the league record to innings without a walk to 72 1/3.

John Smoltz, five years removed from a season in which he won 29 games including the All-Star Game and postseason, returned from Tommy John surgery just in time to replace closer John Rocker, a loose cannon traded to Cleveland on June 22 while the Braves were playing the Mets at Shea Stadium. Smoltz thrived in the relief role, converting all but one of his 11 save chances while posting a 1.59 ERA in 31 games.

Atlanta's clincher came in a crushing 20–3 win over the Florida Marlins on October 5. The game featured a 10-run opening burst—the first time since 1953, their first year in Milwaukee, that a Braves team had scored so many runs in the first inning.

At many points during the year, it looked like Atlanta would implode.

For the second straight spring, Atlanta tried but failed to replace slugging first baseman Andres Galarraga, whose departure for Texas via free agency left a gaping hole at first base. Galarraga asked the Braves ownership for a two-year contract, but the most that it would offer was a one-year deal. A revolving door followed, with Rico Brogna, Ken Caminiti, Dave Martinez, B. J. Surhoff, and Wes Helms all attempting to fill the void.

Losing leadoff man Rafael Furcal before the All-Star break was a bitter pill. Warned that head-first slides were risky, the switch-hitting Dominican dislocated his left shoulder with a head-first slide into second on July 6. Before the trading deadline three weeks later, Brogna had retired and Quilvio Veras was released as the Braves tried to beef up their attack.

General manager John Schuerholz, never one to be left holding the bag, suddenly had to find three new infielders.

To fill Furcal's hole at short, he landed Rey Sanchez, a fine fielder not known for his bat, from Kansas City; acquired Caminiti, a one-time National League MVP, to play first base; and promoted promising second baseman Marcus Giles from the minors. A month later, after Caminiti provided no improvement, the Braves found a first baseman in a most unlikely place.

Julio Franco was hitting so well in the Mexican League that Schuerholz ignored his age—43—and the chorus of criticism he heard from the media. The veteran Dominican, who had been hitting .437 with 18 homers for the Mexico City Tigers, quickly proved to be in better shape than most of his younger teammates. After a September 5 homer that was his first in the majors since 1997, he connected in consecutive games against the Mets on September 28–29.

Franco, Giles, and Sanchez formed a fine down-the-stretch infield with the always reliable Chipper Jones, the switch-hitting slugger who anchored the lineup from the No. 3 hole. En route to a .330 season that included 38 homers, Chipper became the first third baseman to produce six straight 100-RBI seasons.

Andruw Jones had 34 home runs, a team-high 104 RBIs, and another Gold Glove but the star of the September stretch was Brian Jordan. In a six-day span, he had three key homers, including a two-out, ninth-inning grand slam on an 0–2 pitch that beat the New York Mets, 8–5, in Atlanta on September 29. Jordan had previously jolted the Mets with a two-homer game on September 23.

Javy Lopez played a strong supporting role to the attack, slugging 17 home runs, and B. J. Surhoff also reached double digits. Lopez finished strong, batting .377 in September.

Even Giles chipped in, collecting four hits in a game at Wrigley Field on September 9 and poking nine home runs in the 68 games he played following his recall from Triple-A Richmond.

Atlanta's unsung hero was journeyman right-hander John Burkett, formerly a mainstay in San Francisco. He won a dozen games, fanned 187 hitters, and finished third in the league with a 3.04 earned run average. Except for Maddux and Glavine, no other Braves starter won in double figures. Kevin Millwood, a big winner in both 1998 and 1999, missed nearly half the season with an inflamed right labrum. He made only 21 starts, five more than Jason Marquis and Odalis Perez, but all three had their moments.

Not surprisingly, the Braves bullpen bore a heavy workload. Rocker saved 19 games before his trade while Mike Remlinger, Kerry Ligtenberg, and Jose Cabrera all worked more than 50 times. Steve Reed and Steve Karsay, picked up in the Rocker swap, pitched well in setup roles after their arrival.

The Postseason

The first team to reach the playoffs with a losing record at home (40–41), the Braves refused to be intimidated. They humbled the Houston Astros in the Division Series, sweeping the best-of-five match in three straight—Atlanta's fourth first-round sweep since the 1996 postseason.

Thanks in part to eight scoreless innings from Glavine in Game Two, which he won 1–0, Houston scored only six runs in the entire series. Atlanta had the same number of home runs, two of them by Chipper.

Beating the Arizona Diamondbacks, however, would prove a task too formidable even for the experienced Braves. The left-right tandem of Randy Johnson and Curt Schilling, a pair of power pitchers at the top of the Arizona rotation, simply dominated.

Johnson blanked the Braves in the opener, 2–0, before the Braves evened the series with an 8–1 win that featured a Javy Lopez homer in the seventh that broke a 1–1 tie. The two-run blast against Miguel Batista sparked a late Atlanta revival. Lopez had missed the Division Series with a sprained ankle.

Schilling was scintillating in Game Three, fanning a dozen Braves in a 5–1, complete-game win, but bad defense sabotaged Atlanta efforts to win the fourth and fifth games, bowing 11–4 and 3–2, respectively. The Braves coughed up eight unearned runs in the last two games.

Glavine was the only Atlanta pitcher able to defeat Arizona but he and Burkett also suffered defeats. Maddux lost both of his starts, ending the season short of a pennant party.

18

2002: MAULERS IN THE OUTFIELD

Opening Day

Furcal, ss
A. Jones, cf
C. Jones, lf
Sheffield, rf
Castilla, 3b
Surhoff, 1b
Lopez, c
Giles, 2b
Glavine, p

Best Hitter: Chipper Jones
Best Pitcher: John Smoltz
Best Newcomer: Gary Sheffield

The Season

AFTER A SLOW start that left them in fourth place, four-and-a-half games from the top of the National League East on April 30, the Braves caught fire, going 50–17 from May 15 through the end of July, and coasted to a 101–59 record. They were the first NL club to reach triple digits in wins seven times and made Bobby Cox the first manager to pilot 100-win teams five times.

Their combination of power plus pitching was lethal. Aided by newcomers Gary Sheffield, acquired from the Dodgers in January for Brian Jordan and Odalis Perez, and Vinny Castilla, a Colorado

Sheff's Stew

When the Braves traded for Gary Sheffield in 2002, he had two years remaining on his contract plus an option year. But he also had the right to demand a trade because he was in the middle of a multi-year deal. The Braves agreed to drop the option clause in return for his agreeing not to exercise his right to demand a deal after the first year. "There was not one issue with him in the two years he was here," John Schuerholz wrote in his book *Built to Win*. "We knew it was going to be a two-year relationship."

slugger signed as a free agent, Atlanta had a nightly habit of clubbing opponents.

Andruw Jones hit 35 home runs, tops on the team, but Chipper Jones led in average (.327) and runs batted in (100). His willingness to change positions for the good of the team allowed the Braves to sign Castilla, a superior defensive third baseman, and move Chipper to left field, an easier spot for his aching knees. Knowing they had Gold Glove defense in center, the Braves were comfortable deploying Sheffield and Chipper in the corners. Both hit over .300 and had more walks than strikeouts. Sheffield even reached base in 52 straight games, a club record, in July.

Hotter than the weather in August, Sheffield homered in the bottom of the ninth to beat the Cardinals, 2–1, on August 4 and hit a shot leading off the 13th that beat the Astros, 6–5, at Houston five days later.

On August 19, Sheffield and Chipper hit solo home runs in the ninth inning that turned a 6–5 deficit into a 7–6 win against Colorado—the first time in franchise history the Braves ever ended a game that way.

In two Atlanta seasons before joining the Yankees as a free agent, Sheffield delivered even more than the Braves expected. He hit .319 with 64 home runs and 216 runs batted in.

Andruw Jones (left) and Gary Sheffield teamed with Chipper Jones to provide a powerful outfield for the 2002 Braves.

Photo by Bill Menzel.

Andruw Jones did his best work in September. With two-homer games on September 7 and 10, he became the 11th National Leaguer to hit four consecutive home runs. Not content to rest on his laurels, Andruw topped himself with a three-homer game at Philadelphia September 25—the first by a Brave since Jeff Blauser turned the trick in Chicago on July 12, 1992.

Shoulder issues hampered the power production of catcher Javy Lopez, whose home run figures dropped for the third straight year, while Castilla didn't come close to matching the three straight 40-homer seasons he once had in Colorado. But the Braves still scored 708 runs against 565 for their opponents.

One of the reasons was the return of Rafael Furcal, the fleet shortstop who had missed the last half of the previous year following a

Newcomers Vinny Castilla and Gary Sheffield combined with Chipper Jones to provide plenty of power in 2002.

Photo by Bill Menzel.

sliding injury to his shoulder. When he ripped three triples in a game against the Marlins on April 21, the Braves knew he was sound again.

Furcal finished with 47 extra-base hits, 27 stolen bases, and a solid .275 batting average. He also proved a good double-play partner for Marcus Giles when the second baseman's ankle allowed him to play.

Julio Franco and Matt Franco, unrelated teammates with the same surname and same position, shared first base and combined for 12 home runs. Julio Franco, the right-handed half of the platoon, hit .315 over his last 72 games and proved himself amazingly agile for someone believed to be 44. Julio even legged out his first triple since 1997.

Atlanta pitchers rarely had to beg for runs. As a result, Tom Glavine celebrated D-Day on June 6 by winning his 10th game, 3–2 over the Mets. That win pushed the crafty lefty's career record to 234–134 and made the Greg Maddux-Tom Glavine tandem the first teammates to go 100 games over .500 since Christy Mathewson and Joe McGinnity did it with the New York Giants in 1908.

Maddux later joined Cy Young as the only pitchers to win at least 15 games for 15 consecutive years.

Glavine, who had never reached double digits so quickly, went on to lead the team in starts (36) and tie Kevin Millwood for the most wins (18). Maddux won 16 times, a low number for him, while left-handed rookie Damian Moss, a native of Australia, broke into the big leagues with a 12–6 mark. He also became the first Braves pitcher to work seven hitless innings in a game since Maddux did it at Houston on May 28, 1995.

Because the bullpen was even better than the rotation, Bobby Cox beat a regular path from the dugout to the mound. Atlanta starters completed just three games, two of them shutouts, but the staff posted a 3.13 earned run average that led both leagues for the ninth time in 12 seasons.

John Smoltz, in his first full season as a closer, started slowly but wound up saving 55 games, two more than the previous National League record shared by Randy Myers and Trevor Hoffman. At one point, the hard-throwing right-hander saved 25 straight, four more than Mark Wohlers's club record. He passed Wohlers again with his 40th save on August 8. The Braves won each of the final 49 games in which Smoltz worked.

Thanks in large part to Chris Hammond, whose 0.95 earned run average in 76 innings sent researchers to the history books, Atlanta relievers posted a club-record 2.60 ERA. Seven of them, including Smoltz and Hammond, answered the call at least 50 times without sacrificing their statistics. Darren Holmes and Mike Remlinger ended with ERAs of 1.81 and 1.99, respectively.

Hammond had been out of the major leagues for four years and out of professional baseball for three when he decided to make a comeback. By season's end he had become the third pitcher ever to post an ERA of less than 1.00 while pitching at least 75 innings.

Buoyed by a pitching staff that threw 15 shutouts, the Braves coasted to the division crown by 19 games over the second-place Montreal Expos.

The Postseason

The best-of-five Division Series between the Braves and Giants proved to be a nail-biter. Atlanta was favored not only because of its pitching and power but also because it had home-field advantage.

That edge evaporated quickly, however, when Glavine had a rough outing in the opener. Home runs by Sheffield and Lopez narrowed the gap to 8–5 but the Braves couldn't close the deal with the tying run at the plate in the bottom of the ninth. Hopes for a miracle comeback against San Francisco closer Robb Nen faded when Julio Franco lined out to right and Sheffield banged into a double play.

Millwood evened things with a 7–3 win in Game Two behind homers from Lopez and Castilla, sending the series to San Francisco.

A five-run rally in the sixth helped Maddux to a 10–2 win that featured a rare long ball from Keith Lockhart and an expected one from Giants slugger Barry Bonds, who had also connected in the previous game.

Needing only one more win to advance, the Braves could have called on Smoltz, a one-time stalwart starter who had worked only one inning of relief in the series. Because he was not stretched out, however, Bobby Cox went back to Glavine, his left-handed ace, with the belief that he would rebound from his October 2 debacle. Instead, Glavine was even worse, yielding seven earned runs while not surviving the third inning. The 8–3 Giants win reduced the playoff to a winner-take-all game at Atlanta on October 7.

Millwood was no mystery, yielding an RBI single to Reggie Sanders, who had been a bust with the Braves, and a solo homer to Bonds, whose fourth-inning shot gave the Giants a lead they never relinquished. Making the 3–1 loss even more excruciating for the Braves, history repeated itself in the bottom of the ninth.

Atlanta put runners on the corners with nobody out against the hard-throwing Nen—only to strand them there when Sheffield fanned and Chipper Jones hit into a double play. The winning pitcher, Russ Ortiz, would be traded to the Braves two months later.

19

2003: POWER TO BURN

Opening Day
Furcal, ss
Fick, 1b
Sheffield, rf
C. Jones, lf
A. Jones, cf
Giles, 2b
Castilla, 3b
Blanco, c
Maddux, p
Best Hitter: Gary Sheffield
Best Pitcher: John Smoltz
Best Newcomer: Mike Hampton

The Season

ALTHOUGH MOST OF their 14-year title streak was dominated by pitching, the hitters took center stage in 2003.

Six players had 20 home runs—an achievement accomplished previously only by the 1965 Braves during their last year in Milwaukee—and four reached triple digits in runs batted in for the first time in franchise history. The Braves also became the second National League team since 1900 to have five men score at least 100 times each.

Atlanta led the league with a .284 batting average, .475 slugging percentage, 235 home runs, 907 runs scored, and 1,608 hits. A slew of club records fell: runs, hits, slugging, doubles, home runs, and total bases.

Thanks primarily to hitting coach Terry Pendleton, a former batting champion, the '03 Braves made such good contact that their hitters fanned only 933 times, a league low. The last team to have the most home runs and fewest strikeouts in the league had been the 1999 Colorado Rockies, though the Braves had done it five years earlier.

The surprise hero of 2003 was Javy Lopez, healthy again after a serious 2002 leg injury. Suddenly capitalizing on his power potential, he enhanced his free agent value by hammering 43 home runs in just 129 games. Although he had one as a pinch-hitter, the Puerto Rican slugger still finished with one more than Todd Hundley, whose 41 in 1996 had been the record for catchers.

Lopez, in his last season with the Braves before bolting to Baltimore as a free agent, made the National League All-Star team for the third time and mustered enough votes to finish fifth in the voting for Most

Valuable Player. The MVP of the 1996 Championship Series, Lopez concluded his Braves career ranking eighth in franchise history with 214 home runs.

Gary Sheffield, also getting ready to ply the free-agent waters, collected a team-record 132 runs batted in, topping by five Hank Aaron's 1966 Atlanta record. Sheffield also notched his 2,000th career hit on September 20 before finishing the campaign with 39 home runs, three more than Andruw Jones. The remainder of the 20-homer sextet included

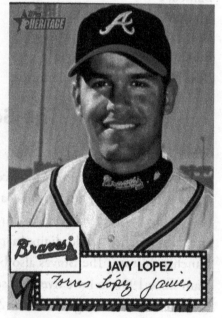

Courtesy of The Topps Company, Inc.

Chipper Jones, Vinny Castilla, and Marcus Giles. The little second baseman also delivered doubles in droves, including a league-record four straight in a nine-inning game on July 27.

Giles, with a franchise-record 49 doubles, and leadoff man Rafael Furcal, a .292 hitter with 25 steals, gave Atlanta's sluggers prolific and productive table setters.

A little guy with a big glove, Giles made only 14 errors in 139 games and showed the benefits of spring training drills with coach Glenn Hubbard, a former Braves second baseman. He led the league in assists and chances "He made play after play after play," Hubbard said of Giles. "You'd watch him and go 'no way he should make that play.' But confidence makes you better too. He knows he can play."

Healed from the ankle injury that cost him six weeks of the 2002 campaign, Giles swung a solid bat, too. He not only hit 21 homers but finished with a .316 average, best ever by an Atlanta second baseman. Not bad for a guy who wasn't picked until the 53rd round of the amateur draft.

With three-quarters of the infield in good hands, manager Bobby Cox only had to worry about one uncertain spot.

First base remained in a state of flux, with free agent signee Robert Fick succeeding Matt Franco as Julio Franco's primary left-handed platoon partner. Two of Fick's 11 home runs came with the bases loaded as he hit .342 with runners in scoring position. Julio Franco was almost as good, producing a .339 mark with men in scoring position and clocking lefties at .351. Matt Franco made his mark, too, with a pair of pinch homers.

Sheffield, Lopez, and the Jones boys all vaulted the 100-RBI plateau as the Braves coasted to the finish line. The team batting average in July was .311, helping the team post a 20–8 record while the pitchers posted an unsightly 4.99 earned run average.

With three 30-homer men for the first time since 1998, Atlanta had 101 wins, good enough for a 10-game cushion in the NL East.

Teamwork

The 2003 Braves kept The Streak going by out-slugging opponents. The team set franchise records with 907 runs scored, 1,608 hits, 321 doubles, 235 home runs, 2,696 total bases, and a .475 slugging percentage. The team batting average of .284 was the best by a Braves team since the 1925 Boston Braves hit .292.

The pitching was far from perfect, however. It didn't help that longtime mainstay Tom Glavine spent the summer in New York after signing with the archrival Mets via free agency. Age also started to furrow the brow of the usually flawless Greg Maddux, whose new $18 million contract forced the club to trade the solid but expensive Kevin Millwood. He went to Philadelphia for minor-league catcher Johnny Estrada, who would later blossom into an NL All-Star.

The team filled the southpaw slot in the rotation with Mike Hampton, obtained in a complicated three-way swap with Colorado and Florida, while further bolstering the front five with Russ Ortiz, villain of the previous postseason. He arrived in a preseason deal that sent southpaw Damian Moss to the Giants.

Ortiz won a career-best 21 games, Hampton rebounded from a two-year Colorado skid to go 14–8, and both newcomers showed prowess at the plate with two homers apiece. Hampton crafted a nine-game midsummer winning streak, tied for best in the league, and Ortiz became Atlanta's first 20-game winner in three years when he blanked Florida, 1–0, in a September 19 home game.

Since Maddux showed signs of age at 37, the additions could not have been timelier.

Maddux, the longtime ace of the staff, went 16–11 but his 3.96 ERA was the highest since he was a rookie with the Cubs in 1987. Although a 3–1 September helped the veteran control artist become the first pitcher to produce 16 consecutive 15-win seasons, he was far from the form that yielded four consecutive Cy Young Awards from 1992 to 1995.

John Smoltz, thriving in his second full year as closer, converted 45 of 49 save opportunities while posting a 1.12 earned run average inflated to that level only when he yielded two earned runs to Philadelphia on September 27, his last outing of the season. In 64 1/3 innings, he allowed 48 hits and eight walks to go with 73 strikeouts.

Though he missed much of the final month, Smoltz joined Eric Gagne as the only relievers to record 100 saves over a two-year span. The Atlanta right-hander also reached 100 career saves in 151 games, the fastest pace in baseball history.

The Braves ranked ninth in the league with their 4.10 staff earned run average but the rotation was rarely as rock-solid as it had been during the first 12 title seasons. Ortiz, Maddux, Hampton, and rookie left-hander Horacio Ramirez won at least a dozen times each and former Astros ace Shane Reynolds almost joined them despite a bloated ERA.

Bobby Cox won by banking on his bats and his bullpen. Smoltz got solid setup work from Kevin Gryboski, Roberto Hernandez, and lefties Ray King, Jung Bong, and August trade acquisition Kent Mercker, author of a 1994 no-hitter as a Braves starter. King's 80 appearances tied for third in the senior circuit.

Fine Fielder

In 2003, Braves pitcher Mike Hampton snapped a streak of 13 straight (10 as a Brave) Gold Gloves by teammate Greg Maddux and became the first and only pitcher to win a Gold Glove and Silver Slugger in the same season.

The Postseason

In a year when Atlanta made hitting its priority, pitching prevailed in the first playoff round. With a 1–2 punch of Kerry Wood and Mark Prior, the Chicago Cubs held Braves bats at bay in all but one contest in a series that went a full five games.

The Braves managed only three hits against Wood and three relievers in the opener, which the Cubs won, 4–2, on a two-run double by their pitcher. Mark DeRosa's two-out, two-run double in the eighth inning of Game Two evened the series.

After Chicago touched Maddux for two first-inning runs in the third game, Prior went all the way on a three-hitter that thrilled the Wrigley Field faithful. The 3–1 win put the Cubs on the brink of the next round.

Anxious to avoid another knockout, Atlanta finally mustered some offense in Game Four. Among its 12 hits were a pair of two-run homers—one from each side of the plate—by Chipper Jones. Russ Ortiz, the first of six Braves pitchers, got the win.

Sheffield sat out the game with a bruised hand but pronounced himself ready for the decisive finale in Atlanta on October 5. He produced the only Atlanta RBI with a sixth-inning single but his mates couldn't touch Wood, who yielded one run on five hits in eight innings. Hampton, working on short rest, was trailing 4–1 when lifted in the seventh.

For the second straight year, the Braves battled to the final game but failed to reap the rewards of the chanting, tomahawk-waving fans at Turner Field. Ironically, the winning manager was ex-Brave Dusty Baker, who managed the Giants past the Braves in the 2002 Division Series.

Atlanta fans had to endure more than the loss of a series; Maddux, Lopez, Sheffield, and Castilla all left town as free agents, forever changing the face of the proud franchise.

20
2004: ROTATION REBORN

Opening Day
Furcal, ss
Giles, 2b
C. Jones, lf
A. Jones, cf
Drew, rf
Franco, 1b
Estrada, c
DeRosa, 3b
Ortiz, p
Best Hitter: J. D. Drew
Best Pitcher: Jaret Wright
Best Newcomer: J. D. Drew

The Season

LONG BEFORE THE 2004 Braves reported to spring training, John Schuerholz performed his Houdini imitation, pulling rabbits out of hats, turning retreads into stars, and saving millions without sabotaging The Streak.

With Time Warner in charge rather than erstwhile owner Ted Turner, corporate accountants ordered Schuerholz to slash $20 million off his payroll. That meant the end of the line for Javy Lopez, Atlanta's slugging catcher for 10 years; cleanup man Gary Sheffield; and future

Hall of Famer Greg Maddux, who had won three Cy Young Awards and contended for many more since joining the Braves in 1993.

Nobody named Greg Maddux, Tom Glavine, or John Smoltz started a game for the 2004 Atlanta Braves. But the team still won the National League East title by 10 games—the same margin as the previous year.

If anything, the revamped pitching staff was even better, recording a 3.74 earned run average that was much improved from 2003. Four different starters won more than a dozen times each, Smoltz saved 44 games, and pitching coach Leo Mazzone was asked almost daily how he resurrected so many veteran arms no one else would touch.

Exhibit A was Jaret Wright, a late-summer waiver wire acquisition from San Diego the previous season, who went 15–8 with a 3.28 ERA that topped the starters in his first full Atlanta campaign.

Returnee Russ Ortiz also won 15, followed by 14-game winner John Thomson, signed as a free agent the previous December, and veteran

Although Greg Maddux and Tom Glavine were gone, Russ Ortiz, John Thomson, and Mike Hampton were all big winners for the 2004 Braves.

Photo by Bill Menzel.

left-hander Mike Hampton, who won 13. Even Paul Byrd, another reclamation project inked as a free agent, added eight wins as the fifth starter—relieving the burden created when tendinitis of the left shoulder sidelined the promising Horacio Ramirez for 109 games. Byrd, slow in his recovery from Tommy John surgery, missed 66.

Like the rotation, the relief corps was rebuilt. Chris Reitsma, acquired from Cincinnati just before the season started, worked 84 times, a club record, and served as the main setup man for Smoltz. Antonio Alfonseca, a huge Dominican right-hander whose hands had six fingers each, answered the call in 79 games. Hard-throwing Juan Cruz averaged almost a strikeout an inning over 50 games. Holdover Kevin Gryboski, a ground ball specialist often inserted when the team needed double plays, made 69 outings and kept his ERA at a tidy 2.84.

Smoltz, in his final season as closer before returning to the Atlanta rotation, had been limited to six spring training games after surgery to clean out elbow scar tissue the previous October. Once the season began, however, he wasted little time showing he was sound again.

For the second year in a row, he didn't get a regular season win but compensated by saving more than 40 games. The first Brave with three straight seasons of at least 30 saves, he averaged 1.43 walks per nine innings, second among NL relievers, and went more than an inning in 15 of the games he saved. The reliable right-hander collected a save in nine straight appearances from July 24 to August 5.

Completing his fourth and final year as a closer, Smoltz ranked second only to Eric Gagne and Trevor Hoffman in successful conversions over that span. He was 154-for-168, a .917 success ratio.

Both the old and the new pitchers had a new catcher. Johnny Estrada, acquired from Philadelphia for Kevin Millwood in a payroll-dumping trade that surprised even the players involved, stepped into the giant shoes of longtime Braves backstop Javy Lopez and made a strong impression.

In his first full season in the majors, Estrada proved Atlanta's most prolific clutch hitter, leading the team with 45 two-out RBIs. When he finished the year with a .314 average, he joined Ted Simmons as the only switch-hitting catchers since 1923 to hit .300. Estrada hit .351 on the road, third in the league, and .329 against right-handed pitchers, placing sixth. Though he could not emulate the home run power of Lopez, who had spent 10 years as the team's top backstop, Estrada was the only Braves player named to the 2004 National League All-Star team.

J. D. Drew and Chipper Jones could have complained; both had 30 homers and 90-plus RBIs. But the brittle third baseman's batting average shrunk for the third straight year, ending at an unsightly .248. It was by far the worst of his career.

Andruw Jones, on the other hand, continued to dazzle on both offense and defense. He had 29 home runs—two of them grand-slams—and 91 runs batted in while supplying his usual spectacular defense in center field.

Clavicle injuries struck the right side of the infield at the same time. While second baseman Marcus Giles was missing two months with a broken right clavicle, rookie first baseman Adam LaRoche missed 31 games with a separated left clavicle. Hamstring injuries also cost Chipper nearly three weeks of playing time early in the season.

Ageless Julio Franco, no relation to the long-lived Spanish dictator of the same last name, provided a perfect right-left platoon partner for LaRoche, whose power would later make him an everyday player. Franco was most potent in the pinch, batting .349 (15-for-43) with two home runs and 16 runs batted in. His on-base percentage was .429 in the role.

Bobby Cox also got the best of bench players Eli Marrero, who finished at .320 in 90 games, and Mark DeRosa, who played everything but the bass fiddle. Nick Green returned from the minors to play several positions and Eddie Perez returned via free agency to give Estrada occasional breathers behind the plate.

The Braves were strong up the middle, where Giles hit .311 with 32 extra-base hits in 102 games and the switch-hitting Furcal stole 29 bases and flashed his rifle arm at shortstop. Furcal even hit 14 homers, one more than LaRoche collected.

Drew, in his first and only Atlanta season, was the team's offensive star. Acquired with Marrero from St. Louis for Jason Marquis, Ray King, and top pitching prospect Adam Wainwright, Drew had a history of heroics when healthy but long stints on the disabled list when not.

Willing to take a chance after the free agent desertion of devastating slugger Gary Sheffield, the Braves placed Drew in right field and kept their fingers crossed. He responded with his best season, and then left for greener pastures once free agency beckoned.

Like Secretariat, the Georgia native started fast out of the gate. In fact, early in the season only he and Estrada were carrying the offense.

The 6'1" left-handed hitter had 67 extra-base hits and a team-best 22-game hitting streak in 145 games, a personal peak. His .436 on-base percentage ranked fourth in the National League.

Drew reached career highs with 158 hits, 31 home runs, 93 runs batted in, 118 runs scored, and 118 walks. He and Marrero earned a combined $6.2 million, roughly half of what the Yankees gave Sheffield to join them after the season.

Marrero, once a catcher, spent most of the year platooning in left field with Charles Thomas. He contributed 10 home runs in 250 at-bats.

"Without [Drew] and Marrero, we don't win this year," said Frank Wren, then assistant general manager. "Pitching is the No. 1 commodity. If you have pitching, you can make deals and keep your team going. Our scouts have done a great job in finding pitchers and we've done a real good job of developing them. That gives us the ability to have the currency that's necessary to make deals. We traded Wainwright, [Joe] Nelson, and [Jung] Bong and still felt we had plenty of depth."

Despite the preseason losses of Sheffield and Lopez, Atlanta still scored runs in bunches, including an 11-run inning against the Mets on April 7 and a 9-run burst against Boston on July 4. They also had an 8-run inning and a pair of 7-run frames.

The Postseason

Atlanta again had home-field advantage in the opening playoff round, which stretched to a full five games, but failed to capitalize.

After tying for the team lead with 15 wins, Jaret Wright took a beating in both the Division Series opener, a 9–3 Houston victory, and the finale, a 12–3 rout. Both games were played at Turner Field, where a field of waving red tomahawks didn't distract the Astros.

Houston's 36 runs scored and 11 home runs in the series were both records for a National League Division Series. The pitching staff that led the league in ERA for the 10th time in 13 years just wasn't there at the end. Without warning, the rotation caved, bursting its balloon of invincibility by yielding 17 runs in 20 1/3 innings,

The offense wasn't much help, fanning 45 times in the best-of-five set.

On the plus side, the Braves got two homers each from Andruw Jones, who went 10-for-19 against Houston pitching in the playoff, and two apiece from the unlikely sources of Johnny Estrada and Rafael Furcal. Furcal's homer was a two-run, 11th-inning shot that clinched Game Two for the Braves by a 4–2 score. Atlanta had trailed, 2–0, entering the seventh.

John Smoltz not only worked three hitless innings from the pen—the second time he made a relief outing of that length—but singled in the ninth for his 12th career postseason hit, a record for pitchers.

Starter Mike Hampton pitched well before leaving in the seventh with tightness in his left forearm. In the very next game, injury interfered with another Atlanta starter. John Thomson re-injured his left oblique after throwing just eight pitches. Paul Byrd was hit hard in long relief as the Braves lost, 8–5.

Atlanta squared the series the next afternoon, however. The team overcame an early 5–2 deficit to win, 6–5, behind the baserunning of Furcal (two steals), the hitting of Adam LaRoche (first postseason homer), and the pitching of Smoltz (two more scoreless frames in relief). The winning run scored when Furcal was hit by a pitch, stole second, and came around on a single by J. D. Drew in the ninth inning.

With the finale scheduled for Turner Field on October 11 and Houston ace Roger Clemens unavailable after working the first five innings of Game Four, the Braves were heavy favorites. But the Astros came out swinging.

They spotted Roy Oswalt a quick 3–0 lead, then erupted for eight runs in the seventh and eighth to ice a 12–3 win. Houston's 17-hit attack was more than enough to send the club to the next round—and send Atlanta home winless for the first time in five NLDS meetings with the Astros.

The two teams alternated wins throughout the series, with the Astros taking the first, third, and fifth games. Houston pitching held Chipper Jones at bay throughout the five-game set. He and Drew, expected to be the bulwarks of the Atlanta attack, combined for no home runs, one run batted in, and a .200 batting average.

No Atlanta starter won a game; both Braves wins went to the bullpen—Antonio Alfonseca in Game Two and Smoltz in Game Four.

Atlanta went home for the winter wondering whether free agency was eroding the team's spirit. Before the year was out, however, the Braves traded for Tim Hudson, the longtime ace of the Oakland Athletics, and Milwaukee closer Dan Kolb, whose presence would allow Smoltz to rejoin the rotation. The team also replaced one free agent, J. D. Drew, with another, Brian Jordan.

All that tinkering, and more, would extend the Atlanta streak to 14 consecutive division titles. But it wouldn't be easy.

21
2005: EIGHTEEN ROOKIES

Opening Day
Furcal, ss
Giles, 2b
C. Jones, 3b
A. Jones, cf
LaRoche, 1b
Estrada, c
Mondesi, rf
Jordan, lf
Smoltz, p
Best Hitter: Andruw Jones
Best Pitcher: Jorge Sosa
Best Newcomer: Jorge Sosa

The Season

AN INJURY HEX that wouldn't evaporate shrouded Turner Field throughout the summer of 2005. But the Braves breached multiple voids by reaching into their rich farm system, scouring the waiver wire, and engineering transactions that turned out even better than they had expected.

After opening the season with over-the-hill veterans Raul Mondesi and Brian Jordan in the outfield corners, Atlanta made much-needed maneuvers in midseason to keep the ship afloat.

Eighteen rookies eventually wore tomahawks but never forced the Braves express onto a siding.

Aaron's Take on 14 Straight

Longtime Braves great Hank Aaron, who became baseball's home run king on April 8, 1974, said in 2014 that he doesn't think any club could win 14 consecutive titles again. "Not the way the game is played today," he said. "It's hard to settle in with great players like Maddux, Glavine, and Smoltz. The agents won't let you do that. If you have a good year, the player goes somewhere else where the money is better. You see a ballplayer today on one club and the next year or so, he may be on another ballclub. I think some of these kids could be great if they get settled in and stay somewhere. Money gets in the way."

The "Baby Braves" won only 90 games, barely sufficient for their 14th consecutive divisional title. The Philadelphia Phillies, who placed second in the NL East, finished two games off the pace.

It was the first time any team had reached postseason play with more than four rookies who had at least 100 at-bats.

Andruw Jones practically carried the club on his broad shoulders. The 28-year-old center fielder hit a club-record 51 home runs and knocked in 128 runs—leading the league in both departments—while finishing fourth in total bases and fifth in slugging. He had 11 outfield assists en route to his eighth straight Gold Glove.

When he hit his 50th home run on September 14, he became the youngest Brave to reach 300 lifetime and the fourth-youngest in baseball history. He was the only man in the majors to hit two walk-off home runs during the 2005 season.

The affable outfielder, who reached the majors as a teenager with enormous potential plus fluency in four languages, erased the old club record of 47 home runs shared by Hall of Famers Eddie Mathews, who did it with the first-year Milwaukee Braves in 1953, and Hank Aaron, who hit a personal-best 47 in 1971 en route to a record 755.

Andruw, armed with an ever-present smile to accompany his booming bat, became the first Brave to lead the majors in home runs since Mathews hit 46 in 1959 and the first Brave to lead the National League since Dale Murphy had 37 in 1985. The youngest Brave and fourth-youngest player to reach 300 career homers, Andruw had nine multi-homer games, a club record, and belted the longest homer by a Brave at Turner Field when he uncorked a 452-foot drive on September 5.

Six days later, he hit his 48th and 49th home runs at Washington in Atlanta's 143rd game. Mathews needed 157 games for his 47, while Aaron played in 139 of the Braves' 162 games in 1971.

After the season, the Curacao product was presented with a brass crown, fit for a king, with a large brass A and a hand-engraved sterling silver plate that read, "Presented by ChopTalk Magazine to Andruw Jones—the Braves' New Season Home Run King 2005."

A strong contender for National League MVP honors, Andruw settled for second place behind Albert Pujols of the Cardinals. A dead pull hitter who never learned to hit the ball to right field, Jones came alive in 2005 after Hall of Famer Willie Mays suggested he widen his stance. He had 27 homers at the All-Star break, made the NL squad for the fourth time, and later became the first Brave since Javy Lopez in 2003 to hit 40 in a season. He hit the 300th home run of his career on September 14 at Citizens Bank Park. That made him the 12th man to reach 300 homers before turning 30.

Keeping up with the Joneses had been tough enough in previous years; in 2005 nobody could keep pace with Andruw. The only teammate with potential fell out of contention quickly.

Even though he missed more than a month with an injured toe ligament, Chipper Jones boosted his batting average nearly 50 points. But he hit just 21 home runs, tying his career-worst total of 1997, because he played only 109 games.

When Chipper was healthy, he and Andruw formed a devastating middle-of-the-order tandem. They homered in the same game eight times, stretching their career total to 50. Not surprisingly, the Braves won 44 of those games for an .880 winning percentage.

Other Atlanta infielders chipped in when Chipper couldn't. Adam LaRoche, whose left-handed power and strong defense made him a solid performer at first base, connected 20 times while double-play partners Marcus Giles and Rafael Furcal contributed 15 and 12, respectively. The switch-hitting Furcal also swiped 46 bases, third in the league, to underline his value as a catalyst and leadoff man.

Old Man River kept rolling along, too; Julio Franco, at 46 the ancient mariner of the majors, became the oldest man to hit a grand slam and the oldest to pinch-hit a home run. Both came in the same at-bat, in the eighth inning on June 27 against the Marlins. His right-handed bat spelled LaRoche on occasion but was also handy off the bench. Franco led the team with 14 pinch-hits.

At the opposite end of the age spectrum was Jeff Francoeur, a 21-year-old outfielder with a winning personality, powerful arm, and promising power.

He homered in his July 7 debut, finishing with 14 in the 70 games he played. The former first-round draft choice hit an even .300 with 45 runs batted in and 13 outfield assists—second in the league. The 6'4", 220-pound right-handed hitter started with such a flourish that he found his face on the cover of *Sports Illustrated*, which dubbed him "The Natural" after the Robert Redford film. Francoeur would eventually fade but Atlanta would not have won without him.

Super Switcher

Chipper Jones was not the only switch-hitting Atlanta infielder with power. Rafael Furcal homered from both sides of the plate twice during the 2005 season.

With five homers in his first dozen games, Francoeur fashioned the fastest start by a Brave since the forgotten Jose Oliva smacked five in his first 11 games during the 1994 season. Hank Aaron needed 32 games to hit five home runs, Dale Murphy needed 83, and Chipper Jones needed 28.

In addition to Francoeur, players who broke into the big leagues with the 2005 Braves—in order of appearance—were Pete Orr, Kyle Davies, Brayan Pena, Kelly Johnson, Andy Marte, Brian McCann, Blaine Boyer, Macay McBride, Joey Devine, Anthony Lerew, and Chuck James.

McCann, a catcher who batted left-handed, hit a solid .278 with five homers in 59 games after his promotion from Double-A Mississippi on June 8. He would blossom into a perennial All-Star, with more staying power than any of the other 18 rookies who cracked the injury-riddled lineup.

Home Grown

On June 15, 2005, every player in the Braves' lineup at Texas came up through their system:

Pete Orr, dh
Marcus Giles, 2b
Kelly Johnson, lf
Adam LaRoche, 1b
Andruw Jones, cf
Ryan Langerhans, rf
Andy Marte, 3b
Brian McCann, c
Wilson Betemit, ss
Kyle Davies, p

Two more left-handed hitters, Kelly Johnson and Pete Orr, also kept the 2005 Braves afloat. Johnson batted third in his first game, on May 29, and finished with nine home runs in 87 games. Orr, a slap hitter, connected just once but tied Francoeur's .300 average. Only switch-hitting infielder Wilson Betemit produced a better result (.305). Both Betemit and outfielder Ryan Langerhans (eight home runs in 128 games) had been up before but were officially 2005 rookies.

Braves fans couldn't identify the players without a scorecard. Brian Jordan, only a shadow of his former self, missed 51 games with knee problems and hardly reminded anyone of his earlier tenure in Atlanta. Eddie Perez missed nearly 100 games with shoulder tendinitis. Johnny Estrada's bad back cost him 14 games and gave McCann more playing time behind the plate.

Chipper's toe kept him on the pines for 37 contests.

The pitchers were hardly immune. Starters Mike Hampton and John Thomson, authors of a combined 27 wins the previous year, missed long stretches that forced the Braves to find replacements. Hampton played hide-and-seek with the disabled list, bouncing on and off with a strained left forearm, strained lower back, herniated disc in his back, and a strained left elbow. Thomson suffered a strained flexor tendon in his right middle finger and sat from May 17 to August 13.

Tim Hudson, acquired in a December deal with the Oakland Athletics, and Jorge Sosa, obtained from Tampa Bay on March 31, were in the right place at the right time.

Gold Glovers

Dynamic defense was a key ingredient in Atlanta's ability to win 14 consecutive division crowns. Starting in 1992, when Terry Pendleton won a Gold Glove for his play at third base, at least one Brave won the award every year through 2007. In nine of those seasons, two Braves won.

So was John Smoltz, who practically pleaded to start again after four years in the bullpen relieved the pressure on his problematic elbow and shoulder.

Skeptics said Smoltz couldn't bounce from starter to closer and back again—especially at the advanced athletic age of 37. The chorus of critics got louder after the articulate Michigan native was pounded in his first game, getting only five outs and giving up seven runs on Opening Day at Miami on April 5.

Five days after that 9–0 fiasco, Smoltz fanned 15 Mets in 7 1/3 innings but lost to Pedro Martinez, who pitched a two-hitter. He righted the ship, however, to post a final record of 14–7 with a 3.06 earned run average. Smoltz worked 229 2/3 innings, his heaviest workload since 1997, in an I-told-you-so season. The losing pitcher for the National League in the All-Star Game, Smoltz became the only man to record an All-Star Game decision in three different decades (he lost in 1989 but won in 1996).

Hudson, in his first National League season, nearly matched Smoltz for consistent excellence during the season. In 29 starts, he went 14–9 with a 3.52 ERA. But even he was not immune from the injury wave, which knocked him out for a month with a strained left oblique.

"His fastball cuts, sails, and sinks," said Fredi Gonzalez, a future Atlanta manager who was then third base coach for Bobby Cox. "Being a former catcher, I can understand how hard it is for anybody to catch him. I was watching the Discovery Channel or the Rodeo Channel late one night and they were talking about the great bull Bodacious that only a few people ever rode. The owner had to retire him because he thought he was going to kill somebody. The cowboys were going, 'He's a tough ride. He bucks and turns.' I'm thinking 'That sounds like Hudson.'"

The owner of a 92–39 mark during his first six seasons in the majors, Hudson became a Brave only because he was entering the final year of his Oakland contract. Frugal A's general manager Billy Beane, knowing he couldn't afford to keep his ace, thought he could lure Atlanta second baseman Marcus Giles as part of a swap. When Atlanta GM John Schuerholz refused to include him, the deal seemed dead. But Beane called back and the rest is history.

Hudson cost the Braves outfielder Charles Thomas and pitchers Dan Meyer and Juan Cruz but was happy to be coming home. On March 1, the Columbus, Georgia, native signed a new four-year contract, with an option for 2010, and won at least a dozen games for Atlanta six times before moving on to San Francisco.

In his first Atlanta season, Hudson spent a month on the sidelines after he was placed on the disabled list June 14 with a strained left oblique. But that gave Sosa a golden opportunity.

A Dominican right-hander used mainly in relief during parts of three seasons with Tampa Bay, he blossomed under the tutelage of Leo Mazzone. In Sosa's 20 starts, the Braves went 15–5 and the pitcher posted a 10–3 mark and 2.62 ERA. He did his best work in September with a 4–0 record and 2.08 earned run average.

Sosa was also superb on the road, where his 9–0 mark was the best of any pitcher who made at least 10 starts. Economical to boot, his road ERA was a minuscule 1.81.

Dubbed "Houdini" by Braves broadcaster Skip Caray, Sosa had a habit of creating and escaping multiple jams during games. Those efforts usually provoked more rocking than usual from Leo Mazzone.

With Hampton and Thomson combining for just nine wins, Mazzone welcomed the return to health of Horacio Ramirez, a left-hander limited by injuries the year before after a fine rookie campaign in 2003. He did his best work in June (4–0, 3.55) and at home (8–1, 3.59).

With Smoltz in the rotation again, Dan Kolb was anointed the new Atlanta closer. For reasons unknown, the magic he manufactured in Milwaukee failed to follow him south.

After saving 39 games and making the NL All-Star team with the Brewers in 2004, Kolb collapsed the minute he donned a tomahawk. He had eight losses, seven blown saves (ironically including several for

---

Untouchable Mark

"I hear insiders and experts talk about unbreakable records. I believe 14 straight titles will never be duplicated. There are too many things that could go wrong."

—Hall of Fame manager Tony La Russa

Smoltz), and a 5.93 earned run average. Often unable to throw strikes, he lost the closer's job first to Chris Reitsma and then to trade deadline acquisition Kyle Farnsworth.

Reitsma led the team with 76 appearances and 15 saves but Farnsworth was nothing short of fantastic after arriving from Detroit in a deadline deal for two younger arms.

He converted all 10 of his save chances while posting a 1.98 ERA in 26 games. The flame-throwing Farnsworth fanned 32 men in 27 1/3 innings pitched. Counting his time with the Tigers, he worked more than 70 games for the fourth straight season.

The bullpen also got a boost from a selection of setup men ranging from Adam Bernero, Blaine Boyer, and Jim Brower to lefties Macay McBride and John Foster.

Atlanta clinched its 14th straight divisional crown when Hudson beat the Rockies, 12–3, at Turner Field on September 27. That set the stage for the sixth playoff meeting between the Braves and the Houston Astros.

The Postseason

The Braves had won four straight postseason matches against the Astros before losing a five-game Division Series in 2004.

Anxious for revenge, they sent Tim Hudson to the mound in the opening game against Andy Pettitte at Turner Field. Pettitte, whom the Braves remembered as a nemesis from the 1996 World Series against the Yankees, prevailed again. Weak work by the Atlanta bullpen made the final score mushroom to 10–5. It had been a 4–3 game before the Astros added to their lead with a run in the top of the seventh and five more in the eighth.

When John Smoltz outpitched Roger Clemens in Game Two, the series was deadlocked. With his elbow aching, the determined Smoltz worked the first seven innings of a 7–1 game. Brian McCann, in the first postseason at-bat of his career, lashed a long three-run home run to back his batterymate. McCann, a left-handed hitter, had been held out of the opener because Houston started a left-handed pitcher.

Sosa, the Game Three starter, pitched well but took the loss when the Braves bullpen suffered a spectacular failure in the bottom of the seventh in Houston on October 8. Reitsma and three other relievers fueled a four-run explosion that was the difference in a 7–3 game.

Facing elimination in four games, the Braves had Hudson on the hill. Pulled after seven with a 5–1 lead, he watched helplessly as Farnsworth imploded for the first time as a Brave.

A perfect 10-for-10 during his two months in Atlanta, Farnsworth loaded the bases in the bottom of the eighth and then, fighting control problems and a home-plate umpire with a small strike zone, tried to throw a fastball past Lance Berkman, who had hit 24 home runs during a regular season shortened by injury.

The switch-hitter lofted a fly ball to left just deep enough to reach the box seats above the left-field scoreboard in the compact ballpark. Brad Ausmus, who had hit only *three* home runs over the 162-game schedule, then hit a two-out, solo shot in the ninth that just cleared the yellow line on the center field wall. Tie score. Extra innings.

The marathon dragged on for 18 innings, with each team emptying its bullpen. The Astros even inserted Clemens, who had been announced as physically unable to pitch, for three innings of scoreless

Lightning Strikes Twice

The ball Chris Burke hit for the pennant-winning home run in the 18th inning of the last 2005 playoff game in Houston was caught by the same fan who caught Lance Berkman's grand slam in the eighth.

relief. Both teams squandered scoring chances, almost suggesting neither wanted the game to end.

Finally, it did—when little-known Chris Burke deposited a Joey Devine pitch almost into the same spot as Berkman's drive 10 innings (and many hours) earlier.

Houston parlayed the momentum of its 7–6 win into its first pennant. The Astros beat the St. Louis Cardinals in a six-game Championship Series and advanced to the World Series against the Chicago White Sox.

The Braves went home, knowing their 14-year streak would never be duplicated but wondering why their winning ways wouldn't translate to more success on the national stage.

22

AFTER THE STREAK

T HE COVER OF the 2005 Atlanta Braves Postseason Media Guide features the numeral 14, in oversized type, under a World Series ring from the team's miraculous '95 campaign.

There are also one-liners, with accompanying photographs, about each title year.

Here's how they read:

1991—"Worst to First" Braves win pennant

1992—Braves celebrate consecutive division titles

1993—Fred McGriff leads Braves to NLCS

1995—Braves win World Series behind MVP Tom Glavine

1996—John Smoltz: NL Cy Young Award

1997—Denny Neagle: National League's only 20-game winner

1998—Braves set a franchise record 106 victories

1999—Chipper Jones: National League MVP

2000—Rafael Furcal: NL Rookie of the Year

2001—Brian Jordan goes on a home run binge

2002—Greg Maddux wins Cy Young with 15th consecutive 15-win season

2003—Javy Lopez sets major-league record for home runs by a catcher

2004—Braves win the division for an unprecedented 13th consecutive season

2005—Andruw Jones sets the Braves home run mark

In 146 seasons of Braves baseball, the team has won 18 pennants, reached the playoffs 27 times, and won four World Series—one each in Boston and Milwaukee, and two in Atlanta. They should have won more.

Between divisional titles in 1969 and 1982, the Braves endured many lean years. History repeated itself, as it often does, after the 14-year title streak ended in 2005.

In 2006, the team dropped to third in the NL East and fell under .500, finishing at 79–83. A year later, the record improved (84–78) but not the final standing. Things were awful in 2008, when the Braves went 72–90 and finished fourth in the five-team division, but better in '09, with an 86–76 final mark that left the team in third place when the curtain fell on the campaign.

With Chipper Jones still at the top of his game, the 2010 Braves went 91–71, second in the East but good enough to claim the wild-card spot for the first time. But Jones fell victim to injury in mid-August and missed the playoffs with a torn ACL that needed surgical repair.

Then there was 2011, a year that could have been historic if not for the final month. In his first year as manager after succeeding the legendary Bobby Cox, former third-base coach Fredi Gonzalez guided his team into title contention all season. Then, seemingly out of nowhere, came a collapse of epic proportions.

The Braves held a 10½-game lead over St. Louis in the wild-card standings in late August and an 8½-game lead as the final month began but lost 18 of their last 27 to hand the wild-card crown to the Cardinals, who finished with a 17–8 spurt. Atlanta lost its final five games, capping the agony on the final day with a 13-inning loss to Philadelphia, the NL East leader, after leading in the ninth. That left the Braves a game behind St. Louis in the wild-card standings.

There was more frustration for Braves fans in 2012, Chipper's last year, when the team couldn't capitalize on home-field advantage in the new, sudden-death wild-card game. Again, the Cardinals were the culprit—along with umpire Sam Holbrook's inexplicable interpretation of the infield fly rule.

A year later, however, resilient Atlanta won its first NL East crown since 2005, the year of historic title run ended. But the high hopes of that October soon came crashing down as The Dodgers dispatched the Braves in a four-game division series.

After they dropped below .500 in 2014, Atlanta's new management team decided to reboot, blaming general manager Frank Wren for doling out dollars to free-agent failures rather than protecting a once-bountiful farm system. With longtime GM John Schuerholz kicked upstairs, John Hart was hired as president of baseball operations and John Coppolella became general manager and executive vice president. That executive troika lasted less than five seasons.

Hart and Coppolella determined that the best way to make the Braves an elite team again was to restock a disappointing farm system by trading high-priced players for prospects—even though more than a few of those veterans were performing at All-Star levels.

Among those traded by the Braves were Evan Gattis, Jason Heyward, Craig Kimbrel, Andrelton Simmons, B.J. Upton (later renamed Melvin Upton, Jr.), Justin Upton, and Alex Wood.

Stripped of virtually all star talent not named Freddie Freeman, the Braves floundered. They not only lost games by the bushel but ran afoul of Commissioner Rob Manfred, who revealed after the 2017 season that the team had violated rules regarding the signing of international free agents. He suspended Coppolella for life and scout Gordon Blakely for a year, fined the team heavily, restricted its participation in the amateur draft and international signings, and released more than a dozen prospects allegedly signed illegally. Hart left too, allowing the team to sign former Toronto Blue Jays general manager Alex Anthopoulos as the new GM in Atlanta.

Organization man Brian Snitker was National League Manager of the Year in 2018, when his youthful Braves were surprise champions of the National League East.

Credit: Getty Images

Although the penalties sent the team reeling, the youthful Anthopoulos added analytics to the tactics employed by manager Brian Snitker, an organization man 20 years his senior who had replaced Fredi Gonzalez after the 2016 Braves started 9–28. The analytics idea worked like a charm—so well, in fact, that Snitker was named National League Manager of the Year.

To the surprise of the entire baseball world, the team once derisively called the Bad-News Braves bounced back into contention with a youthful cast almost too young to vote. The only team in the majors to employ a 20-year-old pitcher in 2018 actually used three of them—and watched each win his first start.

Two of the other kids, Ozzie Albies and Mike Foltynewicz, made the All-Star team, along with veterans Freddie Freeman and Nick Markakis, but the surprise of the year was the rise of 20-year-old left-fielder Ronald Acuña, Jr.

At age 20, the Venezuelan slugger not only reached Atlanta in 2018 but led the team in home runs, including a club-record eight to lead

Mike Foltynewicz became a first-time All-Star in 2018 as ace of an Atlanta pitching staff that won 90 games, most in the National League East.

Credit: Getty Images

off games. Comparisons to Hank Aaron, another 6-foot, 180-pound righthanded hitter, were inevitable. Both had five-letter surnames starting with the first letter of the alphabet, both played for the Braves, and both began their careers in left field.

Led by Acuña, who romped to the Rookie of the Year Award that eluded Aaron, the 2018 Braves strolled to the National League East title—their second since the end of The Streak—by an eight-game margin over the favored Washington Nationals. A cadre of kids, including All-Stars Ozzie Albies and Mike Foltynewicz, teamed with veterans Nick Markakis and Freeman to make the magical season possible.

Though he missed two months, Acuña led the club with 26 home runs en route to the first NL rookie trophy by a Brave since Craig Kimbrel in 2011. Acuña was among four Atlanta regulars aged 24 or under.

The last team to win 90 after losing 90 three years in a row? The "worst to first" Braves of 1991 led by Bobby Cox and John Schuerholz.

The old leaders, tired of languishing in the depths of the division, relished the revival.

Schuerholz moved from general manager to team president in 2007 but still had a say about player development and movement. He later became vice chairman of the board but remained a regular presence at the ballpark, along with Cox.

The old days were definitely gone: no Ted Turner, no Stan Kasten, no SuperStation, and no Pete, Skip, and Ernie. No Turner Field either. The team shifted to a new Cobb County edifice originally named Sun Trust Park in 2017. It is there that management hopes to launch a new dynasty, built on the philosophy that powered the old.

The Baby Braves of 2019, just learning how to walk, seem headed in that direction.

Postseason Update

Even the men responsible for the 14-year streak of consecutive division titles don't believe the Braves can do it again. But the team has made several attempts. Here's a look at how they fared:

2010 Division Series

After missing the playoffs for four years in a row, Atlanta went 91–71 to qualify as the National League's wild-card team. They finished second in the NL East, six games out, but would have done better if Chipper Jones had not been shelved in August with a crippling knee injury. Without Jones in the Division Series against the San Francisco Giants, the Braves lacked both the offense and defense to compete. Tim Lincecum held Atlanta to two hits in Game One, winning, 1-0, after Buster Posey was called safe at second in a disputed call in the fourth and scored on a Cody Ross single. The Braves then won Game Two, 5–4, in 11 innings, on a Rick Ankiel solo homer. But the win was costly, as closer Billy Wagner suffered an oblique injury in the 10th. Though the series moved to Turner Field for Game Three, the error-prone Braves (three more miscues) blew a 2–1 lead in the ninth and lost, 3–2. The same scenario repeated the next day in the last game for manager Bobby Cox. Derek Lowe was the losing pitcher in two of his team's three losses, although iron-handed infielder Brooks Conrad may have deserved the title more. Moved from third to second during the series, the ball kept finding him anyway. Only one previous postseason encounter, the Cincinnati-Oakland World Series of 1972, had its first four games decided by one run.

2012 Wild-Card Game

Before the 2012 season began, Major League Baseball expanded its playoff structure to include two wild-card qualifiers in each league—non-title winners that had the second and third-best winning percentages.

The 2012 Atlanta Braves, whose 94–68 record left them four games out of first place, won home-field advantage because of a record better than the other hopeful, the St. Louis Cardinals [88–74]. Before 52,631 fans in Turner Field, the Braves started Kris Medlen, sometimes called "the poor man's Greg Maddux" because he favored location over velocity. The team had won 23 straight games Medlen had started—a major-league record—but Kyle Lohse ended that streak. With the Braves nursing a 2–0 lead in the fourth, Carlos Beltran singled and Matt Holliday followed with a grounder that looked like a sure double-play ball. But Chipper Jones threw it over the head of Dan Uggla, leaving runners at the corners with nobody out. Allen Craig doubled, Yadier Molina delivered an RBI groundout, and David Freese hit a sacrifice fly, giving the Cards a 3–2 lead they padded later on a Matt Holliday homer and a pair of Atlanta errors in the seventh. In the bottom of that inning, however, the Braves had a run home and looked like they would add more when umpire Sam Holbrook called the infield fly rule—an automatic out—after a ball dropped cleanly between the shortstop and leftfielder. Atlanta left the bases loaded and lost, 6–3, while outhitting St. Louis, 12–6. The Braves had a shot in the ninth, when Uggla came to the plate as the potential tying run, but Jason Motte got him out. Four of the six St. Louis runs in the game were unearned.

2013 Division Series

The Braves not only took their first NL East title since 2005 but led the league with 181 home runs while yielding a fourth-fewest 127. That didn't seem to matter in the NLDS against the Los Angeles Dodgers, who outhomered the Braves in a four-game set. The only bright spots for Atlanta were Mike Minor, who beat Zack Greinke in Game Two to earn his first postseason win; Craig Kimbrel, who earned his first postseason save; Jason Heyward, who hit his first postseason homer; and Chris Johnson, who hit .438 with five runs batted in. Even with Johnson, however, the Braves had a team batting average of .214 and composite ERA of 5.82. Dodgers ace Clayton Kershaw started the first and last games but got a Game Four reprieve when Juan Uribe smacked a two-run homer—the second yielded by David Carpenter in the series—in the eighth inning while a warmed-up Kimbrel was left standing but unused in the Atlanta bullpen. The Braves had leads in every game but the opener.

2018 Division Series

After three straight 90-loss seasons, the Braves won 90 games, good enough for an eight-game bulge over the favored Washington

Nationals in the NL East. They also clinched on September 22, earlier than the winners of the other National League divisions, both of whom had to play title tie-breakers that extended their seasons to 163 games. Still, the Braves proved no match for the Los Angeles Dodgers, a team loaded with power, pitching, and players who could move all over the field like chessmen. Atlanta had ended the regular season with a whimper, losing four of its last five to the Mets and Phillies and scoring just two runs in those four losses. That malaise extended into the playoffs, with the Dodgers posting back-to-back shutouts and hitting five home runs in the first two games. The Braves won only once, in Game Three, when rookie slugger Ronald Acuña Jr. hit a two-out grand slam that sparked a 6–5 win at Sun Trust Park. Los Angeles, fresh from winning its sixth straight NL West crown, sealed the deal the next night, went on to beat the Milwaukee Brewers in a seven-game Championship Series, and advanced to the World Series against the Boston Red Sox.

2019 Division Series

With their hand strengthened by player acquisition and signings, the 2019 Braves looked like they would make a serious bid for their first pennant since 1999.

Heavy-hitting third baseman Josh Donaldson signed a one-year, $23 million contract—the biggest one-year deal ever given a free agent—and former Braves star Brian McCann returned home for a one-year, $2 million pact. In addition, Atlanta product Nick Markakis signed a one-year, $6 million deal in January and, in June, the Braves outbid the Yankees to land free-agent pitcher Dallas Keuchel, a former American League Cy Young Award winner, for a one-year, $13 million contract. But that money might have been better spent on ex-Brave Craig Kimbrel, a closer who chose the Chicago Cubs instead.

Atlanta also insured its future in April by giving Ronald Acuña Jr. an eight-year, $100 million pact and Ozzie Albies a seven-year, $35 million extension. Acuña's deal was the biggest ever bestowed on a player with less than one year of major-league service.

After battling injuries for several seasons, Donaldson delivered with 37 homers, 94 runs batted in, and a .379 on-base percentage but left after the season when the Twins lured him away with an offer richer in years and dollars. Keuchel didn't deliver as advertised, splitting 16 decisions before testing free agency again.

Led by Acuña, who finished with 41 home runs and 37 stolen bases, the Braves went 97–65 to win their 20th division crown, a major-league mark shared with the Yankees. That left them four games ahead of the Washington Nationals, a wild-card winner that went on to win its first world championship.

After splitting the first two games of the Division Series against St. Louis, the Braves won their first road game, 3–1, behind Sean Newcomb, aided by Mark Melancon's second save. But the Cards took Game Four, 5–4 in 10 innings, forcing the best-of-five match back to Atlanta.

With Game Two winner Mike Foltynewicz on the mound, the home team had high hopes of advancing. Matched again against Cardinals ace Jack Flaherty, whom he had beaten by a 3–0 score in St. Louis, Folty faltered from the start. Fueled by shaky defense, Atlanta became the first team to allow 10 runs in the first inning of a playoff game. The final score was 13–1.

2020 Wild-Card, Division, and Championship Series
Even before the Braves reached the new Wild-Card Series, the 2020 season was wild, unpredictable, and almost unplayable.

Thanks to a lethal outbreak of a highly contagious coronavirus called COVID-19, spring training was cut short on March 12, with opening games postponed until July 24—preceded by a second round of spring training. The schedule was cut to 60 games, coupled with changes in both rules and scheduling.

The designated hitter became universal, relief pitchers were required to face at least three batters, both games of doubleheaders were shortened to seven innings, and an automatic runner was inserted at the start of every extra inning to speed up the game. Teams in each league's three divisions played only each other plus opponents from the same division in the opposite league.

In addition, fans were banned from ballparks, with many teams substituting cardboard cutouts and canned crowd noise while broadcasters used video feeds to call road games remotely (from their home broadcast booths).

When the season began, rosters had 30 spots, reduced to 28 two weeks later, and later to 26, expanded by one over the previous maximum.

The Braves didn't need any help: en route to a 35–25 record that left them four games ahead of the Miami Marlins—the only other NL East team with a winning record—Atlanta led the majors with 556 hits, 130 doubles, 338 runs batted in, 1,001 total bases, a .349 on-base percentage, and .832 on-base plus slugging (OPS) mark.

They even scored 29 runs, a National League record and one short of the modern major-league mark, against the Marlins on September 9. Earlier in the month, Marcell Ozuna and Adam Duvall became the first teammate tandem to have back-to-back three-homer games, both against the Red Sox in Fenway Park.

Ozuna, a free agent who had signed a one-year, $18 million pact in January, replaced Josh Donaldson as cleanup man and became the first official DH in Braves history. He wound up leading the league in home runs, runs batted in, and total bases.

The team also signed catcher Travis d'Arnaud, closer Will Smith, and starter Cole Hamels on the free-agent market. Neither Hamels nor Felix Hernandez, who opted out because of COVID, made an impact, but d'Arnaud, Smith, and Ozuna almost pushed the team into the World Series.

With the playoffs expanded to include 16 of the 30 teams—an apparent effort to hike revenues after all teams lost millions with fans banned from ballparks—the Braves used potent pitching to sweep the first two rounds.

In the best-of-three Wild-Card Series, they swept Cincinnati, 1–0 in 13 innings and 5–0 in nine innings. Then they beat the Marlins, 9–5, 2–0, and 7–0 in the best-of-five Division Series. Rookie right-hander Ian Anderson, a late-season addition to the Atlanta roster, pitched scoreless ball to pick up wins in both series.

Things were tougher in the Championship Series, however. Facing the Los Angeles Dodgers, a veteran and versatile team with considerable postseason experience, the Braves won three of the first four, by scores of 5–1, 8–7, and 10–2. But they suffered a rout in Game 3, when rookie Kyle Wright—coming off his shutout of Miami in the NLDS clincher—was knocked out in the first inning. The Dodgers scored a record 11 runs in the opening frame of the game and wound up winning, 15–3.

Dodgers bats and arms were relentless in the last three games, which LA won, 7–3, 3–1, and 4–3. All games were played at Globe Life Field, the Arlington home of the Texas Rangers, with partial attendance allowed (the top crowd was 11,119 for Game 5). An oblique injury to Atlanta slugger Adam Duvall in the first inning of the first game might have made the difference.

Even in defeat, the young and hungry Braves gained valuable experience in the Championship Series—their first since 2001. None of the Atlanta starters, including a promising young left-hander named Max Fried, had ever started a playoff game before 2020.

They would be back.

23
THE MIRACLE BRAVES OF 2021

Opening Day
Acuña Jr., rf
Albies, 2b
Freeman, 1b
Ozuna, lf
d'Arnaud, c
Swanson, ss
Riley, 3b
Pache, cf
Fried, p
Best Hitter: Austin Riley
Best Pitcher: Max Fried
Best Newcomers: Eddie Rosario / Jorge Soler

THE BRAVES LEARNED in 2021 that the road to the World Series runs through Los Angeles. They also learned that navigating the traffic on that road isn't easy.

The Opening Day roster was without Adam Duvall, a slugging outfielder who also brought stalwart defense, and the bullpen trio of Mark Melancon, Shane Greene, and Darren O'Day. All signed elsewhere as free agents after Atlanta slashed payroll to compensate for huge revenue losses caused by the pandemic.

Also gone from the previous year were Hank Aaron, Phil Niekro, and long-time broadcaster Don Sutton, Atlanta icons who passed away before spring training.

When the Braves reported to their spring camp in North Port, Florida, the spectre of COVID-19 was still casting a giant shadow over the game. Not only was fan attendance limited, but so was the number of media members, who were no longer allowed into the clubhouse or onto the field before games.

It was obvious the season was going to be the most challenging in baseball history. That turned out to be especially true for the Atlanta Braves.

The team opened at Citizens Bank Park in Philadelphia, facing one of its most determined title challengers. The Phillies swept the three-game series, which was overshadowed by the news that MLB Commissioner Rob Manfred had decided to move the July 13 All-Star Game out of Atlanta in response to a newly signed Georgia law he said restricted the voting rights of African Americans.

Manfred's decision, which seemed to be made in haste, inflicted another hefty financial hit on the team but also impacted thousands of potential beneficiaries, from hotels and airlines to peanut vendors at Truist Park. Never mind that Atlanta, which is 51 percent African American, has the largest black population of any major-league city.

Cancellation of the Atlanta All-Star Game meant the Braves had to rip off special patches that had been sewn onto the sleeves of their uniforms. It also meant the team had to cancel a special All-Star Game tribute to Aaron, who had spent all but two of his 23 big-league seasons with the franchise, in both Milwaukee and Atlanta.

It was the first of numerous hits that the Braves would suffer as they bid for their fourth consecutive National League East title.

On May 1, catcher Travis d'Arnaud tore a thumb ligament in his catching hand and needed surgical repair that idled him for three months. Just two weeks later, breakthrough starting pitcher Huascar Ynoa punched a bench in frustration and broke his hand. He also needed three months to heal.

The mayday disaster wasn't done. On May 26, Marcell Ozuna broke two fingers when he slid head-first into Red Sox third baseman Rafael Devers during a game in Boston. Less than a week later, Ozuna was arrested and charged in a domestic violence assault against his wife, Genesis, at their home in Sandy Springs, Georgia.

Placed on administrative leave while Major League Baseball conducted its own investigation, the National League's defending home run and RBI king missed the rest of the season.

With the Braves forced to play musical catchers, the pitching rotation staked its own claim for Injury of the Year. Just as he was getting ready to return to the mound, Mike Soroka, a 2019 All-Star who had been the team's Opening Day starter in 2020, tore his Achilles for the second time in 10 months on June 26, shelving him for another calendar year.

Fortunately for Atlanta, the anticipated four-team race for the NL East title never materialized.

The New York Mets, under billionaire new owner Steve Cohen, held first place for most of the first half as the Philadelphia Phillies and Washington Nationals struggled and the Miami Marlins slipped back into the cellar after their sudden surprise during the shortened season.

The Braves, victimized far too often by an undependable bullpen, looked like a submarine trying to skim the surface of .500 but not quite getting there. Then they were hit by a torpedo on July 10.

Star right fielder Ronald Acuña Jr. tore his ACL while trying to catch a long drive by Miami shortstop Jazz Chisholm. The 23-year-old Venezuelan, in just his second full season, had been enjoying an MVP-caliber campaign before the injury and had been elected by fans to start in the 2021 All-Star Game at Denver's Coors Field.

Ronald Acuña Jr. seemed headed for an MVP season when he tore his ACL on July 10, forcing Alex Anthopoulos to acquire four new outfielders. *Credit: Gettty Images*

Rather than throw in the towel on the season, however, Alex Anthopoulos pulled off a half-dozen deals, most of them under the radar, that landed a much-needed veteran catcher (Stephen Vogt), a relief pitcher with closer experience (Richard Rodriguez), and four solid outfielders.

Trading Up

The Braves reached the July 30 trade deadline with a record of 51–52. But six last-minute swaps turned the tide. "We hit every pothole, every bump you could possibly hit this year," Freddie Freeman said, "but still made it to the other side. We've been the best team since the trade deadline and we played like it all the way into the postseason. We got hot and carried it over."

Joc Pederson came first in a deal with the Chicago Cubs. Then the Braves reacquired Adam Duvall, who had pounded them during his four-month stay with the Miami Marlins, plus Jorge Soler, whose 48 home runs for Kansas City in 2019 had led the American League, and Eddie Rosario, a left-handed hitter who had been on the Cleveland injured list with an oblique strain.

All thrived in their new surroundings, allowing the Braves to win 36 of their 54 regular-season games from August 3 until the end of the season two months later. Then they won 11 of 16 postseason games, with Rosario and Soler becoming the first pair of teammates not on the Opening Day roster to win MVP awards in the Championship Series and World Series, respectively.

Atlanta hadn't even topped the .500 mark for the first time until August 6, making them the first world championship team to languish that long (111 days) with a losing record.

Like the Boston Braves of 1914, the upstart Milwaukee Braves of 1957, and the worst-to-first 1991 Atlanta Braves that started the 14-year title streak, it was truly a miracle made in baseball heaven.

First baseman Freddie Freeman raises his arms in joy after recording the final putout of the 2021 World Series, retiring Yuli Gurriel of the Houston Astros at Minute Maid Park on November 2, 2021. It was Atlanta's first world championship since 1995. *Credit: Getty Images*

But it didn't look that way at the start. Freddie Freeman, defending the Most Valuable Player award he had the year before, got off to a dreadful start. So did Marcell Ozuna, who had led all National Leaguers in home runs, runs batted in, and total bases the year before. When promising Austin Riley had trouble shaking the winter cobwebs out of his bat, fans complained loudly

Free-agent signee Charlie Morton, a former Brave lured from Tampa Bay with a one-year, $15 million offer, also had a rough return to Atlanta. And left-handed pitching partner Max Fried, a perfect 7–0 during the 2020 shortened season, didn't look anything like his former self. Closer Will Smith threw too many gopher balls and his bullpen colleagues weren't much better.

On April 25, Atlanta hit rock bottom. Against the Arizona Diamondbacks, a team that would lose 110 games and finish 55 games out of first place in the NL West, the Braves got exactly one hit in 14 innings—two seven-inning games in a doubleheader. After managing one puny single against Zac Gallen in the opener, the Braves went hit-less against veteran left-hander Madison Bumgarner, who got credit for the shutout and complete game but not a no-hitter because the game went seven innings. Never had a Braves team staged such an embarrassing performance on its home turf.

With only one way to go, Atlanta started to regroup. Switch-hitting Ozzie Albies, the shortest player in the National League, became a sudden slugger. Freeman and Riley hiked their averages. And Dansby Swanson, a shortstop known mainly for his defense, showed surprising power.

By season's end, each of the four infielders had more than 25 home runs—the first time any team had done that since the 2007 Florida Marlins.

Freeman hit for the cycle on August 18 and Rosario followed suit on September 19, needing only five pitches to crank out a single, double, triple, and home run.

Big Guns

Atlanta got 59 home runs—a major-league record—from players who began the season with other clubs. Twelve of them came during the 16 postseason games played by the team.

With the offense chugging like a well-oiled locomotive, the pitching also settled into a comfortable groove. Even the bullpen, which posted a 4.58 ERA over the first half, gained enough confidence as the season progressed that it yielded only 3.24 earned runs per game over the second half. By the time the team got to the playoffs, A. J. Minter's mid-season exile to the minors and Will Smith's 11 home run balls seemed like ancient history.

Atlanta roared down the stretch with a .667 winning percentage, trailing only the 100-win Giants and Dodgers, and made quick work of baseball's best teams in the playoffs.

They beat the pitching-rich Brewers in the best-of-five Division Series when Freddie Freeman clubbed an eighth-inning, Game Four homer against hard-throwing Milwaukee closer Josh Hader, a lefty who had blown only one save all season.

Freddie Ties Fred

Freddie Freeman's fifth postseason homer tied a team record owned by Fred McGriff (1996).

Given the gift of home-field advantage in the Championship Series because the Dodgers, with 106 wins, won one game less than the Giants and thus became a wild card, Atlanta needed only six games to dethrone the defending world champions.

Then the Braves surprised the baseball world—including themselves—by burying the hard-hitting Houston Astros in a six-game World Series.

In nine of their 11 postseason wins, Atlanta pitchers limited powerful opponents to two runs or less. Their hitters also rose to the occasion. The Braves hit 11 home runs against the Astros while holding Houston to a pair, both by diminutive Jose Altuve.

Although the Astros had been the highest-scoring team in the majors, averaging more than five runs per game, they couldn't handle Atlanta's talented left-handed relief troika of A. J. Minter, Tyler Matzek, and Will Smith. The starters also starred—rookie Ian Anderson pitched five hitless innings to open Game 3 and lefty Max Fried lasted longer (six innings) than any starter in the 2021 Series.

Stingy Pitchers

Max Fried joined Tom Glavine (1995), John Smoltz (1991), and Lew Burdette (1957) as Braves who pitched at least six scoreless innings in a potential World Series clincher.

It hardly mattered that veteran Charlie Morton fractured his fibula in the second inning of the first game. Signed specifically because of his reputation as a big-game pitcher, Morton tried to soldier on, throwing 16 pitches after the injury, but finally left the big stage.

Brian Snitker never left, however. A failed minor-league catcher given a coaching job by Hank Aaron when the Hall of Fame outfielder was Atlanta's farm director, Snitker lasted 45 years, serving as minor-league manager, major-league coach, and loyal employee who rode a career elevator that seemed to make most of its stops going down—at least for him.

He was in the system but not the majors when the 1995 Braves won the World Series under Bobby Cox but coached for Cox and Fredi

Gonzalez between stints in the bushes. Given a chance as interim manager after Gonzalez was fired in 2016, Snitker won the first of four straight NL East crowns just two years later. He even survived a front-office shakeup that brought in Anthopoulos, an analytics-oriented executive 20 years his junior.

Somehow, the Old School guy and the *wunderkind* hit it off, with a Manager of the Year award and World Series ring to follow. The oldest manager in the National League at 66, Snitker took a page from the Cox playbook, asking only that his young charges showed up on time and played hard. He stayed out of their hair and let them do their thing.

Snitker's reward, long in coming, was his first journey to the World Series—matched against ex-Brave Dusty Baker, second-oldest active manager in the majors at age 72 (Tony La Russa is 77). They had the oldest combined age of any managers in the history of the Fall Classic.

Like Snitker, Baker also had a Hank Aaron connection. Mentored by the superstar, he was even in the on-deck circle for Atlanta on April 8, 1974, the date Aaron broke Babe Ruth's lifetime home run record.

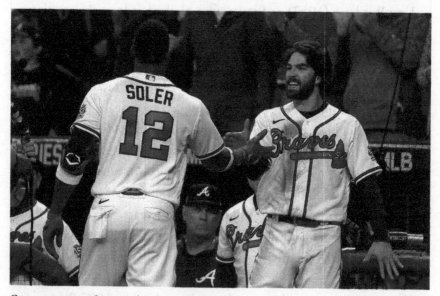

Consecutive seventh-inning home runs by Dansby Swanson and Jorge Soler in the fourth game of the World Series turned a 2–1 deficit into a 3-2 victory at Truist Park on October 30. *Credit: Getty Images*

The home runs flew for the Braves in the postseason. In six World Series games, for example, Soler had three go-ahead homers, including a towering three-run shot in the third inning of the decisive sixth game against Houston right-hander Luis Garcia. Before that shot, which went out of Minute Maid Park with the roof open and onto the street below, he became the first man to lead off a World Series with a home run and added a Game Four solo shot that narrowly cleared the left-field fence in Truist Park. At 6'5" and 245 pounds, he was hardly a typical leadoff man but then again, neither was Acuña.

Soler, who had tested positive for COVID before the playoffs started, got into only 11 games but connected when it counted. Duvall, Pederson, and Rosario also had three postseason homers but Freeman had five, tops on the team, and knocked in 11 runs, tied with Rosario for best among the Braves. Atlanta had 23 postseason homers, tops among the 10 playoff teams, and had a +9 home run differential, tied for the largest by any team in a World Series, with the 1956 Yankees, who hit 12 to 3 by the Dodgers.

Duvall, a low-average, high-power hitter whose eyes light up with men on base, had the only postseason grand slam, in the first inning of the fifth game. But the Braves lost that early 4–0 lead in the "bullpen game" by a 9–5 score. Duvall ended the season as the league leader in runs batted in (113) and the winner of a Gold Glove for his play in right field (though he spent the bulk of the postseason in center to make room for Rosario in left and Soler in right). Duvall, Freeman, Austin Riley, and Ozzie Albies all topped the 30-homer plateau.

Rosario, who cost the Braves only rotund pinch-hitter Pablo Sandoval, had been so hot in the preceding NL Championship Series that opposing manager Dave Roberts conceded, "We couldn't figure him out."

Thanks to a pair of four-hit games, he solved the difficult Dodgers pitching staff for 14 hits, tying a major-league record for any post-season series, and three home runs. In six games, he hit .560 (14-for-25) with a .607 on-base percentage, 1.040 slugging average, six runs

Adam Duvall and Eddie Rosario each hammered three home runs for the Braves in postseason play, enabling Atlanta to win 11 of 16 games. *Credit: Getty Images*

scored, and nine runs batted in. He had four hits and an RBI in Game Two, another RBI in Game Three, two homers and four RBI in Game Four, plus two hits each in the last two games. One of those was the three-run, fourth-inning homer in Game Six that put the Braves up, 4–1, in a game they won, 4–2.

Meanwhile, the injured Acuña accompanied the Braves on the road, sitting in the dugout and serving as a good-luck charm. He must have helped: Braves pitching paralyzed Yordan Alvarez, Most Valuable Player of the American League Championship Series. Fried pitched the game of his life after Michael Brantley stepped on his ankle in the first inning of the final game. And the much-maligned Will Smith went 2–0 with six saves, a 0.00 ERA, and .139 opponents' average in 11 postseason appearances.

In the on-field celebration that followed Game Six, one notable figure was missing. Alex Anthopoulos, architect of the miracle team, was nowhere to be found. It was later announced that he had tested

Freddie Freeman, whose five postseason homers tied a Fred McGriff club record, shares a victory hug with Braves manager Brian Snitker. *Credit: Getty Images*

positive for COVID, completing the circle of sickness and injury that surrounded but did not suffocate the 2021 Braves.

They won fewer games (88) than any of the playoff teams during the regular season but got hot when the weather warmed and never cooled off—even when a misty rain fell throughout World Series Games Three and Four at Truist Park.

By the end of Game Six, the Braves saw nothing but rainbows.

Pearl Man

Joc Pederson's penchant for wearing pearls during games led to brisk sales of pearls to Braves fans. During the team's victory parade, Pederson threw necklaces to spectators as if they were Mardi Gras beads.

Three days after the end of the World Series, the Braves staged a parade that started in downtown Atlanta, at the spot where Hank

Aaron's 715th home run ball landed, and snaked its way toward their new ballpark in Cobb County. The World Series trophy was passed around from one player to another. With schools given a special holiday, crowds swelled to more than a million people.

"I can't wait to take this trophy back and show Bobby Cox," said Snitker, who was in the stands when the Cox-led Braves won the first Atlanta world championship in 1995.

The Hall of Fame manager, at the helm for the entire 14-year title run, was confined to his home while recuperating from a stroke.

Snitker is now on a title run of his own. When the 1995 Braves won the World Series, they did it in the year of their fourth straight division title. The 2021 Braves also went all the way in their fourth title year.

Somewhere above the fray, Hank Aaron was enjoying the festivities. With his famous 44 numerals emblazoned into the Truist Park outfield grass, the Braves won 44 games before the All-Star break and 44 games after the All-Star break, winning the World Series in the 44th week of the year.

Braves manager Brian Snitker, in the organization 45 years, with the World Series trophy his team won by defeating the hard-hitting Houston Astros at Minute Maid Park on November 2, 2021. *Credit: Getty Images*

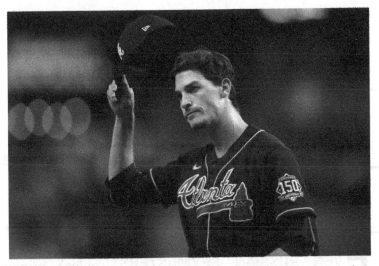

Max Fried yielded four hits, no walks, and no runs during a six-inning scoreless outing in the decisive Game 6 of the 2021 World Series, played at Houston's Minute Maid Park on November 2. *Credit: Getty Images*

Freddie Freeman hit a franchise-record five home runs during the 2021 postseason, helping the Atlanta Braves roll up an 11–5 record against the Milwaukee Brewers, Los Angeles Dodgers, and Houston Astros. *Credit: Dan Schlossberg*

24

COOPERSTOWN

EVEN RUSSIAN SPYMASTERS couldn't manipulate the machinery that governs election to the Baseball Hall of Fame.

Only 1 percent of anyone who played Major League Baseball ever gets a plaque in Cooperstown.

Since election requires 75 percent of the vote, and since totals are invariably skewed by writers who fail to fill out all 10 slots on their ballots, some of the biggest legends have endured unexpectedly long waits.

Superstar pitchers Carl Hubbell, Lefty Grove, and Grover Cleveland Alexander finally got in on their third attempt. Joe DiMaggio needed four, Rogers Hornsby five, Hank Greenberg nine, and Duke Snider 11. Neither Gil Hodges, who had the most RBI during the '50s, nor Dale Murphy, a two-time MVP who had the most total bases in the '80s, found their way in.

That's why electing six men in five years was such a feather in the cap for the Atlanta Braves.

Pitchers Greg Maddux and Tom Glavine, along with manager Bobby Cox, were among the six-member Class of 2014. One year later, starter-reliever John Smoltz joined them. Then it was John Schuerholz, architect of the 14-year title run, in 2017 and finally Chipper Jones, face of the franchise between Murphy and Freddie Freeman, one year later.

Maddux, Glavine, Smoltz, and Jones were all selected on the first ballot, while Cox and Schuerholz was named by the Veterans Committee.

The only pitcher with 200 wins and 150 saves, John Smoltz smiles as he receives his plaque from Baseball Hall of Fame president Jeff Idelson.

Credit: Getty Images

Maddux got 97.2 percent of the vote, the tenth best percentage at the time, while Jones ranked right behind him at 97.16 percent.

Glavine got 91.94 percent—a better figure than Pedro Martinez and Christy Mathewson but just a shade behind Jim Palmer. Smoltz, who split his time between the rotation and the relief corps, finished with 82.9 percent, well above the 75 percent he needed.

Once players are picked, nobody remembers those percentages. But they do remember the induction ceremonies—especially those of the tomahawk-tinged Class of 2014.

Tom Glavine

Early in his speech, Glavine said, "I'd like to take an extra minute to thank Greg and Bobby. It's hard to imagine that a day like this could get any better but for me, it does—to have the opportunity to go into the

Hall of Fame with two guys who had such a profound impact on me as a person and on my career... And I can't tell you how good [Bobby] was at pumping [us] up all the time, how many times I'd pitch a bad game, read his comments in the newspaper the next day, and think, 'Hey, what game were you watching and how did I not win?' Bobby, thank you so much for all your guidance. I appreciate everything you did for me."

The well-spoken southpaw also singled out Leo Mazzone, one of three men, along with Cox and Smoltz, to wear Atlanta colors throughout the 14-year streak.

"Leo, when you first came to Atlanta and said you wanted me to throw twice between starts, I thought you were crazy. My arm already hurt at the time, so I wasn't really sure what throwing more was going to do to me. But boy, did that help!"

The lefty also thanked one-time Braves owner Ted Turner for bringing Cox, Schuerholz, and former team president Stan Kasten into the organization and for providing the resources to get players who contributed to the unprecedented title run.

For Glavine, the best examples he had were his parents, Fred and Millie. "When I was a kid," said the Massachusetts native, "I wanted to be a professional athlete: Red Sox or Bruins. I loved Bobby Orr, Carl Yastrzemski, Carlton Fisk, and Jim Rice, but my parents have always been my role models."

Glavine also paid tribute to his wife Chris, five children, sister Deb, and brothers Fred and Mike.

Greg Maddux

Like Glavine, Maddux mentioned his brother Mike. A one-time pitcher who became a highly-respected pitching coach, Mike Maddux was a few years older.

"I was very fortunate to have a brother I could learn from," said Maddux, who worked more than 5,000 innings with no arm problems. "Everything I was about to do on and off the field, he had already done."

As good a prankster as he was a pitcher, Maddux couldn't resist teasing Smoltz, a golfing buddy who was covering the 2014 inductions for MLB Network. "After many near-misses, we finally got our ring in '95, which was great to share with our coaches, teammates, and the city of Atlanta," he said.

"I'm honored to be on the dais with Bobby Cox. He led us to the promised land and taught us how to play winning baseball and to enjoy our time away from the park. Thank goodness David Justice hit that homer when he did and Glav threw one more clutch game.

After winning the 1995 world championship, Maddux said, he spent the next seven years winning division titles, watching his family grow up, and watching John Smoltz's hairline recede. He also called Smoltz one of his favorite teammates and said he deserved a spot in Cooperstown too.

Smoltz was not the only one on the receiving end of a Maddux punchline. He mentioned how he would chuckle—a least under his breath—when his catchers would get hit in the face by foul tips.

The veteran control artist also conceded he perfected his patented changeup 24 years after first learning it from current Braves pitching coach Rick Kranitz. "It just goes to show you that no matter how old you are, you're still looking to get better," he said.

The mercurial Maddux disappointed Atlanta fans by rejecting the "A" logo for the cap on his bronze bust in the Hall of Fame gallery. "People ask me why my Hall of Fame plaque has no logo," he said. "I spent 12 years in Chicago and 11 in Atlanta, but both places are very special to me. Without experiences in both cities, I would not be standing here today."

Mantra From Maddux

Greg Maddux once gathered a group of young pitchers at the Braves spring training camp. "You know why I'm a millionaire?" he said. "It's because I can throw my fastball where I want to. You know why I have beachfront property in L.A.? Because I can change speeds." With that, he walked away, feeling he fulfilled Leo Mazzone's request for a lecture to the kids.

John Smoltz

One year later, Smoltz was standing there. Because he retired a year after Maddux and Glavine, Smoltz had to wait to join them in the hallowed Hall. Once he got in, however, he gave the Braves the only trio of starters in Cooperstown who spent at least a decade together as teammates.

He also broke other new ground: he was the first player elected to the Hall of Fame after his career was interrupted by Tommy John surgery. Just as John missed the 1974 campaign to undergo the ulnar collateral ligament reconstruction surgery on his elbow, Smoltz sat out the 2000 season for the same reason. At 34, he wondered whether he would ever make it back.

Smoltz did return to the starting rotation, but not right away. He spent three-and-a-half years in the Atlanta bullpen, performing at a high level but working far fewer innings than he did as a starter. With millions watching his induction on MLB Network, Smoltz said the surgery can turn a patient into *The Six Million Dollar Man*: better, faster, and stronger. But he also said parents should not rush teenagers to undergo the procedure.

"I'd be remiss if I did not talk about Tommy John," said Smoltz, whose half-dozen injuries also included bone spurs, bone chips, elbow inflammation, multiple elbow sprains, tendinitis, and shoulder surgery. To compensate for the pain, he even changed his delivery, dropping from overhand to three-quarters delivery, and flirted with a knuckleball.

"I've been given an opportunity as the only player inducted into the Hall of Fame after Tommy John surgery. It's an epidemic—something that is affecting our game. It's something that I thought would cost me my career but thanks to Dr. James Andrews and all those before him, performing the surgery with such precision has caused it to be almost a false-read, like a band-aid you put on your arm."

Smoltz admitted that he never pestered Maddux and Glavine about Induction Weekend. "I stayed away from asking them Hall of Fame questions for a lot of reasons," he said. "I didn't want to do anything until this day came but there will be a variety of questions that I'll have as time goes on. I enjoyed last year so much that I can't put into words the appreciation I have for the Hall. I couldn't believe how many people were there, how unique and neat that town is, and how nice it was that I got a chance to play golf by myself in an hour and 40 minutes while they were at dinner. It was like a little slice of heaven."

So is Cooperstown, a Central New York hamlet with one traffic light, one flagpole, and a tiny, oblong diner squeezed into a small patch of real estate on Main Street, the only major thoroughfare in a town of 1,200 permanent residents—many of whom rent their homes and driveways during Induction Weekend.

"This is an honor I could not have anticipated when I started playing baseball and even today," said the longtime pitcher, who got 455 of the 549 votes cast for the Class of 2015. "I'm not comfortable with titles but I'm relishing this one and I will for the rest of my life."

Responding to the good-natured ribbing by Maddux and Glavine from the same pulpit one year earlier, Smoltz pulled out a black wig and put it on as the crowd outside the Clark Sports Center roared. But that didn't stop the teasing. After all, Chipper Jones wanted a turn too.

Three years later, he got it. Jones capped his induction speech by saying, "Smoltzie always pitched like his hair was on fire. That makes sense when you look at him now."

One year after Greg Maddux and Tom Glavine teased him about his bald head, John Smoltz drew laughs at his Hall of Fame induction by donning a wig.
Credit: Getty Images

Chipper Jones

The 2018 induction of Jones, the nation's top amateur draft choice in 1990, doubled the number of No. 1 picks who reached the Hall of Fame. Ken Griffey, Jr., drafted in 1987 and elected in 2016, was the first.

As in 2014, there were six new inductees that year. But Jones spoke first, an unfamiliar leadoff spot for a man who batted third for his entire career with the Braves. Organizers were worried that the lanky Floridian might have to make an early exit because pregnant wife Taylor had a due date that coincided with the July 29 induction.

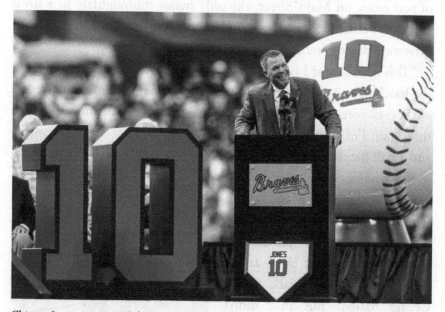

Chipper Jones was so good during a 19-year career spent entirely with the Braves that his Number 10 was retired by the team.
Credit: Getty Images

"We decided to name him Cooper in honor of this occasion," Jones said of his soon-to-be seventh child. One of the others is named Shea because of Chipper's prowess at producing big numbers against the New York Mets at their longtime home, Shea Stadium.

Chipper the Switcher

Even though he did things few other switch-hitters could match, Chipper Jones said it wasn't easy. "Trying to keep both swings up to big-league standards is rough," said Jones, whose Braves career stretched from 1993 to 2012. "It's a constant mind-game. Sometimes you're hitting it good righthanded and can't find it going the other way. You're going to have a month where both ways don't feel real good. And you're going to have a month where nobody can get you out. It was a constant roller-coaster ride."

With Taylor still expecting the next morning, Jones joined the other Class of 2018 inductees in an hour-long informal roundtable and thrilled the Doubleday Field crowd by taking a few swings at pitches thrown by his father, Larry Wayne Jones Sr. He wasn't wearing his familiar No. 10 Braves jersey, but the lefthanded swing was unmistakable.

The image of the former third baseman in the Hall of Fame gallery was also unmistakable. Unlike rushed photos taken for driver's licenses, the bronze Chipper Jones relief had the slugger's approval. "It's pretty good," he said. "They could have done worse. I've had some bobble-heads that looked like I was in a train wreck. But that one was pretty good. I liked it."

Chipper's Heroes

Chipper Jones became a switch-hitter because of Mickey Mantle. "I didn't get to see Mickey play," he said, "but I heard tales of his greatness. He was the reason my dad made me a switch-hitter at such an early age. My heroes were the guys I grew up watching who played my position: Cal Ripken Jr., Ozzie Smith, and Barry Larkin."

The outdoor crowd of 53,000, undulating in the Central New York sun, also liked Chipper. He admitted later that he kept his composure by averting his eyes from the video highlights clip that preceded his speech and later from his family members in the front row of the VIP section.

Among those he thanked, in addition to his family, friends, and coaches, were Bobby Cox and Willie Stargell.

Heart of Dixie

It's rare these days, but Chipper Jones spent his entire 19-year career with just one team. "I'm a Southern kid who grew up in the South," he said. "The Atlanta Braves and all their farm teams are here. My family and friends are here. So many times I played with guys who left, came back, and said, 'The grass isn't greener on the other side. I wish I had never left.'"

Addressing Cox, one of 51 incumbent Hall of Famers seated behind him, Jones said, "Bobby, you believed in me before I truly believed I belonged in the big leagues. On Opening Day of 1995, you put me in the three-hole in front of Fred McGriff and David Justice. You knew that hitting me in front of those two dudes would get me a lot of fast-balls—and it worked."

Stargell, like Cox, changed Chipper's life. "He picked up my bat and said, 'Son, I pick my teeth with bigger pieces of wood than this.' He suggested I swing with the biggest bat I could get around on a 90 mile-per-hour heater. I swung that heavy bat until the day I retired."

On a more serious note, Jones acknowledged Hank Aaron, the 85-year-old Braves icon, who drew a prolonged standing ovation from the crowd, and closed by thanking his fans with the sign-language gesture for "I love you."

The Mathews Legacy

Before Chipper Jones journeyed from Braves third baseman to Hall of Fame member, Eddie Mathews made the same trip. According to John Schuerholz, "I saw Eddie play from afar. I know what a great player he was and how he led the Braves. But having been with Chipper up close and personal, side-by-side for 19 years, he was a true leader in bringing his teammates along with him and having guys play well enough to win 14 consecutive division championships. [Chipper's] place in that lineup, in the clubhouse, and in the dugout had a lot to do with that. And Eddie was the same way."

Bobby Cox

Cox was also grateful to his fellow inductees. "I am truly humbled to stand here before you in Cooperstown with two men who pitched for me and two managers who made my life as a manager so challenging [Joe Torre and Tony La Russa]," Cox said during his speech. "To Tom Glavine and Greg Maddux, and I have to mention the third member of the Big Three in John Smoltz, I can honestly say I would not be standing here today if it weren't for you guys."

To Braves opponents, it always seemed that one of them was pitching—and sometimes two, since Smoltz spent three years as Atlanta's closer. The pitchers helped Cox's teams compile six 100-win seasons and win 2,504 games in 29 seasons—all but four with the Braves in two separate stints.

In a video that preceded Cox's speech, Glavine praised Cox for his preparation abilities.

Tim Hudson, whose nine-year Atlanta tenure began in the last year of the title streak, explained to the media why Cox had such a superb reputation as a players' manager. "He was a manager who felt like a teammate, a friend, and a father figure. I'm proud that I played for one of the best managers a player could ever ask for."

Maddux won the only World Series ring of his career under Cox. "Bobby taught us to play winning baseball and enjoy our time away from the park," he said, noting that the manager encouraged his pitchers to swap stories, secrets, and pitching philosophies on the golf course.

Between two stints as Braves manager, Bobby Cox also spent five years as Atlanta's GM.
Credit: Getty Images

According to Smoltz, "A small part of Bobby Cox changes you as a baseball player. Twenty years with the man changes your life."

Chipper Jones, the lifelong Brave, best explained how Cox reached Cooperstown: "He never played an inning for the Atlanta Braves. He never threw a pitch and he never got a hit. But he was responsible for more than 2,000 wins."

The Sporting News picked him as National League Manager of the Year eight times. "It's really been a great ride for all these seasons, every one with a changing cast of characters," said Cox, who endured dual knee replacements—probably caused in part by endless trips onto the field to argue with umpires (he had a record 158 regular-season and three postseason ejections).

"I'll never forget the '91 season and the '95 season when we went to the World Series and got all the way past Cleveland."

Bobby's Way

Asked about his managing philosophy, Bobby Cox said, "I was my own manager. I had no 'book' on the subject. I didn't pattern myself after anybody." In 29 seasons, all but four with the Braves, he won 15 division crowns, five pennants, one world championship, and one wild-card title.

John Schuerholz

It was Schuerholz whose acquisitions made that run possible and allowed him to become the first general manager to win world championships in both leagues. He often had to be his own talent scout and accountant, balancing a limited budget with one eye on arbitration cases and the other on the potential demands of newly-acquired players.

"In over 50 years of baseball," the longtime executive told the Cooperstown crowd, "I've had the great honor of attending many of these inductions. I sat out there where you're seated today, watching in awe and admiration as the greats of the game were recognized and honored. I really liked my seat out there on that lawn. But I must confess that I love my new seat up here on this stage a lot more."

Raised in a blue-collar Baltimore neighborhood, Schuerholz played stickball against the walls of brick factory buildings while his father played three years of minor-league ball before breaking his leg. He attended an Orioles tryout camp but never hooked on, becoming a teacher instead. But the love of baseball wouldn't quit and Schuerholz wrote a blind letter to the local ballclub. He wound up working with Frank Cashen, Harry Dalton, and Lou Gorman before jumping to the expansion Kansas City Royals with Gorman. At 41, he became the youngest GM in the game.

Schuerholz watched the first professional game played by future Hall of Famer George Brett, then 17, and befriended Kansas City baseball legend Buck O'Neil, whom he later hired as a scout. After putting together the 1985 Royals team that won a surprise world championship, he jumped to the Braves after a chance meeting with then-Braves president Stan Kasten. He never complained about inheriting Bobby Cox.

It turns out, the tandem of Cox and Schuerholz shared the same philosophy. "As my father and grandfather and many smart baseball people have often reminded me, pitching is what you win with," Schuerholz said. "We won in 1995 with pitching. Cleveland was the best team we faced all year. They were an offensive juggernaut. They led the world in almost every offensive category. They were the marauders of the American League that year. They were built on hitting and we were built on pitching."

The resulting 1995 world championship flag is the third in franchise history: one each in Boston (1914), Milwaukee (1957), and Atlanta (1995). Schuerholz and Cox, who still consult often, yearn for more.

Schuerholz has strong attachments to the game.

"I'm 76 years old," he said during his speech, "and I've been in the game

Two of the big reasons the Braves reached the 2018 playoffs were switch-hitting second baseman Ozzie Albies (1) and slugging outfielder Ronald Acuña Jr., who was NL Rookie of the Year at age 20.

Credit: Getty Images

more than 50 years. But my heart still beats with baseball. The first thing I do every morning is catch up on the games played the night before."

Still a Braves partisan, he has switched his allegiance from Maddux, Glavine, and Smoltz to Acuña, Albies, and Freeman. But he still relishes the myriad of magical moments created by the future Hall of Famers he brought to the team.

Five for the Future

Like most Braves fans, Schuerholz believes Chipper's 2018 induction will not be the last from the teams of the streak. Gary Sheffield and Andruw Jones remain on the writers' ballot while Fred McGriff, Leo Mazzone, and Dale Murphy could be chosen by one of the four Veterans Committees.

According to Schuerholz, who watched them every day, "Andruw Jones was the best center fielder in baseball for 10 straight years. To have those skills and tools and to use them to help your team win for 10 years [is pretty impressive]. He was the best combination offensive and defensive centerfielder in the game for more than a decade. He played a few extra years that probably deterred some of the voters but if they measured him on the pinnacle of those 10 years, he had a remarkable decade. I think many will look at him as a worthy candidate.

Jones Over Justice

When the 1996 Atlanta Braves lost regular rightfielder David Justice to a dislocated shoulder, they promoted 19-year-old Andruw Jones ahead of schedule. He got a hit in his debut on August 15, homered for the first time the next night, and started 22 games down the stretch. Then, after playing just 31 games in the majors, he homered in each of his first two World Series at-bats at Yankee Stadium. Justice never played for the Braves again.

"As for McGriff, if you look at the totality of his career, the consistency of production, his character, and his contributions to the game, there's nobody that presents those assets better than Fred McGriff has."

McGriff remains the classic case of a Hall of Fame wannabe: he just missed 500 home runs, didn't reach 3,000 hits, and never won an MVP award. But he had as many home runs (493) as Lou Gehrig, ranks in the Top 50 in career runs batted in, and was a feared and dangerous clutch hitter. One well-known authority, Joe Posnanski of MLB.com, wrote on January 16, 2018, "The Hall of Fame would be better with the Crime Dog in it."

Both McGriff and Sheffield, unlike Jones and Mazzone, had relatively short tenures in Atlanta.

McGriff played parts of five seasons for the Braves and was a key cog in the 1995 world championship team. While playing for eight teams in 22 seasons, Sheffield surfaced in Atlanta for just two years—both during the streak—but was there long enough to set a single-season club record for runs batted in (132 in 2003).

Andruw Jones was one of five outfielders to win ten consecutive Gold Gloves but was also a prodigious slugger who homered in his first two World Series at-bats.

Credit: Getty Images

Two years later, Andruw Jones hit a club-record 51 home runs, fell just four short of Sheffield's RBI mark, and played the best center field since Willie Mays (maybe even better, according to Bobby Cox and several others who saw him every day).

In the field, Jones operated on instinct; he would start running for the ball before it was pitched.

He had the range for center, the arm for right, and the speed to cover more territory than the Manifest Destiny. After stealing 56 bases in one minor-league season, he topped 20 in each of his first four big-league campaigns.

With Ozzie Smith, Luis Aparicio, Bill Mazeroski, and other glovemen already ensconced in Cooperstown, there should be room for Andruw too—especially since he also provided power (454 home runs).

Andruw's Dad

Henry Jones, father of Andruw, was a catcher for Curacao's national team during the '70s—a time when the island wasn't heavily scouted by big-league clubs. He did pass the torch to his son, giving him his first glove at age three and his first bat at age four. Seven years later, Andruw went to Japan with a traveling All-Star team. He signed at 16, getting a bonus of $46,000 from the Braves.

That's the reason *New York Post* baseball writer Ken Davidoff placed Andruw third on his Hall of Fame ballot the first time Jones became eligible. "He played at a high level for just 11 years and much of his value came from his phenomenal center field defense that would pass any eye test and gets substantiated by the analytics," Davidson wrote.

The writer complained that 10 ballot spots and a 10-year tenure on the ballot (down from 15) were too limiting. His 2018 ballot included both Chipper and Andruw Jones but not Vladimir Guerrero, who was chosen anyway, or Sheffield, whom he also labeled a Hall of Famer.

On the surface, Sheffield's .292 lifetime batting average, 509 home runs, nine All-Star appearances, and three strong runs at MVP awards all seem Hall-worthy. But his defensive metrics, both as an infielder and later as an outfielder, were shaky—making him almost the opposite of Andruw Jones, a gifted fielder but career .254 batter, in the eyes of some voters.

Playing for eight different teams, and running into controversy at more than one stop, also hurts Sheffield, while McGriff's nomadic career (six teams in 19 seasons) might also make voters hesitate. But Braves fans see it differently.

They also believe Mazzone should be the first coach to crack the Hall of Fame gallery. One of three Braves, along with Cox and Smoltz, to wear Braves colors throughout the 14-year streak, Mazzone was responsible not only for Maddux, Glavine, and Smoltz but also for a raft of lesser pitchers plucked off the proverbial scrap heap and resurrected by the fast-talking coach. Almost all of those pitchers,

During his two-year tenure with the Braves, Gary Sheffield produced a 132-RBI season, breaking Hank Aaron's single-season club RBI record.

Credit: Getty Images

from Russ Ortiz to Jaret Wright, did far better under Mazzone than they did before they arrived or after they left.

Ask Mazzone and he'll say that Johnny Sain, another ex-Brave, deserves to be the first coach in Cooperstown. Outspoken, opinionated, and set in his ways, Mazzone mirrors the personality of Sain, whose penchant for producing 20-game winners was offset by a fiercely independent streak that ruffled multiple managers. Whether their old-school approach would thrive in an age of analytics is subject to conjecture. But nobody can argue with their record.

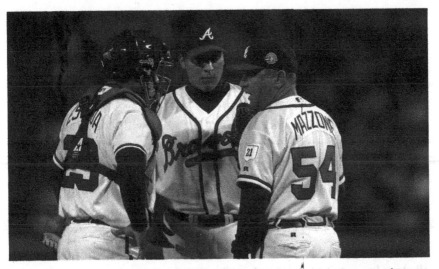

Leo Mazzone, here conferring with catcher Johnny Estrada and pitcher Russ Ortiz, served as Atlanta pitching coach throughout the 14-year title streak, making him a Cooperstown candidate.

Credit: Getty Images

When Mazzone met Sain, he was cooking TV dinners in a trailer parked outside the Braves spring training camp in West Palm Beach.

It was in West Palm Beach where Dale Murphy moved from a scatter-armed catcher to first base, right field, and center field. Although Bobby Cox traded him to Philadelphia in his last major deal as Atlanta's general manager, Murphy will always identify as a Brave.

The National League's version of Cal Ripken Jr., Murphy never smoked, drank, or cursed because of his Mormon faith. His work ethic was just as powerful, since he was a durable player who almost never missed a game during his peak seasons.

He played in 740 consecutive games from 1982 to '85, won consecutive National League MVP awards, and just missed another when he led the league in home runs, slugging, and total bases in 1984. He finished with 398 home runs—one behind first-ballot inductee Al Kaline—and more total bases during the '80s than any other player, including George Brett, Dave Winfield, Paul Molitor, Mike Schmidt, and Eddie Murray. Only Schmidt had more home runs during the decade and only Murray had more runs batted in. But Murphy was

299

first in extra-base hits and runs scored. He won two RBI crowns (two more than Willie Mays) and two home run crowns (two more than Stan Musial).

Murphy also won five Gold Gloves—five more than Jim Rice, who also had fewer homers. Other than suspected steroids abuser Barry Bonds, Murphy is the only National Leaguer with consecutive MVP trophies not enshrined in Cooperstown.

"I would love to see Dale Murphy in the Hall of Fame," said Bobby Cox, who saved the career of the young slugger, troubled by bad knees, moving him out from behind the plate. "He went from catcher to first base to left field to center field and became a Gold Glove winner. He was MVP twice. And his character, what he did for communities and all that, has to add in somewhere."

Dale Murphy won consecutive National League MVP awards in 1982 and 1983 but won't reach Cooperstown unless a Veterans Committee elects him.

Credit: Getty Images

Aaron added another point in Murphy's favor. "One thing that always taught me a lot about a ballplayer," he said, "was how he ran the bases. One of the most valuable things a player can do for a team is to go from first to third on a single. Murphy did that. He almost never got thrown out. When he saw a ball hit, he just knew he was going to get to third base. He had that baseball instinct you can't teach."

That instinct also helped Murphy at the plate, where he showed surprising discipline for a slugger. In 1987, his last great season, he reached career peaks with 44 home runs and a .417 on-base percentage. Within a year, however, his knees started barking again, causing a deep decline in production and performance. The Murphy balloon burst—just as the Andruw Jones balloon would burst 20 years later.

The youngest man to win consecutive National League MVP awards, Murphy has been enshrined in the Atlanta Braves Hall of Fame for more than 15 years. Cooperstown should be next—especially if electors pay attention to *baseball-reference.com* statistics that place him higher than the average Hall of Famer in three of four comparative categories.

His No. 3 is retired by the team, along with the numbers of Aaron (44), Cox (6), Glavine (47), Chipper Jones (10), Maddux (31), Eddie Mathews (41), Phil Niekro (35), Smoltz (29), and Warren Spahn (21). The jerseys of Andruw Jones (25), McGriff (27), Sheffield (11), and Mazzone (54) could join them soon.

When Derek Jeter, Larry Walker, and ex-Brave Ted Simmons were inducted on September 8, 2021, the Hall of Fame had 333 members, including 263 former players, 38 executives, 22 managers, and 10 umpires. Writers and broadcasters receive separate recognition via awards voted on by special panels.

BIBLIOGRAPHY

BOOKS

Bodley, Hal. *How Baseball Explains America*. Chicago: Triumph Books, 2014.

Boyle, Timm. *The Most Valuable Player in Baseball*. Jefferson, NC: McFarland, 2003.

Caruso, Gary. *The Braves Encyclopedia*. Philadelphia: Temple University Press, 1995.

Castle, George. *Throwbacks—Old School Baseball Players in Today's Game*. Dulles, VA: Brassey's Inc., 2003.

Chuck, Bill and Jim Kaplan. *Walkoffs, Last Licks, and Final Outs*. Chicago: ACTA Sports, 2008.

Cohen, Richard M., David S. Neft, and Michael L. Neft. *The Sports Encyclopedia Baseball 2007*. New York: St. Martin's Griffin, 2007.

Decatur, Doug. *Traded—Inside the Most Lopsided Trades in Baseball History*. Chicago: ACTA Sports, 2009.

Dewey, Donald and Nicholas Acocella. *Total Ballclubs—The Ultimate Book of Baseball Teams*. Wilmington, DE: SPORT Media Publishing, 2005.

Glavine, Tom with Nick Cafardo. *None But the Braves—A Pitcher, a Team, a Champion*. New York: HarperCollins, 1996.

Goldberg, Robert and Gerald Jay Goldberg. *Citizen Turner—The Wild Rise of an American Tycoon*. New York: Harcourt Brace, 1995.

Klapisch, Bob and Pete Van Wieren. *The Braves—An Illustrated History of America's Team*. Atlanta: Turner Publishing, 1995.

Krabbenhoft, Herman O. *Leadoff Batters of Major League Baseball*. Jefferson, NC: McFarland, 2006.

Kuenster, John. *Heartbreakers—Baseball's Most Agonizing Defeats*. Chicago: Ivan R. Dee, 2001.

Lopez, Javy with Gary Caruso. *Behind the Plate—A Catcher's View of the Braves Dynasty.* Chicago: Triumph Books, 2012.

Lyons, Douglas B. *100 Years of Who's Who in Baseball.* Guilford, CT: Lyons Press, 2015.

Mazzone, Leo: *Tales from the Mound.* Champaign, IL: Sports Publishing, 2006.

Neary, Kevin and Leigh A. Tobin. *Major League Dads—Baseball's Best Players Reflect on the Fathers Who Inspired Them.* Philadelphia: Running Press, 2012.

Purdy, Dennis. *The Team by Team Encyclopedia of Major League Baseball.* New York: Workman, 2006.

Rosenberg, I. J. Bravo! *The Inside Story of the Atlanta Braves' 1995 World Series Championship.* Marietta, GA: Longstreet Press, 1995.

_____. *Encore! The Inside Story of the Atlanta Braves' Second Consecutive National League Championship.* Marietta, GA: Longstreet Press, 1992.

_____. Miracle Season! *The Inside Story of the 1991 Atlanta Braves' Race for Baseball Glory.* Atlanta:Turner Publishing, 1991.

Schlossberg, Dan: *Baseball Bits—The Best Stories, Facts, and Trivia from the Dugout to the Outfield.* Alpha, NJ: Alpha Books, 2008.

_____. *Baseball Gold*—Mining Nuggets from Our National Pastime. Chicago: Triumph, 2007.

_____. George Brett, John Delcos, Tony Gwynn, and Bob Nightengale. *Chipper Jones—A Brave Legend in the Making.* Dallas: Beckett Publications, 2000.

_____. *The 300 Club—Have We Seen the Last of Baseball's 300-Game Winners?* Olathe, KS: Ascend Books, 2010.

_____. Michael Gershman, Pete Palmer, David Pietrusza, and John Thorn. *Total Braves.* New York: Penguin Books, 1996.

Schuerholz, John. *Built to Win, Inside Stories and Leadership Strategies from Baseball's Winningest GM.* New York: Warner Books, 2007.

Shanks, Bill. *Scout's Honor—The Bravest Way to Build a Winning Team.* New York: Sterling and Ross, 2005.

Silvia, Tony. *Fathers and Sons in Baseball Broadcasting.* Jefferson, NC: McFarland, 2009.

Sink, Richard. *Chop to the Top! The Behind-the-Scenes Look at the Team and the Town it Turned Upside Down.* Cornelius, NC: Tomahawk Press, 1992.

Smoltz, John. *Starting and Closing.* New York: William Morrow, 2012.

Stark, Jayson. *Wild Pitches—Rumblings, Grumblings, and Reflections on the Game I Love.* Chicago: Triumph, 2014.

Weiss, Peter. *Longshots—The Most Unlikely Championship Teams in Baseball History.* Holbrook, MA: Bob Adams, 1992.

Wendel, Tim. *Down to the Last Pitch: How the 1991 Minnesota Twins and Atlanta Braves Gave Us the Best World Series of All Time.* Cambridge, MA: Da Capo, 2014.

Westcott, Rich. *Great Stuff—Baseball's Most Amazing Pitching Feats.* New York: Sports Publishing, 2014.

Whitaker, Lang. *In the Time of Bobby Cox—The Atlanta Braves, Their Manager, My Couch, Two Decades, and Me.* New York: Scribner, 2011.

Van Wieren, Pete. *Of Mikes and Men—A Lifetime of Braves Baseball.* Chicago: Triumph Books, 2010.

Wilkinson, Jack. *100 Things Braves Fans Should Know and Do Before They Die.* Chicago: Triumph Books, 2011.

Zack, Bill. *Tomahawked—The Inside Story of the Atlanta Braves' Tumultuous Season.* New York: Simon & Schuster, 1993.

BROADCASTS

Braves Banter [iTunes and BlogTalkRadio.com]

PUBLICATIONS

Atlanta Braves Media Guides [1991–2006]
USA TODAY Sports Weekly
USA TODAY

WEBSITES

Baseball-almanac.com
Baseball-Reference.com
MLB.com
SABR.org

APPENDIX

During the Streak (1991–2005)

Members of the Atlanta Braves with special achievements during the 14-year title run:

Most Valuable Players
1991 Terry Pendleton
1999 Chipper Jones

World Series MVP
1995 Tom Glavine

Championship Series MVP
1991 Steve Avery
1992 John Smoltz
1995 Mike Devereaux
1996 Javy Lopez
1999 Eddie Perez

All-Star Game MVP
1994 Fred McGriff

Cy Young Awards
1991 Tom Glavine
1993 Greg Maddux

1994 Greg Maddux
1995 Greg Maddux
1996 John Smoltz
1998 Tom Glavine

Rookie of the Year Award
2000 Rafael Furcal

Manager of the Year Awards
1991 Bobby Cox
2004 Bobby Cox
2005 Bobby Cox

Gold Gloves
1992 Terry Pendleton
1993 Greg Maddux
1994 Greg Maddux
1995 Greg Maddux, Marquis Grissom
1996 Greg Maddux, Marquis Grissom
1997 Greg Maddux
1998 Greg Maddux, Andruw Jones
1999 Greg Maddux, Andruw Jones
2000 Greg Maddux, Andruw Jones
2001 Greg Maddux, Andruw Jones
2002 Greg Maddux, Andruw Jones
2003 Mike Hampton, Andruw Jones
2004 Andruw Jones
2005 Andruw Jones

Three-Homer Games
1992 Jeff Blauser (July 12)
2002 Andruw Jones (September 25)

40-Homer Seasons
1993 David Justice (40)

1998 Andres Galarraga (44)

1999 Chipper Jones (45)

2003 Javy Lopez (43)

2005 Andruw Jones (51)

No-Hitters
1991 Kent Mercker, Mark Wohlers, and Alejandro Pena (September 11)

1994 Kent Mercker (April 8)

20-Win Seasons
1991 Tom Glavine (20–11)

1992 Tom Glavine (20–8)

1993 Tom Glavine (22–6), Greg Maddux (20–10)

1997 Denny Neagle (20–5)

1998 Tom Glavine (20–6)

1999 Tom Glavine (21–9)

2003 Russ Ortiz (21–7)

40-Save Seasons
2002 John Smoltz (55)

2003 John Smoltz (45)

2002 John Smoltz (44)

15-Strikeout Game
1992 John Smoltz (May 24)

All-Star Selections
1991 Tom Glavine

1992 Tom Glavine, John Smoltz, Ron Gant, Terry Pendleton

1993 Tom Glavine, John Smoltz, Steve Avery, David Justice, Jeff Blauser

1994 Greg Maddux, Fred McGriff, David Justice

1995 Greg Maddux, Fred McGriff
1996 Tom Glavine, Greg Maddux, John Smoltz, Mark Wohlers, Chipper Jones, Fred McGriff
1997 Tom Glavine, Greg Maddux, Denny Neagle, Chipper Jones, Javy Lopez, Kenny Lofton, Jeff Blauser
1998 Tom Glavine, Greg Maddux, Chipper Jones, Javy Lopez, Andres Galarraga, Walt Weiss
1999 Kevin Millwood, Brian Jordan
2000 Tom Glavine, Greg Maddux, Chipper Jones, Andruw Jones, Andres Galarraga
2001 John Burkett, Chipper Jones
2002 Tom Glavine, Mike Remlinger, Andruw Jones
2003 John Smoltz, Russ Ortiz, Javy Lopez, Andruw Jones, Gary Sheffield, Rafael Furcal, Marcus Giles
2004 Johnny Estrada
2005 John Smoltz, Andruw Jones

Comparing the Record

From 1991 through 2005, the Atlanta Braves finished first 14 times in a row—a professional sports record.

At the time their streak ended, no other team had come close to duplicating that feat.

Three teams had done it nine times: the 1957–65 Boston Celtics, 1982–90 Los Angeles Lakers, and 1995–2003 Colorado Avalanche. The NFL mark of seven straight was held by the 1973–79 Los Angeles Rams.

The Braves also had 14 straight postseason appearances, three more than the New York Yankees of 1995–2005. Next in line were the 1949–53 and 1960–64 Yankees, both with five, and the 1971–75 Oakland A's and 1995–99 Cleveland Indians, also with five.

The Yankees also rank second to the Braves with eight consecutive division titles from 1998 to 2005.

The Los Angeles Dodgers won eight straight before their streak ended in 2021. Even though they won 106 games, they finished one game behind the San Francisco Giants in the National League West title chase.

Building a Winner

During their 14-year title streak, the Atlanta Braves were World Series winners in 1995. Here's how that team was built:

Amateur Free Agent Draft

	Draft	Phase	Round
STEVE AVERY	JUNE 1988	REGULAR	1ST
JEFF BLAUSER	JUNE 1984	SECONDARY	1ST
BRAD CLONTZ	JUNE 1992	REGULAR	10TH
TOM GLAVINE	JUNE 1984	REGULAR	2ND
CHIPPER JONES	JUNE 1990	REGULAR	1ST
DAVID JUSTICE	JUNE 1985	REGULAR	4TH
RYAN KLESKO	JUNE 1989	REGULAR	6TH
MARK LEMKE	JUNE 1983	REGULAR	27TH
KENT MERCKER	JUNE 1986	REGULAR	1ST
MIKE MORDECAI	JUNE 1989	REGULAR	7TH
MARK WOHLERS	JUNE 1988	REGULAR	8TH

Acquired by Trade

	From	Date	For
MIKE DEVEREAUX	CHI. (AL)	8/25/95	ANDRE KING
MARQUIS GRISSOM	MON.	4/6/95	ROBERTO KELLY
			TONY TARASCO
			ESTEBAN YAN
			CASH
FRED McGRIFF	S.D.	7/18/93	MELVIN NIEVES
			VINCENT MOORE
			DONNIE ELLIOTT
ALEJANDRO PENA	FLA.	8/31/95	PTBNL
		9/15/95	(CHRIS SEELBACH)
LUIS POLONIA	N.Y. (AL)	8/11/95	TROY HUGHES
JOHN SMOLTZ	DET.	8/13/87	DOYLE ALEXANDER

Signed as Free Agent

	From	Date
RAFAEL BELLIARD	PITT.	12/18/90
PEDRO BORBON	CHI. (AL)	8/25/89
GREG MADDUX	CHI. (NL)	12/9/92
GREG McMICHAEL	CLEV.	4/16/91
CHARLIE O'BRIEN	N.Y. (NL)	11/29/93
DWIGHT SMITH	BAL.	4/12/95

Signed as Non-Drafted Free Agent

	Date
JAVIER LOPEZ	11/6/87
EDUARDO PEREZ	9/27/86

Source: ATLANTA BRAVES

Atlanta Braves Title Clinch Dates During the Streak

Year	Division	Date Clinched	Games Played* (Record)	Final	Final Games Ahead
1991	West	October 5	161 (94–67)	94–68	1.0
1992	West	September 29	156 (94–62)	98–64	8.0
1993	West	October 3	162 (104–58)	104–58	1.0
1995	East	September 13	129 (81–48)	90–54	21.0
1996	East	September 22	155 (93–62)	96–66	8.0
1997	East	September 22	156 (98–58)	101–61	9.0
1998	East	September 14	151 (96–55)	106–56	18.0
1999	East	September 26	156 (99–57)	103–59	6.5
2000	East	September 26	157 (94–63)	95–67	1.0
2001	East	October 5	160 (87–73)	88–74	2.0
2002	East	September 9	142 (90–51)	101–59	19.0
2003	East	September 18	153 (95–58)	101–61	10.0
2004	East	September 24	154 (90–64)	96–66	10.0
2005	East	September 27	158 (90–68)	90–72	2.0

*Games completed and record at the end of the day on "clinch day."

Source: Atlanta Braves

Braves World Series Homers During the Streak

Date	Game	Player	Pitcher	Site
10/22/1991	3	DAVID JUSTICE	SCOTT ERICKSON, MIN	ATL
10/22/1991	3	LONNIE SMITH	SCOTT ERICKSON, MIN	ATL
10/23/1991	4	TERRY PENDLETON	JACK MORRIS, MIN	ATL
10/23/1991	4	LONNIE SMITH	CARL WILLIS, MIN	ATL
10/24/1991	5	DAVID JUSTICE	KEVIN TAPANI, MIN	ATL
10/24/1991	5	LONNIE SMITH	DAVID WEST, MIN	ATL
10/24/1991	5	BRIAN HUNTER	CARL WILLIS, MIN	ATL
10/26/1991	6	TERRY PENDLETON	SCOTT ERICKSON, MIN	MIN
10/17/1992	1	DAMON BERRYHILL	JACK MORRIS, TOR	ATL
10/22/1992	5	DAVID JUSTICE	JACK MORRIS, TOR	TOR
10/22/1992	5	LONNIE SMITH	JACK MORRIS, TOR	TOR
10/21/1995	1	FRED MCGRIFF	OREL HERSHISER, CLE	ATL
10/22/1995	2	JAVY LOPEZ	DENNIS MARTINEZ, CLE	ATL
10/24/1995	3	FRED MCGRIFF	CHARLES NAGY, CLE	CLE
10/24/1995	3	RYAN KLESKO	CHARLES NAGY, CLE	CLE
10/25/1995	4	RYAN KLESKO	KEN HILL, CLE	CLE
10/26/1995	5	LUIS POLONIA	OREL HERSHISER, CLE	CLE
10/26/1995	5	RYAN KLESKO	JOSE MESA, CLE	CLE
10/28/1995	6	DAVID JUSTICE	JIM POOLE, CLE	ATL
10/20/1996	1	ANDRUW JONES	ANDY PETTITTE, NYA	NYA
10/20/1996	1	ANDRUW JONES	BRIAN BOEHRINGER, NYA	NYA
10/20/1996	1	FRED MCGRIFF	BRIAN BOEHRINGER, NYA	NYA
10/23/1996	4	FRED MCGRIFF	KENNY ROGERS, NYA	ATL
10/23/1999	1	CHIPPER JONES	ORLANDO HERNANDEZ, NYA	ATL

Information courtesy of David Vincent, SABR

10 Best Trades During the Streak

Rank	Date	Braves Get	Braves Trade
1.	7/18/93	Fred McGriff	Donnie Elliott, Melvin Nieves, Vince Moore
2.	4/1/91	Otis Nixon, Boi Rodriguez	Jimmy Kremers, Keith Morrison
3.	1/15/2002	Gary Sheffield	Brian Jordan, Odalis Perez, Andy Brown
4.	11/10/98	Bret Boone, Mike Remlinger	Denny Neagle, Michael Tucker, Robbie Bell
5.	4/6/95	Marquis Grissom	Roberto Kelly, Tony Tarasco, Esteban Yan
6.	12/17/2002	Russ Ortiz	Damian Moss, Manuel Mateo
7.	8/28/96	Denny Neagle	Ron Wright, Corey Pointer, Jason Schmidt
8.	12/16/2004	Tim Hudson	Charles Thomas, Dan Meyer, Juan Cruz
9.	11/18/2002	Mike Hampton	Tim Spooneybarger, Ryan Baker
10.	3/31/2005	Jorge Sosa	Nick Green

Also by Dan Schlossberg

The 300 Club: Have We Seen the Last of Baseball's 300-Game Winners?
The Baseball Almanac
Baseball Bits
The Baseball Book of Why
The Baseball Catalog
Baseball Gold
The Baseball IQ Challenge
Baseball Stars of 1985
Baseball Stars of 1986
Baseball Stars of 1987
Called Out But Safe: a Baseball Umpire's Story (also by Al Clark)
Designated Hebrew: the Ron Blomberg Story (also by Ron Blomberg)
Hammerin' Hank: the Henry Aaron Story
Making Airwaves: 60 Years at Milo's Microphone (also by Milo
    Hamilton)
Miracle Over Miami
*The New Baseball Bible: Notes, Nuggets, Lists & Legends From Our
    National Pastime*
Pitching
The Wit & Wisdom of Baseball

INDEX

Note: Photographs and illustrations are indicated by page numbers in *italics*.

A

Aaron, Hank, 39, 83, 96, 100, 108, 150, 204, 215, 232, 245-246, 248, 259, 263, 269, *271*, 275- 276, 279-280, 300-301

Acuña, Ronald, Jr., 258-259, 264, 268, 270, *271*, 277, *278*, *294*, 295

African American, 269

Albies, Ozzie, 258-259, 264, 268, 273, 277, *294*, 295

Alexander, Doyle, 29, 56

Alexander, Grover Cleveland, 282

Alfonseca, Antonio, 239, 243

All-Star Game, 269, 270, 280, 298

Altuve, Jose, 275

Alvarez, Yordan, 278

American League, 272

American League Championship Series, 278

Anderson, Ian, 266, 275

Andersen, Larry, 158

Anderson, Sparky, 34

Andrews, Dr. James, 286

Ankiel, Rick, 260

Anthopoulos, Alex, 257, 271, 276, 278

Aparicio, Luis, 297

Arizona Diamondbacks, 223, 273

Assenmacher, Paul, 136

Atlanta Braves Hall of Fame, 301

Avery, Steve, 29, 35, 42, 45, 49-50, 55, 60, 80, 120, 122-123, 125-127, *127*, 136, 140, 154-155, 157, 165, 168-169, 173, 181

B

Bagwell, Jeff, 91, 110, 164, 190, 206

Baker, Dusty, 236, 276

Baltimore Orioles, 3, 22, 293

Bartholomay, Bill, 5

Baseball Hall of Fame, 280, 282, 285, 288, 295, 297, 298

Batista, Miguel, 223

Batiste, Kim, 157

Bautista, Danny, 175, 196

Baylor, Don, 31, 107, 110

Beane, Billy, 250-251

Bedrosian, Steve, 154-155

Belcher, Tim, 102

Belinda, Stan, 141-142

Bell, Derek, 190

Bell, Mike, 120

Bell, Robbie, 200

Belle, Albert, 46

Belliard, Rafael, 6, 30, 73, 118, 120, 124, 134, 138, 153, 166, 169, 175,181, 189

Beltran, Carlos, 61

Benitez, Armando, 208

Berenguer, Juan, 7, 53-54, 120, 123, 137

Berkman, Lance, 107, 253-254

Bernero, Adam, 252
Berra, Yogi, 139
Berry, Halle, 138, 163
Berryhill, Damon, 139, 141, 144, 148, 153, 157, 162
Betemit, Wilson, 248-249
Bichette, Dante, 90
Bielecki, Mike, 146, 173, 187
Biggio, Craig, 47, 190
Bisher, Furman, 6
Black, Bud, 93
Blakely, Gordon, 257
Blauser, Jeff, 29, 49, 121, 124, 134, 136, 138, 141, 144, 148, 150, 153, 157, 159-160, 166, 172, 174-175, 184, 188-189, 191, 193, 226
Boggs, Wade, 48, 53, 181
Bonds, Barry, 9, 40, 41-43, 48, 72, 87, 96, 100-101, 124, 137, 141-142, 152, 156, 229-230, 300
Bong, Jong, 235, 241
Boone, Bret, 17-18, 33, 200-201, 203-204, 206, 209
Borbon, Pedro, Jr., 166, 174, 188
Borowski, Joe, 174
Boston Beaneaters, 135
Boston Braves, 190, 272
Boston Red Sox, 270
Boston Celtics, 26
Bowden, Jim, 22
Boyer, Blaine, 248, 252
Braddy, Paul, 118
Brantley, Michael, 278
Bream, Sid, 3, 6, 18-19, 30, 61, 73, 117-121, 124, 126, 130, 134, 137, 140-142, 148, 153, 162
Brett, George, 293, 299
Brock, Chris, 187
Brogna, Rico, 220-221
Brooklyn Dodgers, 180
Brower, Jim, 252
Brown, Andrew, 17
Brown, Kevin, 192, 199
Built to Win (Schuerholz), 9, 225

Bumgarner, Madison, 273
Burdette, Lew, 40, 154, 275
Burke, Chris, 254
Burkett, John, 50-52, 216, 220, 222-223
Burroughs, Jeff, 150
Byrd, Paul, 51, 187, 239, 242

C
Cabrera, Francisco, 59, 61, 120-121, 141-144, 145, 162
Called Out But Safe: a Baseball Umpire's Journey (Clark), 27
Caminiti, Ken, 139, 198, 205-206, 221-222
Caray, Chip, 135
Caray, Harry, 135
Caray, Skip, 23, 50, 135, 142, 251, 260
Cardenal, Jose, 182
Carlton, Steve, 71
Carpenter, David, 262
Carr, Chuck, 191
Carter, Jimmy, 24, 118
Carty, Rico, 150
Casals, Pablo, 4
Cashen, Frank, 293
Castilla, Vinny, 19, 34, 111, 111, 147, 224-226, 227, 229, 231, 233, 236
Castillo, Tony, 17
Cather, Mike, 191, 197
Cepeda, Orlando, 150
Chambliss, Chris, 37
Charlton, Norm, 197
Chen, Bruce, 197
Chicago Cubs, 87, 93, 95, 134-136, 154, 161, 188, 198, 203, 217, 234, 236, 264, 271
Chicago White Sox, 5, 166, 254
Chisholm, Jazz, 270
Cincinnati Reds, 11, 17, 45-46, 121, 135, 161, 167-168, 175, 203, 239, 266
Clark, Al, 27
Clark Sports Center, 287

Clark, Will, 42, 219

Clemens, Roger, 209, 243, 253

Cleveland Indians, 11, 18, 62, 74-75, 91, *176*, 180, 192, 272, 292, 294

Cloninger, Tony, 183

Clontz, Brad, 166, 174, 187

Cobb County, 250, 280

Coble, Drew, 129

Cohen, Steve, 270

Colbrunn, Gregg, 189, 196

Colorado Rockies, 11, 76-77, 155, 167, 194, 224-226, 232, 234, 252

Conrad, Brooks, 261

Cooperstown, 282, 287, 291, 297, 301

Coors Field, 270

Coppolella, John, 257

Corrales, Pat, 31, 33

Costas, Bob, 4

COVID-19, 265, 269, 277, 279

Cox, Bobby, 4-5, 11, 13-14, 17, 26-36, 28, *32, 36,* 37-38, 40, 43-46, 48, 50, 54-56, 59, 65-66, 72-73, 81, 85-86, 93, 97, 99, 102, 108-111, 114, 118-119, 133, 135-136, 138, 141, 146, 159, 165, 170, 173, 177, 182, 189, 196, 205, 213, 216, *218,* 224, 228-229, 233, 235, 240, 250, 256, 259-260, 280, 282-285, 290-294, *292,* 297-99, 300-301

Craig, Allen, 261

Crawford, Jerry, 33

Crime Dog, 296

Cruz, Juan, 18, 239, 251

Curtis, Chad, 209

Cy Young Award, 13, 40, 42-43, 52, 58, 63, 65, 71-72, 76-78, 85, 87, 90-92, 95, 122, 133-134, 154, 162, 173, 186, 196, 203, 228, 235, 238, 263

D

Dalton, Harry, 293

d'Arnaud, Travis, 268, 270

Dark, Alvin, 150

Davidoff, Ken, 297

Davies, Kyle, 248

Davis, Jody, 120

Denver, 270

DeRosa, Mark, 236-237, 240

Detroit Tigers, 56

Devereaux, Mike, 166, 168

Devers, Rafael, 270

Devine, Joey, 248, 254

Dibble, Rob, 121

Dierker, Larry, 176

DiMaggio, Joe, 22, 112

Donaldson, Josh, 263, 265

Doubleday Field, 289

Drabek, Doug, 61, 140-141

Drew, J. D., 15, 18, 237, 240-241, 243

Duvall, Adam, 265-266, 268, 271, 277, *278*

Dye, Jermaine, 18, 172, 174, 178, 181-182

Dykstra, Lenny, 67, 152, 158

E

Eckersley, Dennis, 58

Elliott, Donnie, 17

Embree, Alan, 18, 187, 197

Estrada, Johnny, 15, 32, 234, 237, 239-242, 244, 249, *299*

Evans, Darrell, 97

Everett, Carl, 206

F

Fall Classic, 276

Farnsworth, Kyle, 252-253

Fick, Robert, 231, 233

Fisk, Carlton, 284

Flaherty, Jack, 264

Florida (Miami) Marlins, 12, 35, 103, 166, 191-193, 227, 247, 265-266, 270, 273

Foltynewicz, Mike, 258-259, *259,* 264

Fonda, Jane, 24, 127, 142, 163

Ford, Whitey, 71

Foster, John, 252

Franco, Julio, 3, 19, 222, 227, 229, 233, 237, 240, 247

Franco, Matt, 227, 233

Freeman, Freddie, 257-259, 268, 271, *272*, 273-274, 277, *279*, *281*, 282, 295

Freeman, Marvin, 8, 51, 137, 144, 154

Freese, David, 261

Fregosi, Jim, 157

Fried, Max, 267-268, 273, 275, 278, *281*

Furcal, Rafael, 27, 210, 213, *213*, 214, 220-221- 224, 226-227, 231, 233, 237, 240-244, 247, 255

G

Gaetti, Gary, 178

Gagne, Eric, 235, 239

Gagne, Greg, 130

Galarraga, Andres, 3, 1, 49, 108, 146, 194-195, 199, 201, 210-211, *211*, 217, 221

Gallen, Zac, 273

Gant, Ron, 11, 88, 117, 120, 123-124, 126, 129-130, 134, 138-141, 146, 148, 150, *151*, 153, 159, 162, 178

Garr, Ralph, 100, 124, 175

Garcia, Luis, 257

Gehrig, Lou, 22, 296

Giles, Marcus, 34, 220, 222, 224, 227, 231, 237, 240, 244, 247-248, 251

Gladden, Dan, 128, 131

Glavine, Tom, 8, 13, 15-17, 29-31, 40-45, 47-50, 56, 65-66, 68, 70-84, *72*, *74-75*, *79*, *81-82*, 85, 91-93, 95, 104, 114, 117, 119, 122-123, 129, 133-134, 136, 140, 144, *153*, 154-155, 157, 161, 163-165, 169-170, 172-173, *176*, 178-179, 181-182, 186-187, 190-192, 194, 196-199, 201, 203, 206-207, 209-210, 216-217, 219, 221-224, 228-229, 234, 238, *238*, 245, 255,

264, 275, 282-287, 291, 295, 298-299, 301

Gold Glove, 277, 300

Gonzalez, Fredi, 32, 250, 256, 258, 275-276

Gorman, Lou, 293

Grace, Mark, 14

Graffanino, Tony, 189, 194-195, 200

Green, Nick, 240

Greenberg, Hank, 282

Greene, Shane, 268

Greene, Tommy, 158

Gregg, Eric, 12, 191-192

Greinke, Zack, 262

Griffey, Ken, Jr., 261, 288

Grissom, Marquis, 15, 17-18, 160, 163, 166-167, 172, 175-177, 179, 181-182, 186

Grove, Lefty, 282

Gryboski, Kevin, 235, 239

Guerrero, Vladimir, Sr., 297

Guillen, Ozzie, 195, 208

Gurriel, Yuli, 272

Gwynn, Tony, 12, 43, 66, 111, 120

H

Hader, Josh, 274

Hamels, Cole, 266

Hammonds, Chris, 228-229

Hampton, Mike, 19, 32, 51-52, 191, 205, 231, 234-236, *238*, 239, 242, 249, 251

Harper, Brian, 130

Hart, John, 257

Heath, Mike, 7

Helms, Wes, 221

Henke, Tom, 144

Hernandez, Felix, 266

Hernandez, Jose, 204

Hernandez, Livan, 12, 192

Hernandez, Orlando, 209

Hernandez, Roberto, 235

Heyward, Jason, 257, 262

Hitchcock, Sterling, 199

Hodges, Gil, 282
Hoffman, Trevor, 228, 239
Holbrook, Sam, 262
Holliday, Matt, 261
Holmes, Darren, 228.
Horner, Bob, 37, 97
Hornsby, Rogers, 282
Houston Astros, 60, 71, 122, 139,
    164, 190, 205-206, 223, 225, 242-
    243, 252-254, 272, 275
Howell, Jay, 154
Hubbard, Glenn, 233
Hubbell, Carl, 282
Hudson, Tim, 18, 32, 111, 243, 249-
    253, 291
Hundley, Todd, 232
Hunter, Brian, 3, 103, 119, 124, 126,
    129, 131, 137

I
Idelson, Jeff, *283*

J
Jackson, Danny, 157
Jackson, Darrin, 99
James, Chuck, 248
Jarvis, Pat, *176*
Jenkins, Ferguson, 95, 154
Jeter, Derek, 113, 217, 301
Jocketty, Walt, 10
John, Elton, 164-165
John, Tommy, 215, 286
Johnson, Charles, 191-192
Johnson, Chris, 262
Johnson, Ernie, Sr., 23
Johnson, Kelly, 248-249
Johnson, Randy, 85, 113, 211, 223
Johnson, Walter, 8, 165
Jones, Andruw, 12, 19-20, 27, 34,
    176-177, *177*, 179-180, 182, 188,
    194-195, 198, 201, 204, 208, 210,
    212, *212*, 217, *218*, 220, 222, 224-
    226, *226*, 231-232, 237, 240, 242,
    244-248, 256, 295-298, *296*

Jones, Chipper, 11-12, 16-17, 32, 57,
    96-114, *104-105, 108, 111, 113*,
    160-164, 166-168, 172, 174, 178,
    184, 188-189, 191-192, 194-195,
    198, 201, 202, 204, 208-212, 217,
    220, 222-225, *226-227*, 230-231,
    233, 236-237, 240, 243-244, 246-
    249, 255, 256, 260-261, 282, 287-
    292, *288*, 295-296, 301
Jones, Clarence, 133
Jones, Henry, 297
Jones, Larry Wayne, Sr., 289
Jordan, Brian, 17, 20, 178, 201, 204-
    205, 207-208, 210, 214, 220, 224,
    243-244, 249, 255
Joyner, Wally, 18
Justice, David, 15, 18, 29, 74, 117,
    119-122, 126, 130, 134-135, 137-
    138, 140-141, 148, 150, *151*, 152,
    153, 155, 160, 163-164, 166, 168,
    170, *170*, 172, 174, 186, 213, 284,
    290, 295

K
Kaat, Jim, 54
Kahn, Roger, 51
Kaline, Al, 299
Kansas City Royals, 3, 18, 30, 221,
    272, 293
Karros, Eric, 178
Karsay, Steve, 223
Kasten, Stan, 4-5, 24, 30, 53, 63,
    103, 118, 260, 284, 294
Kelly, Roberto, 17, 160, 166
Kelly, Tom, 131
Kershaw, Clayton, 262
Keuchel, Dallas, 263-264
Kile, Darryl, 190
Kimbrel, Craig, 257, 259, 262, 264, 279
Kiner, Ralph, 123
King, Carolyn, 118
King, Jeff, 141
King, Ray, 18, 235, 241
Klesko, Ryan, 18, 66, 146, 162-163,

165-166, 169, 172, 174-175, 178-179, 182, 184, 188, 190-192, 194, 196, 198, 201, 204

Knoblauch, Chuck, 130-131

Kolb, Dan, 243, 251

Koufax, Sandy, 20, 90

Kranitz, Rick, 285

Kremers, Jimmy, 7, 17

Kruk, John, 157

L

La Russa, Tony, 34, 242, 276, 291

Langerhans, Ryan, 248-249

Larkin, Barry, 90, 289

Larkin, Gene, 131

LaRoche, Adam, 146, 240-241, 243-244, 247-248

Larsen, Don, 75, 275

LaValliere, Mike, "Spanky," 140, 142

Layne, Jerry, 47-48

Leibrandt, Charlie, 15, 20, 122-123, 129, 136, 146-147

Leiter, Al, 208

Leius, Scott, 128-129

Lemke, Mark, 29, 49, 98, 124, *128*, 129, 132, 138, 141, 148, 153, 160, 163, 166, 172, 175, 178-179, 184, 188

Lerew, Anthony, 248

Leland, Jim, 34, 141

Leyritz, Jim, 181, 187

Ligtenberg, Kerry, 4, 20, 53-54, 188, 197-199, 202, 215, 223

Lincecum, Tim, 260

Llewellyn, Jack, 59

Lockhart, Keith, 18, 186, 192, 195, 200

Lofton, Kenny, 18, 33, 46, 169, 184, 186, 189

Lohse, Kyle, 261

Lolich, Mickey, 76

Lopes, Davey, 216

Lopez, Javy, 15, 20, 34, 95, 153, 160, 162, 165-166, 168-169, 172, 175, 177-179, 184-185, 188, 195, 198,

201, 204-206, *206*, 214, 220, 222-224, 226, 229, 232, *232*, 236-237, 239-241, 246, 255

Los Angeles Dodgers, 17, 25, 28, 46, 63, 73, 76-77, 101, 105-106, 120-122, 155, 161, 167, 177-178, 262, 266, 274, 277

Lowe, Derek, 261

M

Mack, Connie, 26

Maddux, Greg, 8-10, 12-13, 15-17, 30-31, 34, 40-44, 47-51, 54, 65-66, 68, 72, 78, 80-81, 85-95, *86, 89, 94*, 103, 114, 134, 147-148, 153, 154-155, 157, 159-169, 172-173, 175, 178-180, 182, 184, 186-187, 190-192, 194, 196-199, 203, 205-207, 209-210, 214, 216-217, 219-223, 228-229, 231, 234-236, 238, 238, 245, 255, 282-287, 291-292, 295, 298, 301

Maddux, Mike, 89-90, 284

Major League Baseball, 261

Maldonado, Candy, 144

Manfred, Rob, 257, 269

Mangan, Ed, 6

Mantle, Mickey, 71, 108, 112-113, 180, 289

Manzanillo, Josias, 164

Mardi Gras, 279

Marichal, Juan, 197

Markakis, Nick, 258-259, 263, 279

Marquis, Jason, 18, 53, 223, 241

Marrero, Eli, 18, 240-241

Marsh, Randy, 140, 192

Marte, Andy, 248

Martin, Billy, 34

Martinez, Dave, 221

Martinez, Dennis, 197, 199

Martinez, Pedro, 113, 250, 283

Martinez, Ramon, 177

Mathews, Eddie, 97, 105, 204, 245-246, 291, 301

Mathewson, Christy, 228, 283
Matthews, Gary, 29
Mattingly, Don, 53
Matzek, Tyler, 275
Mauch, Gene, 34
Mays, Willie, 34, 100, 124, 177, *218*, 246, 297, 300
Mazeroski, Bill, 297
Mazzone, Leo, 13, 30-31, 37-55, 39, 56, 78, 93, 159, 238, 251, 274, 284, 295-296, 298-299, *299*
McBride, Macay, 248, 252
McCann, Brian, 248-249, 253, 263
McCarthy, Joe, 31
McGinnity, Joe, 228
McGlinchy, Kevin, 203, 208
McGraw, John, 26
McGriff, Fred, 3, 9-10, 12, 17, 43, 62, 148-150, *150-151*, 153, 155, 157, *158*, 160, 162-163, 166-167, 169, 172, 174, 178-180, 184, 188, 255, 263, 274, *279*, 290, 295-296, 298
McGuirk, Terry, 16, 24-25, 30
McGwire, Mark, 202
McMichael, Greg, 53-54, 154, 157, 166, 173-174, 178
McSherry, John, 140
Medar, Ralph, 93
Medlen, Kris, 261
Melancon, Mark, 264, 268
Merced, Orlando, 141
Mercker, Kent, 48, 50, 54, 99, 120, 137, 161, 165, 235
Mexican League, 3, 19, 222
Mexico City Tigers, 222
Meyer, Dan, 18, 251
Millan, Felix, 204
Millwood, Kevin, 15, 41, 43, 187, 196-197, 201, 203, 205-209, 216, 219, 222, 228-230, 234, 239
Milwaukee Braves, 5, 40, 135, 137, 171, 174, 221, 231, 246, 272
Milwaukee Brewers, 216, 243, 251, 274
Minaya, Omar, 14

Minneapolis Loons, 4
Minnesota Twins, 73, 128-131, 274
Minor, Mike, 262
Minter, A. J., 274-275
Mitchell, Keith, 119
Mitchell, Kevin, 45, 103
MLB Network, 285-286
Molina, Yadier, 261
Molitor, Paul, 299
Mondesi, Raul, 244
Montreal Expos, 7, 17, 35, 119, 121, 136, 139, 165, 172, 175, 177, 229
Moore, Vince, 16
Morandini, Mickey, 87, 159
Mordecai, Mike, 166, 172, 175, 189
Morris, Hal, 99
Morris, Jack, 9, 59-60, 63, 101, 129-132, 144
Morrison, Keith, 17
Morton, Charlie, 273, 275
Moss, Damian, 17, 41, 228, 234
Motte, Jason, 262
Mulholland, Terry, 203, 216
Murdoch, Rupert, 25
Murphy, Dale, 12, 29, 37, 83, 96, 101, *108*, 110, 118, 124, 150, 165, 204, 24, 248, 282, 295, 299-301, *300*
Murray, Eddie, 112, 113, 299
Musial, Stan, 300
Myers, Randy, 228

N
Neagle, Denny, 17, 40, 43, 173, 179, 181, 186, 192, 196-197, 199-200, 203, 255
Nen, Robb, 229-230
Newcomb, Sean, 264
New York Mets, 16-17, 35, 83, 109, 126, 131, 161, 164, 196, 199, 201, 206-209, 214, 217, 221-222, 228, 241-242, 288
Nied, David, 147

Niekro, Phil, 29, 122, 136, 165, 274, 269, 301
Nieves, Melvin, 17
Nixon, Otis, 7, 17, 21, 73, 119-120, 123-124, 131, 136-139, 146, 148, 153, 162, 201, 204, 214
Nixon, Russ, 30
Nomo, Hideo, 105, 178

O

O'Brien, Charlie, 95, 163, 166, 168
O'Day, Darren, 268
O'Neil, Buck, 293
O'Neill, Paul, 182
Oakland Athletics, 18, 243, 249-250
Office, Rowland, 175
Oleud, John, 207
Oliva, Jose, 248
Olson, Greg, 21, 60, 118, 14, 126, 134, 138-139, 153
Orr, Bobby, 284
Ortiz, Russ, 17, 40, 51, 230, 234, 236-238, *238*, 298, *299*
Osborne, Donovan, 179
Oswalt, Roy, 243
Ozuna, Marcell, 265-266, 268, 270, 273

P

Pache, Cristian, 268
Palmer, Jim, 283
Pederson, Joc, 271, 277, 279
Pena, Alejandro, 17, 54, 99, 120, 123, 126, 131, 135, 137, 146, 161, 166
Pena, Brayan, 248
Pendleton, Terry, 6, 9, 19, 30, 53, 73, 90-91, 96-114, *98*, *104*, 117-120, 123, 129-130, 133-134, 137, 141, 148-150, 157, 175, 202, 232, 249
Perez, Eddie, 95, 146, 166, 175, 189, 194, 196, 198, 205-206, *206*, 207, 210, 214, 240, 249
Perez, Odalis, 17, 197-198, 223-224

Perry, Gerald, 20, 214
Pettitte, Andy, 62-63, 180-181, 252
Philadelphia Athletics, 21-22
Philadelphia Phillies, 62, 154, 156, 161, 220, 226, 239, 245, 256, 269, 270, 299
Piazza, Mike, 154, 207-208
Piniella, Lou, 100
Pittsburgh Pirates, 43, 45, 60-61, 73, 96, 124-126, 139-140, 176, 192
Plank, Eddie, 71
Pole, Dick, 93
Polonia, Luis, 163, 166, 169, 175, 182
Poole, Jim, 170
Posey, Buster, 260
Posnanski, Joe, 296
Pratt, Todd, 208
Presley, Jim, 120
Pride, Curtis, 196
Prior, Mark, 236
Puckett, Kirby, 129-131
Pujols, Albert, 246

R

Ramirez, Horacio, 34, 41, 235, 239, 251
Reardon, Jeff, 61, 134, 136-137, 144, 146
Reed, Steve, 223
Reitsma, Chris, 239, 252-253
Remlinger, Mike, 17, 52, 200, 203, 207-209, 215, 223, 228
Reynolds, Shane, 205-106, 235
Reynoso, Armando, 147
Rice, Jim, 284, 300
Riley, Austin, 268, 273, 277
Rijo, Jose, 154
Ripken, Cal, 22, 299
Ripken, Cal, Jr., 12, 103, 111, 289
Rivera, Mariano, 54
Roa, Joe, 17
Roberts, Dave, 277
Roberts, Robin, 78
Rocker, John, 14-15, 33, 53-55, 58,

197, 203-207, 214-215, *215*, 221, 223

Rodriguez, Richard, 271

Rogers, Kenny, 208-209

Rosario, Eddie, 268, 272-273, 277, *278*

Ross, Cody, 260

Ruth, Babe, 22, 27, 276

S

Sain, Johnny, 37-38, 40, 48, 298-299

San Diego Padres, 17-18, 43, 149, 186, 199, 238

San Francisco Giants, 11, 17, 22, 42-43, 62, 77, 87, 135, 149, 155, 163, 193, 217, 236, 260, 274

Sanchez, Rey, 221-222

Sandberg, Ryne, 91

Sandoval, Pablo, 277

Sanders, Deion, 21, 33, 102, 118-119, 123-124, 131, 134, 136, 138, 146-147, 149, 153, 157, 210

Sanders, Reggie, 18, 214, 230

Schilling, Curt, 157, 223

Schmidt, Jason, 173, 187

Schmidt, Mike, 299

Schourek, Pete, 167

Schuerholz, Jerry, 22

Schuerholz, John, 3-25, *7*, 2, 30, 35, 46, 59, 72, 97, 102, 111, 118-119, 128, 133, 166, 215, 217, 221-222, 225, 237, 251, 257, 259-260, 279, 282, 284, 291, 293-295

Seanez, Rudy, 197, 203, 214

Sheffield, Gary, 15, 17, 21, 34, 224-225, *226-227*, 229-233, 236-237, 241, 295, 296, 298, *298*

Shiell, Jason, 18

Simmons, Andrelton, 257

Simmons, Ted, 240, 301

Simon, Randall, 204

Smiley, John, 81, 164

Smith, Dwight, 166, 175

Smith, Janet Marie, 186

Smith, Lee, 162

Smith, Lonnie, 21, 100-101, 120, 124, 128-131, 137-138, 144, 146

Smith, Ozzie, 289, 297

Smith, Pete, 42, 136

Smith, Reggie, 106

Smith, Will, 266, 273-275, 278

Smith, Zane, 126

Smoltz, John, 8, 13, 15-17, 29-31, 40-43, 45, 47, 49, 53, 56-69, *57*, *62, 64, 67, 69*, 73, 80, 85, 91, 101, 114, 117-118, 122-123, 125-126, 129, 131, 136-137, 139-141, 144, *153*, 154, 157, 161, 163, 165, 169, *169*, 172-173, *173*, 177-182, 184, 186-187, 190-191, 196, 198-199, 203, 206-209, 214-215, 221, 224, 228, 231, 235, 238-239, 242-245, 250-251, 253, 275, 282, *283*, 284, 286, 287, *287*, 291-292, 295, 298, 301

Snider, Duke, 282

Snitker, Brian, 258, 275, 276, 279-280, *279-280*

Snyder, Paul, 4, 6, 29, 106, 177

Soler, Jorge, 268, 272, *276*, 277

Soroka, Mike, 270

Sosa, Jorge, 244, 249, 251, 253

Sosa, Sammy, 244, 249, 251, 253

Sotomayor, Sonia, 160

Spahn, Warren, 40, 42, 67, 70-71, 78, 81, 85, 136, 154, 301

Spehr, Tim, 190

Sprague, Ed, 61, 144

Springer, Russ, 197, 208

Sroba, Joe, 124

St. Louis Cardinals, 9, 1, 18, 22, 63, 77, 97-98, 161, 178-179, 195, 217, 241, 246, 254, 256, 261, 264

Stanton, Mike, 54-55, 123, 131, 137, 154

Stargell, Willie, 290

Stark, Jayson, 33, 113

Starting and Closing (Smoltz), 31, 68

Stengel, Casey, 26

Surhoff, B. J., 214, 220-222, 224
Sutton, Don, 34, 89, 269
Swanson, Dansby, 268, 273, *276*

T

Tales From the Braves Mound
  (Mazzone), 52
Tampa Bay Rays, 51, 249, 251, 273
Tanner, Chuck, 174
Tapani, Kevin, 129, 198
Tarasco, Tony, 17, 166
Taylor, Dean, 7
Tenace, Gene, 180
Texas Rangers, 266
Thomas, Andres, 120
Thomas, Charles, 18, 241, 251
Thome, Jim, 46, 75, 169
Thomson, John, 32, 51, 238, *238*,
  242, 249
Torborg, Jeff, 35
Toronto Blue Jays, 9, 27, 29, 37, 61,
  132, 144, 146, 215, 257
Torre, Joe, 26, 29, 140, 182-183, 291
Trammell, Alan, 56, 108
Traynor, Pie, 112
Treadway, Jeff, 99, 117, 124, 138, 146
Tucker, Michael, 17-18, 184-186,
  188, 193-194, 198, 200
Turner, Ted, 4, 16, 23-25, 29, 37, 40,
  75, 118, 127, 132, 142, 163, 184,
  237, 284

U

Uggla, Dan, 261-262
Upton, B. J., 257
Upton, Justin, 257
Uribe, Juan, 262

V

Valdez, Merkin, 17
Valentine, Bobby, 208
Van Poppel, Todd, 106
Van Slyke, Andy, 127, 136, 141-142
Van Wieren, Pete, 7, 23, 136, 179, 260

Veeck, Bill, 23
Ventura, Robin, 207-208
Veras, Quilvio, 18, 210, 213, 220-221
Verna, Chris, 137
Vogt, Stephen, 271

W

Wade, Terrell, 173, 187
Wagner, Billy, 261
Wainwright, Adam, 5, 18, 241
Wakefield, Tim, 140
Walk, Bob, 140
Walker, Jamie, 18
Walker, Larry, 49, 301
Waner, Paul, 112
Washington Nationals, 246, 259, 262,
  264, 270
Weaver, Earl, 34
Weiss, Walt, 186, 194-195, 201, 204,
  207, 210, 213
Williams, Bernie, 181
Williams, Gerald, 186, 196, 204,
  206, 208
Williams, Jimy, 31, 131
Williams, Mitch, 101, 13, 157
Williams, Ted, 71
Winfield, Dave, 146, 299
Wohlers, Mark, 47, 53, 75-76, 99
  120, 123, 137, 154, 158, 161,
  164, 166-168, 170, 173-174, 177-
  179, 181, 185, 187, 191, 197,
  202, 228
Wood, Alex, 257
Wood, Kerry, 236
Woodall, Brad, 173
World Series
  1948, 168
  1957, 96
  1958, 125
  1972, 261
  1987, 159
  1991, 8-9, 21, 30, 60, 74, 83,
    127-129, 131-132, 168, 188
  1992, 33, 139, 146-147

1993, 42
1995, 46, 62-63, 74-75, 77-78, 90, 110, 169-170, 176
1996, 12, 33, 64, 183, 187, 252, 295
1997, 192
1999, 49, 59, 110
2021, 268, 272, 275, 276, 279-280
Wren, Frank, 241, 257

Wright, Jaret, 241, 298
Wright, Kyle, 266

Y
Yan, Esteban, 17, 166
Yastrzemski, Carl, 284
Yost, Ned, 19, 33, 135
Young, Andrew, 215
Young, Cy, 228
Ynoa, Huascar, 270

1993, 47
1995, 46, 62-63, 74-75, 77-78,
90, 110, 169, 170, 176
1996, 17, 33, 64, 184, 187,
242, 293
1997, 193
1999, 49, 59, 110,
2021, 269, 272, 275, 276

Xerb, Daniel, 257, 257

Wright, John 281, 298
Wright, Kyle 266

Yanchenkov, 77, 186
Yascovitch, Olaf 294
Yost, Fred, 19, 93, 135
Young, Andrew, 315
Young, Ca 228
Yoo, Marcus 279